Lab Manual for

MCTS Guide to Microsoft® Windows 7 (Exam #70-680)

Lab Manual for
MCTS Guide to Microsoft® Windows 7 (Exam #70-680)

Byron Wright
Leon Plesniarski

COURSE TECHNOLOGY
CENGAGE Learning™

Australia • Brazil • Japan • Korea • Mexico • Singapore • Spain • United Kingdom • United States

COURSE TECHNOLOGY
CENGAGE Learning™

MCTS Lab Manual for Guide to Microsoft Windows 7 (exam # 70-680)
Byron Wright and Leon Plesniarski

Vice President, Editorial: Dave Garza

Executive Editor: Stephen Helba

Acquisitions Editor: Nick Lombardi

Managing Editor: Marah Bellegarde

Product Manager: Natalie Pashoukos

Developmental Editor: Jill Batistick

Editorial Assistant: Sarah Pickering

Vice President, Marketing: Jennifer Ann Baker

Marketing Director: Deborah S. Yarnell

Marketing Manager: Erin Coffin

Marketing Coordinator: Erica Ropitsky

Production Director: Wendy Troeger

Production Manager: Andrew Crouth

Senior Content Project Manager: Andrea Majot

Senior Art Director: Jack Pendleton

For product information and technology assistance, contact us at
Cengage Learning Customer & Sales Support, 1-800-354-9706

For permission to use material from this text or product, submit all requests online at **cengage.com/permissions**
Further permissions questions can be emailed to
permissionrequest@cengage.com

Microsoft ® is a registered trademark of the Microsoft Corporation.

Library of Congress Control Number: 2011933983

ISBN-13: 978-1-111-30978-7

ISBN-10: 1-111-30978-7

Course Technology
20 Channel Center Street
Boston, MA 02210
USA

Cengage Learning is a leading provider of customized learning solutions with office locations around the globe, including Singapore, the United Kingdom, Australia, Mexico, Brazil, and Japan. Locate your local office at: **international.cengage.com/region**

Cengage Learning products are represented in Canada by Nelson Education, Ltd.

For your lifelong learning solutions, visit **www.cengage.com/coursetechnology**

Purchase any of our products at your local college store or at our preferred online store **www.cengagebrain.com**

Visit our corporate website at **cengage.com**.

Printed in the United States of America
1 2 3 4 5 6 7 12 11

Byron and Leon would like to thank the entire team that we have worked with at Cengage Learning. In particular we would like to thank Jill Batistick and Natalie Pashoukos, who patiently worked with us as we missed a few deadlines during the writing process.

Leon would like to thank his loving wife, Angela, and his boys, Tyler and Terry, for sharing their family time with all the people who will use this book as part of their greater education.

Byron would especially like to thank Tracey, Sammi, and Michelle for allowing him to maintain a sense of perspective when deadlines loom.

TABLE OF CONTENTS

INTRODUCTION

The objective of this lab manual is to provide hands-on activities that help you prepare for the Microsoft Certified Technical Specialist (MCTS) Exam 70-680: TS: Windows 7, Configuring. This manual is intended to be used with the companion Course Technology book *MCTS Guide to Microsoft® Windows 7* (ISBN 978-1-111-30977-0).

The activities in this lab manual can be completed by students in a classroom or through individual study with access to the proper equipment. For the optimal hands-on experience, students will complete the activities both in the main textbook and in this lab manual. Certain labs in this manual depend on successful completion of the labs in the companion book. Ideally, these labs will be performed in a virtual machine environment so that students do not require multiple sets of computer hardware or lab partners. However, there is no reason the labs cannot be completed using multiple physical computers connected to a LAN.

Saving Your Work

The labs are written with the assumption that students will complete all the steps. It is also assumed that in a virtualized environment, students will save their work at the end of each chapter.

Features

This lab manual includes the following features to provide a successful learning experience:

- **Time required.** The estimated time to complete the steps is shown before each lab.
- **Lab objectives.** The learning objectives for each lab are stated at the beginning of the lab.
- **Description.** Each lab activity is described within the context of the learning objectives.
- **Step-by-step instructions.** Detailed steps are provided to complete each lab, with notations as appropriate.
- **Certification exam objectives.** Relevant exam objectives are listed at the beginning of each chapter.
- **Review questions.** Questions are included to reinforce a student's understanding of the chapter material.

Computer Requirements

A minimum of three computers are required to complete all labs. You can use virtual machines or physical computers. Each machine has the following minimum requirements:

- **CPU.** Minimum 1 GHz for x86 CPU or 1.4 GHz for x64 CPU
- **Memory.** Minimum 1 GB of RAM (2 GB recommended for x64)
- **Disk space.** 40 GB hard disk
- **Video.** Monitor supporting a resolution of 1024x768. DirectX 9-capable graphics processor with WDDM support (recommended).
- **Drives.** A DVD-ROM drive
- **Networking.** Network interface card with an Internet connection. A switch or hub is necessary if using physical computers.
- **Peripherals.** A keyboard and mouse

Software Requirements

Microsoft Windows 7 Enterprise for each computer. Other versions can be used, but some labs may not be possible to perform. For example, the Parental Controls feature is not available in business versions of Windows 7. Students perform the installation of all necessary software during the *MCTS Guide to Microsoft Windows 7* labs. Each lab provides a brief overview of the software required.

Software used during this course can be obtained at the following locations:

- Windows 7 Enterprise 90-day Trial:
  http://technet.microsoft.com/en-us/evalcenter/cc442495.aspx

- Windows Automated Installation Kit for Windows 7:
  http://www.microsoft.com/downloads/details.aspx?FamilyID=696dd665-9f76-4177-a811-39c26d3b3b34&displaylang=en

- Windows Server 2008 R2 Trial:
  http://www.microsoft.com/windowsserver2008/en/us/trial-software.aspx

Lab Setup

Successful completion of all labs requires three different computers. All of these computers are created and configured in the main book (*MCTS Guide to Microsoft Windows 7*). The computers required are as follows:

- User*x*-PC. This Windows 7 computer is the main computer used in each lab.

- A partner with a Windows 7 computer.

- DC*y*. This Windows Server 2008 R2 computer is configured as a domain controller. This computer is used only to complete Chapter 13, "Enterprise Computer" labs.

Note that various labs in this manual require access to Internet resources. If you are running virtual machines, the virtual machines require Internet access.

Lab Manual for
MCTS Guide to Microsoft® Windows 7 (Exam #70-680)

INTRODUCTION TO WINDOWS 7

Labs included in this chapter:

- Lab 1.1 Discovering Essential Computer Specifications
- Lab 1.2 Observing Processes and Services with Windows Task Manager
- Lab 1.3 Observing Thread and Kernel Activity with Windows Task Manager
- Lab 1.4 Investigating Windows CardSpace

Microsoft MCTS Exam #70-680 Objectives

Objective	Lab
Configure devices	1.1
Monitor systems	1.2, 1.3
Configure Internet Explorer	1.4

Lab 1.1: Discovering Essential Computer Specifications

Objectives

The object of this activity is to identify CPU, RAM, hard drive, and network specifications and identities for a computer running Windows 7. Identification will be done using various system utilities included with Windows 7.

Materials Required

This lab requires the following:

- A physical computer or virtual machine running Windows 7 that is configured as User*x*-PC or as specified by your instructor

Estimated completion time: **15 minutes**

Activity Background

A friend has asked you to come with him to look at a used computer he is thinking about buying. He would like to compare the computer's hardware specifications to one recently advertised in a local store flyer. He is not sure how to identify what components the used computer comes with and has asked you to identify the type of CPU, the size of the hard drive, the operating system version, the amount of RAM, and the type of network cards installed. You sit down at the computer and discover it is running Windows 7.

Activity

1. Log on to User*x*-PC.

2. Click **Start**, point to **All Programs**, and then click to select and expand the **Accessories** submenu.

3. In the Accessories submenu, click **Run**.

4. In the Open dialog box, type the command **winver**, and then click the **OK** button to open the About Windows window.

5. Write down the following details, and then click **OK** to close the window:

   a. Installed version of Windows _____

   b. Who this copy is licensed to _____

6. Click **Start** and select **Control Panel** from the Start menu.

7. In the Control Panel window, click **System and Security**.

8. In the System and Security window, click **System**.

9. Write down the following details:

   a. Windows edition _____

   b. Processor _____

   c. Installed memory (RAM) total _____

   d. Installed memory (RAM) usable _____ (only present on 32-bit versions)

   e. System type _____

   f. Computer name _____

g. Workgroup _____

h. Windows activation status _____

10. In the System window, click the **Device Manager** link.

11. In the Device Manager window, click the **Disk drives** arrow to expand that category.

12. For the first disk drive listed under Disk drives, double-click the name of the drive to open the drive's properties.

13. Select the **Volumes** tab in the drive's Properties window.

14. Click the **Populate** button and wait while the disk and volume information is retrieved. Write down the following for the drive, and then click **OK**.

a. Disk _____

b. Type _____

c. Partition style _____

d. Capacity _____

e. For each volume listed on that disk, write down the following:

i. Volume name _____

ii. Drive letter _____

iii. Capacity _____

15. In the Device Manager window, click the **Processors** arrow to expand that category.

16. Write down the name of the processor listed under the Processors category: _____.

17. In the Device Manager window, click the **Network adapters** arrow to expand that category.

18. Write down the name of each network adapter listed under the Network adapters category: _____.

19. Close the Device Manager window.

20. In the System window, click the **Advanced system settings** link.

21. In the System Properties window, click the **Hardware** tab and note the buttons to launch Device Manager and the Device installation Settings Wizard.

22. In the System Properties window, click the **Computer Name** tab. Note and record the following:

a. Full computer name _____

b. Workgroup _____

23. Close the System Properties window.

24. Close the System window.

25. Click **Start**, point to **All Programs**, click **Accessories**, and then click **Run**.

26. In the Open dialog box, type the command **msinfo32**, and then click the **OK** button to open the System Information window.

27. The System Summary screen will be displayed when the System Information utility is first started. Write down the following details from the right-side detail pane:

a. OS Name _____

b. System Name _____

c. Processor _____

d. User Name _____

e. Installed Physical Memory _____

f. Total Physical Memory _____

28. In the left pane of the System Information window, click the plus symbol next to Components to expand that category.

29. Click the plus symbol next to the Storage category below Components.

30. Click the **Drives** category below Storage and wait for the system information to refresh on the right pane of the System Information window.

31. Write down, for each unique drive listed, the following details:

a. Drive letter _____

b. Description _____

c. File System (if present) _____

d. Size (if present) _____

e. Free Space (if present) _____

32. Click the **Disks** category below Storage, and then write down the following for each disk drive:

a. Description _____

b. Model _____

c. Size _____

33. Close the System Information window.

Certification Objectives

Objectives for MCTS Exam #70-680: Windows 7, Configuring:

- Configuring Hardware and Applications: Configure devices

Review Questions

1. Which utility identified in the activity clearly identified the licensee for this copy of Windows?

a. System Information

b. Device manager

c. Advanced system settings

d. Winver

2. Which utility can identify in a single pane the disk drive model installed in the computer and the volumes that the disk drive contains?

a. Msinfo32

b. Device Manager

c. System

d. System Configuration

3. The RAM installed in the computer is detailed in which utility? (Select two.)

a. System Information

b. System Properties

c. Device Manager

d. Winver

4. Which Control Panel applet identifies if the operating system currently installed is either 32-bit or 64-bit?

5. Your friend is wondering if the computer discussed in the lab includes a wireless network card. What two utilities can identify the types of network adapters installed in the computer?

Lab 1.2: Observing Processes and Services with Windows Task Manager

Objectives

The objective of this activity is to use Task Manager to observe the activity of processes, threads, and services running on Windows 7.

Materials Required

This lab requires the following:

- The physical computer or virtual machine running Windows 7 that was previously configured as User*x*-PC or as specified by your instructor

Estimated completion time: **20 minutes**

Activity Background

The senior IT administrator for your company has left a user's computer with you for further inspection. The user has been complaining that she cannot print. Your boss wants you to confirm that the print spooler service is running. The print spooler service is responsible for managing the flow of data between applications and printers available to the computer's users when they print to them. If the print spooler service is running, you can restart it to confirm that is operating properly.

Activity

1. Log on to User*x*-PC.

2. Click **Start**, point to **All Programs**, and then click to select and expand the **Accessories** submenu.

3. In the Accessories submenu, click the **Command Prompt**.

4. In the Command Prompt window, type the command **taskmgr** and press **Enter** to start the Windows Task Manager.

5. Click the **Processes** tab, if necessary.

6. Click the **Show processes from all users button**. The Windows Task Manager window will refresh to list all processes currently running on the computer.

7. Click the **Services** tab.

8. In the **Name** column, find and click the **Spooler** service to select it. Write down the following details for the Spooler service:

   a. PID _____

   b. Description _____

   c. Status _____

9. The PID (process ID) uniquely identifies an active process running on the computer. Right-click the **Spooler** service and select **Stop Service** from the pop-up menu. Write down the following details for the Spooler service:

   a. PID _____

   b. Status _____

10. Right-click the **Spooler** service and select **Start Service** from the pop-up menu. Write down the following details for the Spooler service:

    a. PID _____

    b. Status _____

11. Right-click the **Spooler** service and select **Go to Process**. The selected tab will change to the Processes tab. Note that the name of the currently selected process is spoolsv.exe.

12. Click the **View** menu in Windows Task Manager, and select the **Select Columns** menu item.

13. In the Select Process Page Columns window, click the **PID (Process Identifier)** check box, and then click **OK** to close the window.

14. New columns will appear on the Processes tab. Write down the PID for the spoolsv.exe process:

    a. PID _____

15. Right-click the **spoolsv.exe** process and select **End Process** from the pop-up menu.

16. When you are prompted by Windows Task Manager to confirm that you want to end the process, click the **End process** button to confirm. Note that, after a brief refresh, the spoolsv.exe process name is no longer listed under the Processes tab.

17. Click the **Services** tab.

18. In the **Name** column, find and click the **Spooler** service to select it. Write down the following details for the Spooler service:

    a. PID _____

    b. Status _____

19. Right-click the **Spooler** service and select **Start Service** from the pop-up menu. Write down the following details for the Spooler service:

    a. PID _____

    b. Status _____

20. Leave Windows Task Manager open for the next lab.

Certification Objectives

Objectives for MCTS Exam #70-680: Windows 7, Configuring:

- Monitoring and Maintaining Systems that Run Windows 7: Monitor systems

Review Questions

1. When a service is stopped, what process ID (PID) is reported by Windows Task Manager?

2. Which Windows Task Manager tab allows you to start and stop the process associated with a service?

3. Each time a service is started, the process associated with it is assigned a well-known process ID (PID) value that uniquely identifies the service. True or False?

4. If the process associated with a service stops running, the status of the service becomes
_____.

    a. Unknown

    b. Running

    c. Disabled

    d. Stopped

5. Consider the situation in which the option to Show processes from all users is disabled and the user right-clicks the Spooler service in the Services tab and selects Go to process from the pop-up menu. What process name will be highlighted in the Processes tab when the view changes to the Processes tab? Note that the mouse cursor will highlight any service it hovers over; this should not be confused with a highlighted item that does not change with the mouse cursor's position.

Lab 1.3: Observing Threads and Kernel Activity with Windows Task Manager

Objectives

The objective of this activity is to apply a Windows 7 image to a new computer.

Materials Required

This lab requires the following:

- The physical computer or virtual machine running Windows 7 that was previously configured as User*x*-PC or as specified by your instructor
- Completion of Lab 1.2

Estimated completion time: **20 minutes**

Activity Background

The senior IT administrator for your company has returned a user's computer to you for further inspection. The user has been complaining that performance has been very slow when she manually triggers a defragmentation scan of the computer's C: drive. Your boss has asked you to confirm that the disk defragmentation service runs within expectations.

The disk defragmentation service is responsible for reorganizing blocks of file data stored on disk drives to improve performance when reading or writing file data. This computer was purchased along with 100 similar units three months ago. Some units have been experiencing a system flaw that triggers two symptoms. The first noted symptom is that the number of threads started by the disk defragmentation service will continuously increase while the service is active. The second symptom is that the computer CPU will spend almost 100 percent of its CPU cycles running in privileged kernel mode. You must confirm that neither symptom is occurring on this computer.

Activity

1. Log on to User*x*-PC.

2. In Windows Task Manager, click the **Processes** tab, if necessary. Check the **Show processes from all users** check box, if necessary.

3. Click the **Services** tab.

4. Click the view menu and select the **Refresh Now** menu item.

5. In the Name column, find and click the **defragsvc** service to select it. Write down the following details for the defragsvc service:

   a. PID (If blank, record that it is blank.) _____

   b. Description _____

   c. Status _____

6. Click the **Performance** tab. Note the CPU Usage and CPU Usage History visual graphs displayed on the tab, as shown in Figure 1-1. The green indicators represent the total CPU activity displayed in the last second and over the last few seconds, respectively.

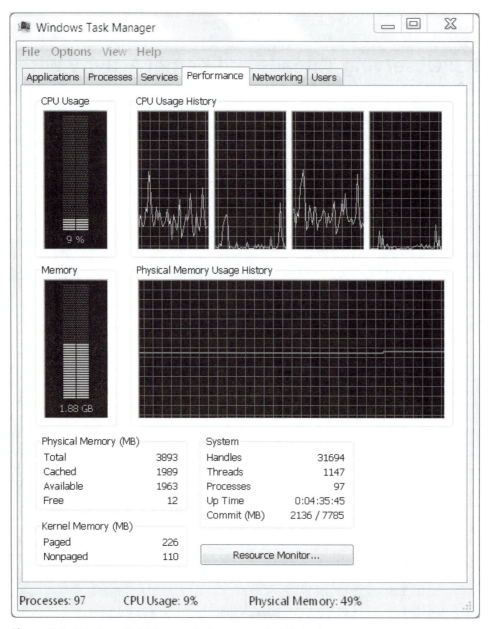

Figure 1-1 Windows Task Manager Performance tab default view
© Cengage Learning 2012

7. Click the **View** menu and select the **Show Kernel Times** menu item. This changes the CPU Usage and CPU Usage History indicators to show total CPU activity. Kernel activity is also displayed in a different color (red), as seen in Figure 1-2. Kernel activity shows how much time the CPU is spending in privileged kernel mode.

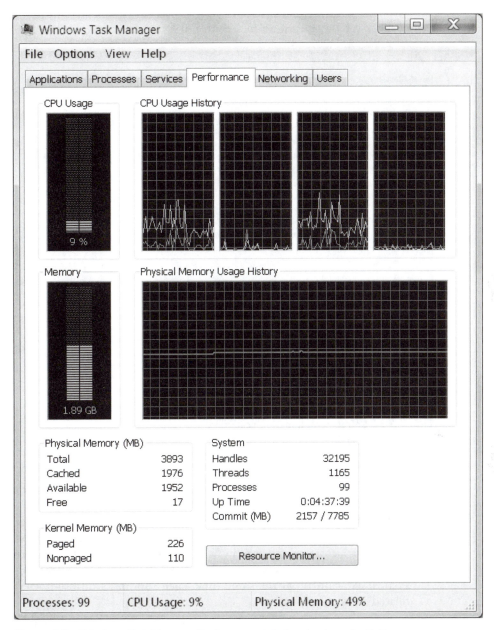

Figure 1-2   Windows Task Manager Performance tab showing kernel activity
© *Cengage Learning 2012*

8. Click the **Processes** tab.

9. Click the **View** menu in Windows Task Manager, and select the **Select Columns** menu item.

10. In the Select Process Page Columns window, check the **Threads** check box, if necessary, and then click **OK** to close the window.

11. Click the **Services** tab Locate, and click the **defragsvc** service to select it.

12. Launch the disk defragmentation utility, as detailed in the following steps:

    a. Click **Start**, and then select **Computer** from the Start menu.

    b. Right-click the icon for **C:** and select **Properties** from the pop-up menu.

    c. In the (C:) Properties window, select the **Tools** tab.

    d. Click the **Defragment now** button to start the defragmentation graphical utility, as shown in Figure 1-3.

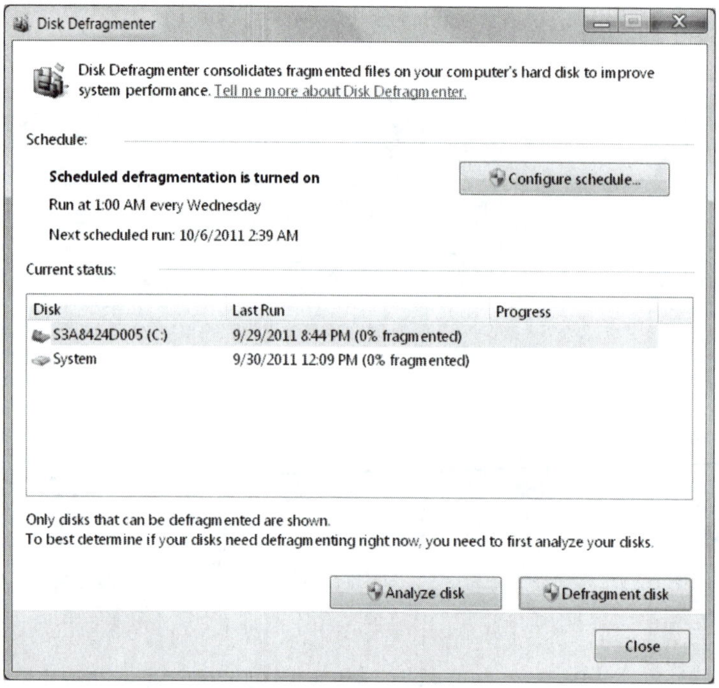

Figure 1-3 Defragmentation graphical utility
© Cengage Learning 2012

13. Switch to the Windows Task Manager window. Notice that the disk defragmentation service is now running and has a process PID associated with it. Write down the PID: _____.

14. Right-click the **defragsvc** service in the Services tab, and select **Go to process** from the pop-up menu. Note that the process name is identified as svchost.exe. Svchost.exe is a generic process name used by Windows to identify services that run from dynamic-link libraries (DLLs) instead of specific executable program files. Multiple instances of svchost.exe can run at the same time, each running a different service or a group of related services.

15. Switch to the Command Prompt window. Type the command **tasklist /SVC /FI "PID EQ #"** but replace # with the PID noted for the defragmentation service. (See Step 13.) For example, if the PID were found to be 5780, the command to type would be *tasklist /SVC /FI "PID EQ 5780"*.

16. Press **Enter** to run the tasklist command; this will display a list of currently running processes matching the filter criteria (i.e., services hosted in the process with a process ID matching 5780 in the prior example).

17. Read the output from the tasklist command and note the service named in the displayed results.

18. Switch to the Windows Task Manager, select the **Processes** tab if required, and note the number of active threads listed in the **Threads** column for the highlighted process that is responsible for the defragmentation service (svchost.exe).

19. Click the **Performance** tab. Note the current CPU and kernel activity in the visual graphs.

20. Switch to the Disk Defragmenter window and start the disk fragmentation for C, as follows:

    a. In the Disk Defragmenter window, click to select the **(C:)** drive in the list of disks below Current status.

    b. Click the **Analyze disk** button.

21. Switch to the Windows Task Manager window. Notice the change in CPU and kernel activity displayed in the graphs.

22. Switch to the **Processes** tab and note the number of threads now active for the defragmentation process. The number of threads has increased.

23. When the disk fragmentation process completes, click the **Close** button for the Disk Defragmenter window.

24. In Windows Task Manager, switch to the **Services** tab. Note that the defragsvc is still highlighted and the service's status is listed as Running.

25. Wait at least four minutes and note that the defragsvc will automatically stop itself when no further action is required to manage disk defragmentation.

26. Remove the PID (Process Identifier) and Threads columns from the list of selected Processes page columns in Windows Task Manager, as detailed in the following steps:

    a. On the **Processes** tab, click the **View** menu and click **Select Columns**.

    b. Deselect the **PID (Process Identifier)** check box.

    c. Deselect the **Threads** check box.

    d. Click **OK**.

27. On the **Performance** tab, click the **View** menu and click **Show Kernel Times** to disable the display of kernel times.

28. Close all open windows.

Certification Objectives

Objectives for MCTS Exam #70-680: Windows 7, Configuring:

- Monitoring and Maintaining Systems that Run Windows 7: Monitor systems

Review Questions

1. What option must be enabled in Windows Task Manager to display operating system processes?

2. In Windows Task Manager, which tab would you use to identify which program was utilizing too much CPU time?

    a. Applications

    b. Processes

    c. Services

    d. Performance

3. Which command-line utility displays a text-based list of details about currently running processes?

   a. taskmgr

   b. tasklist

   c. taskkill

   d. tasksched

4. Your computer seems to be running slowly. When you look at active processes in Windows Task Manager, one process is taking up to 95 percent of the CPU's attention. That process is identified with the name svchost.exe and a PID of 8345. What command would you type at a command-line prompt to discover the identity of the service or services hosted by this instance of svchost.exe?

5. After enabling the display of kernel time, on which Windows Task Manager tab would you see the kernel time displayed?

   a. Performance

   b. Processes

   c. Services

   d. Applications

Lab 1.4: Investigating Windows CardSpace

Objectives

The objective of this activity is to familiarize yourself with Windows CardSpace and the basic identity services it can provide.

Materials Required

This lab requires the following:

- The physical computer or virtual machine running Windows 7 that was previously configured as User*x*-PC or as specified by your instructor

Estimated completion time: **20 minutes**

Activity Background

Your company has developed several new Web sites to service customer banking inquiries. The developers of the Web site are planning on obtaining a high-assurance certificate for their Web sites. They have asked you to test their Web site in its early stages, using Windows CardSpace on your Windows 7 computer. They will issue managed identities at a later date, but for now you must be able to connect with personally created identities.

You are not familiar with Windows CardSpace, and you must confirm the process required to create a personal identity, back it up, delete it, and finally recover it. You also must review how Windows CardSpace can protect your locally stored identities from other users or applications that might obtain local access to your machine.

Activity

1. Log on to User*x*-PC.

2. Click **Start** and in the Search programs and files box, type **notepad** and press **Enter**. Type a sentence of at least 10 words into the Notepad editor window.

3. Press and hold the **ALT** key while repeatedly pressing the **TAB** key to confirm that you can cycle through applications. Release ALT and TAB when the desktop is displayed.

4. Click **Start**, click **Control panel**, and click **User Accounts and Family Safety**.

5. Click **Windows CardSpace**.

6. Add a personal identity card, as detailed in the following steps:

    a. Click the **Add a card** task link.

    b. Click **Create a Personal card**.

    c. Complete the following fields:

        i. Card Name: ANMP Bank

        ii. First Name: *your name*

        iii. Last Name: Student

        iv. Email Address: billg@microbiz.local

        v. Home Phone: (905) 555-1212

        vi. Date of Birth: 8/16/1991

    d. Click the **Save** button to create the identity card. Note that the CardSpace window displays an icon representing the identity card with the card's name below it.

7. Back up the identify cards in CardSpace, as detailed in the following steps:

    a. Click the **Back up cards** task link. A list of cards that could be backed up is displayed; make sure there is a check mark in the top-left corner of the "ANMP Bank" identity card icon.

    b. Click the **Continue** button.

    c. Click the **Browse** button to specify the name of the CardSpace backup file. Note that the default location to create the file is in the current user's Documents library.

    d. In the Filename field, type the name **UserACardSpace**. In the Save as type drop-down list below the filename field, note the file extension used to identify a CardSpace backup file.

    e. Click the **Save** button to confirm the backup filename and location displayed by the Backup Wizard.

    f. Click the **Continue** button. In the Type password and Retype password fields, enter the text **password**.

    g. Click the **Back Up** button.

8. Lock the identity card with a PIN, as detailed in the following steps:

    a. Double-click the **ANMP Bank** card to preview the card's details.

    b. Click the **Lock card** task link.

    c. In the New PIN and Confirm new PIN field, type the text **A9315c**, and then click the **Lock** button. Note the minimum PIN length and that the PIN can contain letters (case-sensitive), numbers, and symbols.

9. Open a locked identity card, as detailed in the following steps:

    a. Exit Windows CardSpace and then reopen it.

    b. Double-click the **ANMP Bank** card and, when prompted, enter the correct PIN you used in Step 8c to open it.

    c. Once you have confirmed that you can open the identity card, exit Windows CardSpace and then reopen it.

10. Delete all identity cards from Windows CardSpace, as detailed in the following steps:

    a. Click the **Delete all cards** task link. Read the warning notifying you that all cards will be deleted from this user's account.

    b. Check the **Yes, I want to delete all cards and card history** check box, and then click the **Delete All** button.

    c. Confirm that all identity cards are gone. Exit Windows CardSpace.

11. Recover CardSpace cards from a backup file, as detailed in the following steps:

    a. Click **Start**, and then click **Computer** to open a file browser window.

    b. Under Libraries, click **Documents** to browse the list of files in the current user's document library.

    c. Locate and double-click the file **UserACardSpace**.

    d. When prompted by CardSpace for the file password, enter the password used in Step 7f.

    e. Click the **Continue** button. Note the information message and then click the **Install and Exit** button.

12. Edit a CardSpace identity card, as detailed in the following steps:

    a. Open Windows CardSpace from Control Panel again.

    b. Double-click the **ANMP Bank** identity card icon. Notice there is no prompt for a PIN this time.

    c. Click the **Edit** button and modify the Home Phone value to **(401) 555-8383**.

    d. Click the **Save** button to save your changes.

13. Press and hold the **ALT** key while repeatedly pressing the **TAB** key. Note that you cannot cycle through running applications. Release the ALT and TAB keys. Note that the desktop background around the CardSpace window itself is dimmed, indicating that the CardSpace utility is running in a protected process space that regular applications and services do not have access to.

14. Close all open windows and shut down your computer.

Certification Objectives

Objectives for MCTS Exam #70-680: Windows 7, Configuring:

- Configuring Hardware and Applications: Configure Internet Explorer

Review Questions

1. Why was a PIN not required when editing the home phone number within the ANMP Bank identity card?

2. Why would the Windows CardSpace utility prevent you from using ALT+TAB to switch applications and run in a protected space?

3. All identity fields must be filled in to complete a CardSpace identity card. True or False?

4. In the lab, you assigned both a PIN and a password to protect CardSpace information. What was each used for?

CHAPTER TWO

INSTALLING WINDOWS 7

Labs included in this chapter:

- Lab 2.1 Creating a Customized Windows PE Boot CD

- Lab 2.2 Creating a Windows 7 Image

- Lab 2.3 Applying a Windows 7 Image

- Lab 2.4 Performing an Unattended Installation of Windows 7

Microsoft MCTS Exam #70-680 Objectives

Objective	Lab
Capture a system image	2.1, 2.2
Prepare a system image for deployment	2.2
Deploy a system image	2.3
Perform a clean installation	2.4

Lab 2.1: Creating a Customized Windows PE Boot CD

Objectives

The object of this activity is to create a Windows PE boot CD that has been customized to load an updated network card driver.

Materials Required

This lab requires the following:

- A physical computer or virtual machine running Windows 7 that is configured as User*x*-PC or as specified by your instructor
- The Windows Automated Installation Kit for Windows 7 already installed
- A CD or DVD burner if the installation is being performed on a physical computer

Estimated completion time: **15 minutes**

Activity Background

Windows PE is used to perform the imaging process when an image is captured from a configured reference computer and deployed to new computers. The image of Windows PE that is included as part of the Windows Automated Installation Kit includes a large number of hardware drivers. However, it is possible that Windows PE will not have appropriate hardware drivers for newer network cards or storage controllers.

Activity

1. Log on to User*x*-PC.

2. Download and extract a network card driver for your computer. If possible, identify the network card in your computer, download the latest driver from the manufacturer's Web site, and extract the driver to C:\Network. An example of steps for a Broadcom network card driver follow. These steps can be used regardless of the network card in your computer because adding an additional unused driver will not impact the ability to finish this activity.

   a. Open Internet Explorer.

   b. In the address bar, type **http://www.broadcom.com/support/ethernet_ nic/netxtreme_desktop.php** and press **Enter**.

   c. Scroll down and click **Windows 7 (32 bit)**.

   d. Scroll down to the bottom of the Broadcom License Agreement, and click **Accept**.

   e. In the File Download window, click **Save**.

   f. In the Save As window, click **Save** to accept the default settings. This saves the file win_vista_2k8_32-14.2.0.5a.zip in the Downloads folder of User*x*.

   g. In the Download complete window, click **Open**.

   h. In the Internet Explorer Security window, click **Allow**.

   i. In the Windows Explorer window, double-click **win_vista_2k8_32** to view the contents of the folder.

   j. Press **Ctrl + a** to select all files and then press **Ctrl + c** to copy the files to the Clipboard.

   k. In the left pane of the Windows Explorer window, expand **Computer** and click **Local Disk (C:)**.

   l. In the toolbar, click **New folder**, type **Network**, and press **Enter**.

m. Double-click **Network** to open the folder.

n. Press **Ctrl + v** to paste the network driver files into the C:\Network folder.

o. Close all open windows.

3. Click **Start**, point to **All Programs**, click **Microsoft Windows AIK**, right-click **Deployment Tools Command Prompt**, and click **Run as administrator**.

4. In the User Account Control window, click **Yes**.

5. Type **copype.cmd x86 C:\modbootcd** and press **Enter**. This command creates the necessary folder structure for the 32-bit version of Windows PE in the C:\bootcd folder. For a 64-bit version of Windows PE, use the option amd64 instead of x86.

6. Type **copy C:\modbootcd\winpe.wim C:\modbootcd\ISO\sources\boot .wim** and press **Enter**. This command copies and renames the bootable image of Windows PE. The ISO folder is the content that is used to create the ISO file.

7. Type **copy "C:\Program Files\Windows AIK\Tools\x86\imagex.exe" C:\modbootcd\ISO** and press **Enter**. Notice that ImageX is being copied from an architecture-specific directory. You need to ensure that the version of ImageX matches the architecture selected when you ran copype.cmd.

8. Add an updated network card driver to the boot.wim file, shown in Figure 2-1, as detailed in the following steps:

a. Type **Dism /Get-WimInfo /WimFile:C:\modbootcd\ISO\sources\boot .wim** and press **Enter**. This lists names and index numbers of images in the WIM file. Only one image is present in the WIM file.

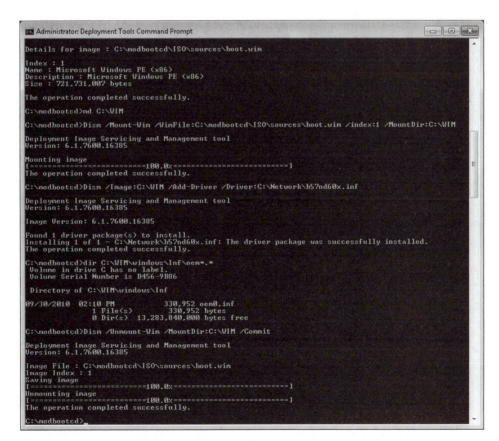

Figure 2-1 Adding a network card driver to Windows PE

© Cengage Learning 2012

b. Type **md C:\WIM** and press **Enter**.

c. Type **Dism /Mount-Wim /WimFile:C:\modbootcd\ISO\sources\boot .wim /index:1 /MountDir:C:\WIM** and press **Enter**.

d. Type **Dism /Image:C:\WIM /Add-Driver /Driver:C:\Network\b57nd60x .inf** and press **Enter**. The INF file used to add the driver varies depending on the driver you have downloaded from the manufacturer of the network card. Verify the name of the INF used by your network card driver in the C:\Network folder.

e. Type **dir C:\WIM\windows\Inf\oem*.*** and press **Enter**. This displays the name of the inf file you added to the driver store.

f. Type **Dism /Unmount-Wim /MountDir:C:\WIM /Commit** and press **Enter**.

9. Type **oscdimg -n -bC:\modbootcd\etfsboot.com C:\modbootcd\ISO C:\ modbootcd\WinPEboot.iso** and press **Enter**. This command creates WinPEboot .iso by using the contents of the ISO folder and etfsboot.com. For EFI-based computers (instead of BIOS), you need to substitute efisys.bin for etfsboot.com.

10. If you are using a physical computer, burn **C:\modbootcd\WinPEboot.iso** to a CD or DVD for use in the next activity. If you are using virtual machines, copy **C:\modbootcd\WinPEboot.iso** to the host computer so that you can mount the ISO file as a CD in the next activity.

11. Close all open windows.

Certification Objectives

Objectives for MCTS Exam #70-680: Windows 7, Configuring:

- Deploying Windows 7: Capture a system image

Review Questions

1. Which utility is used to add drivers to a WIM image?

2. When do you need to add additional network drivers to a WIM image?

3. What type of file describes a network card driver and provides instructions about installation of that driver to Windows 7?

4. Why is it important to use the /commit option after modifying a WIM image?

5. Why is it important to review the index numbers present in a WIM file?

Lab 2.2: Creating a Windows 7 Image

Objectives

The objective of this activity is to make an image of a configured Windows 7 computer that can be applied to other computers.

Materials Required

This lab requires the following:

- A physical computer or virtual machine running Windows 7 that is configured as User*x*-PC or as specified by your instructor. The computer is referred to as UserA-PC in this lab.

- A second physical computer or virtual machine running Windows 7 that is configured as User*x*-PC or as specified by your instructor. Your instructor may pair you with a partner for this lab. This computer is referred to as UserB-PC in this lab.

- The bootable CD/ISO created in Lab 2.1

Estimated completion time: **60 minutes**

Activity Background

In most large organizations, imaging is used to configure new computers. This allows the organization to have a standard configuration that is applied to all computers. A standard configuration simplifies troubleshooting and makes it easier to respond to help desk requests from users. In addition, an image can include applications, which avoids the need to manually install applications on each computer after the operating system is installed.

This activity uses two computers that are referred to as UserA-PC and UserB-PC.

Activity

1. Log on to UserB-PC.

2. Change the current network on UserB-PC to a work network to lower security settings and allow file sharing on the network, as detailed in the following steps:

    a. Click **Start** and click **Control Panel**.

    b. Under Network and Internet, click **View network status and tasks**.

    c. In Network and Sharing Center, under View your active networks, click **Public network**.

    d. In the Set Network Location window, click **Work network**.

    e. Click **Close**.

    f. Close all open windows.

3. Create a share for storing images accessed over the network, as detailed in the following steps:

    a. Click **Start**, click **Computer**, and then double-click **Local Disk (C:)**.

    b. In the toolbar, click **New folder**, type **WIMshare**, and press **Enter**.

    c. Right-click **WIMshare**, point to **Share with**, and click **Specific people**.

    d. In the File Sharing window, in the drop-down list, click **Everyone**, and then click **Add**.

    e. In the Permission Level column, next to Everyone, select Read/Write, and then click **Share**.

    f. Take note of the UNC path to the shared folder and then click **Done**.

    g. Close all open windows

4. Log on to UserA-PC

5. Download and install Open Office, as detailed in the following steps:

    a. On the taskbar, click **Internet Explorer**.

    b. In the address bar, type **http://www.openoffice.org** and press **Enter**.

    c. Click **I want to download OpenOffice.org** and then click **Download now!**.

d. Wait a few moments for the download to begin automatically. You may need to allow Internet Explorer to download the file by clicking a yellow security bar that appears at the top of the Web page.

e. In the File Download – Security Warning window, click **Run**. This is a large file and may take several minutes to download.

f. In the User Account Control window, click **Yes** to allow the installation.

g. In the OpenOffice.org 3.2 Installation Preparation window, click **Next** and then click **Unpack**.

h. In the OpenOffice.org 3.2 – Installation Wizard window, click **Next**.

i. On the Customer Information page, click **Next**.

j. On the Setup Type page, click **Next**.

k. On the Ready to Install the Program page, click **Install**.

l. On the Installation Wizard Completed page, click **Finish**.

m. Close all open windows.

6. Place the Windows PE boot CD in UserA-PC.

7. Run Sysprep to prepare the computer to be imaged, shown in Figure 2-2, as detailed in the following steps:

a. Click Windows Explorer on the taskbar.

b. In the Address bar, type `C:\Windows\System32\sysprep` and press **Enter**.

c. Double-click **sysprep**.

d. In the System Cleanup Action box, select **Enter System Out-of-Box Experience (OOBE)**. This option is used to prepare a computer for delivery to an end user.

e. Check the **Generalize** check box. This option removes computer-specific information such as SID and computer name.

f. In the Shutdown Options box, select **Shutdown**. This turns off the computer after Sysprep is complete, so that an image can be captured from it.

g. Click **OK** and wait a few minutes for Sysprep to complete and your computer to shut down.

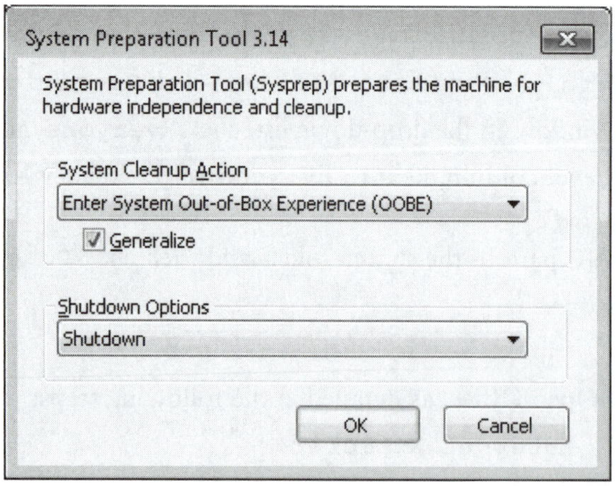

Figure 2-2 Sysprep
© Cengage Learning 2012

8. Start UserA-PC and boot from CD. The specific steps for booting from CD will vary depending on the computer you are using.

9. When prompted, **Press any key to boot from CD or DVD**.

10. At the command prompt, type **net use Z: \\UserB-PC\WIMshare /user:UserB -PC\UserB** and press **Enter**.

11. When prompted for the password, type **password** and press **Enter**.

12. Type **E:\ImageX.exe /capture D:\ Z:\Win7.wim "Win7"** and press **Enter**, as shown in Figure 2-3.

13. Turn off UserA-PC.

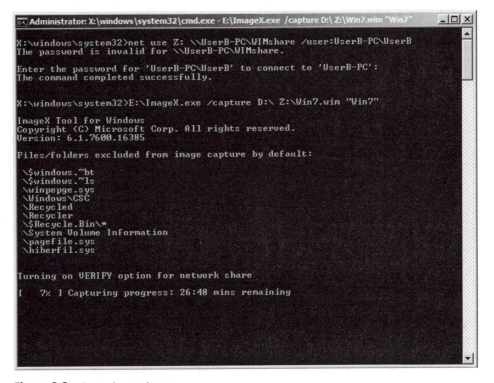

Figure 2-3 Capturing an image
© *Cengage Learning 2012*

Certification Objectives

Objectives for MCTS Exam #70-680: Windows 7, Configuring:

- Deploying Windows 7: Capture a system image
- Deploying Windows 7: Prepare a system image for deployment

Review Questions

1. Why is it important to run Sysprep before taking an image of a computer running Windows 7?

2. Can applications be included as part of a image?

3. Which command is used to create a drive mapping to a network share in Windows PE?

4. Which options need to be specified for ImageX when capturing an image?

5. In this lab, you created an image and stored it on a network share. Are there other locations in which you could store an image?

Lab 2.3: Applying a Windows 7 Image

Objectives

The objective of this activity is to apply a Windows 7 image to a new computer.

Materials Required

This lab requires the following:

- A physical computer or virtual machine running Windows 7 that is configured as Userx-PC or as specified by your instructor. The computer is referred to as UserA-PC in this lab.

- A second physical computer or virtual machine running Windows 7 that is configured as Userx-PC or as specified by your instructor. Your instructor may pair you with a partner for this lab. This computer is referred to as UserB-PC in this lab.

- The bootable CD/ISO created in Lab 2.1

- Product key for Windows 7

- Lab 2.2 completed

Estimated completion time: **60 minutes**

Activity Background

After a standardized image is created and stored in a network location, it can be applied to new computers or as an alternative to upgrading existing computers. The image deployment process destroys all existing data on the computer. Diskpart is used to prepare the disk to accept the image.

Activity

1. Start UserA-PC and boot from CD. The specific steps for booting from CD will vary depending on the computer you are using.

2. When prompted, press any key to boot from CD or DVD.

3. At the command prompt, type **diskpart** and press **Enter**.

4. Type **select disk 0** and press **Enter**.

5. Type **clean** and press **Enter**. This removes existing disk partitions.

6. Create a system partition, shown in Figure 2-4, as detailed in the following steps:

    a. Type **create partition primary size=300** and press **Enter**.

    b. Type **format quick fs=ntfs label="System"** and press **Enter**.

    c. Type **assign letter="S"** and press **Enter**.

    d. Type **active** and press **Enter**.

7. Create a partition for the operating system and applications, as detailed in the following steps:

    a. Type **create partition primary** and press **Enter**.

    b. Type **format quick fs=ntfs label="Windows"** and press **Enter**.

    c. Type **assign letter="W"** and press **Enter**.

8. Type **exit** and press **Enter**.

9. Type **net use Z: \\UserB-PC\WIMshare /user:UserB-PC\UserB** and press **Enter**.

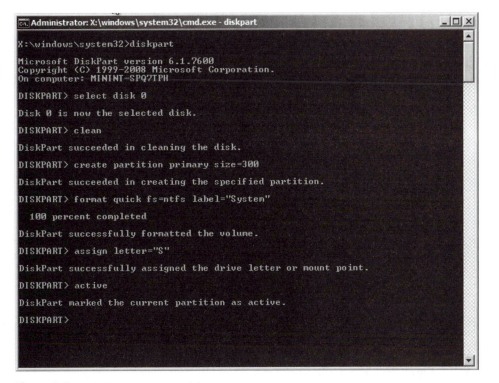

Figure 2-4   Creating a system partition
© Cengage Learning 2012

10. When prompted for the password, type **password** and press **Enter**.

11. Type **E:\ImageX.exe /apply Z:\Win7.wim "Win7" W:** and press **Enter**.

12. Type **bcdboot W:\Windows\ /l en-US** and press **Enter**. This creates the boot sector and copies the system files to the system partition. You can review the files created on the system partition by changing to the drive letter S: and using the **dir /ah** command, which shows hidden files.

13. Type **exit** and press **Enter**.

14. Click **Next** to accept the default settings for Country or region, Time and currency, and keyboard layout.

15. In the Type a user name box, type **NewUserA**.

16. In the Type a computer name box, type **UserA-PC** and then click **Next**.

17. On the Set a password for your account page, in the Type a password and Retype your password boxes, type **password**.

18. In the Type a password hint box, type **Just a simple password** and then click **Next**.

19. If prompted for a product key, type the product key provided by your instructor and then click **Next**.

20. Select the **I accept the license terms** check box and then click **Next**.

21. On the Help protect your computer and improve Windows automatically page, click **Use recommended settings**.

22. Click **Next** to accept the existing time zone information.

23. Click **Public network**.

24. Click the **Start** button. Notice that you are automatically logged on as NewUserA

25. Log off and then log on as **UserA**.

26. Remove NewUserA, as detailed in the following steps:

    a. Click **Start** and then click **Control Panel**.

    b. Under User Accounts and Family Safety, click **Add or remove user accounts**.

    c. Click **NewUserA** and then click **Delete the account**.

    d. In the Delete Account window, click **Delete Files**.

    e. In the Confirm Deletion window, click **Delete Account**.

    f. Close the Manage Accounts Window.

27. Reverse the Lab 2.2 changes on UserB-PC, as detailed in the following steps:

    a. Click **Start** and click **Control Panel**.

    b. Under Network and Internet, click **View network status and tasks**.

    c. In the Network and Sharing Center, under View your active networks, click **Work network**.

    d. In the Set Network Location window, click **Public network**.

    e. Click **Close**.

    f. Close all open windows.

Certification Objectives

Objectives for MCTS Exam #70-680: Windows 7, Configuring:

- Deploying Windows 7: Deploy a system image

Review Questions

1. Why is Windows PE used to perform the imaging process?

2. Is it necessary to create new partitions as part of the imaging process?

3. When Windows PE boots, the X: drive has the Windows PE system files. Why are you running ImageX from the E: drive?

4. When you create partitions as part of the imaging process, which drive letters should you assign to those partitions?

5. Which utility is used to make the hard drive bootable after partitioning is complete?

Lab 2.4: Performing an Unattended Installation of Windows 7

Objectives

The objective of this activity is to perform an unattended installation of Windows 7. Such an installation requires no user interaction.

Materials Required

This lab requires the following:

- A physical computer or virtual machine running Windows 7 that is configured as User*x*-PC or as specified by your instructor

- The Windows Automated Installation Kit for Windows 7 already installed

- A distribution share already created at C:\wininstall\sources with the installation files for Windows 7 copied there

- A spare computer or virtual machine on which to perform the unattended installation
- If performing the unattended installation on a physical computer, a USB key to hold the autounattend.xml file

Estimated completion time: **60 minutes**

Activity Background

In a smaller organization, you may not want to invest the time and effort to create a standardized operating system image. To simplify the deployment process without creating an operating system image, you can automate the installation of Windows 7, including disk partitioning operations. Setup.exe searches removable storage to find an autounattend.xml file during setup.

Activity

1. Log on to User*x*-PC.

2. Click **Start**, point to **All Programs**, click **Microsoft Windows AIK**, and click **Windows System Image Manager**.

3. Select a catalog file that matches the edition of Windows 7 being installed, as detailed in the following steps:

   a. In the Windows Image page, right-click the root node, and click **Select Windows Image**.

   b. In the Select a Windows Image window, browse to **C:\wininstall\sources**, click the catalog file (for example, install_Windows 7 Professional.clg) that matches your version of Windows 7, and click **Open**.

4. Create a new answer file, as detailed in the following steps:

   a. In the Answer File pane, right-click **Untitled** and click **New Answer File**.

   b. If prompted to save changes, click **No**.

5. Add required windowsPE settings to the answer file, as detailed in the following steps:

   a. In the Windows Image pane, expand **Components**, right-click *arch*_**Microsoft-Windows-International-Core-WinPE**_*version*_**neutral**, and click **Add Setting to Pass 1 windowsPE**. You need to select the appropriate settings for the processor architecture you are using. If you are installing the 64-bit version of Windows 7, then use the amd64 settings. If you are installing the 32-bit version of Windows 7, then use the x86 settings.

   b. In the Answer File pane, under 1 windowsPE, expand *arch*_**Microsoft-Windows-International-Core-WinPE**_*version*_**neutral**.

   c. In the right-pane, to the right of UILanguage, type **en-us** as shown in Figure 2-5.

   d. In the Answer File pane, click **SetupUILanguage**.

   e. In the right-pane, to the right of UILanguage, type **en-us**.

   f. In the Windows Image pane, right-click *arch*_**Microsoft-Windows-Setup_**_*version*_**neutral**, and click **Add Setting to Pass 1 windowsPE**.

   g. In the Answer File pane, expand *arch*_**Microsoft-Windows-Setup_**_*version*_**neutral**, and expand **UserData**.

   h. In the right-pane, to the right of AcceptEula, select **true**.

   i. In the Answer File pane, click **ProductKey**, and then in the right pane, next to Key, type your product key.

   j. In the Answer File pane, expand **ImageInstall**, and then click **OSImage**.

   k. In the right pane, next to InstallToAvailablePartition, select **true**.

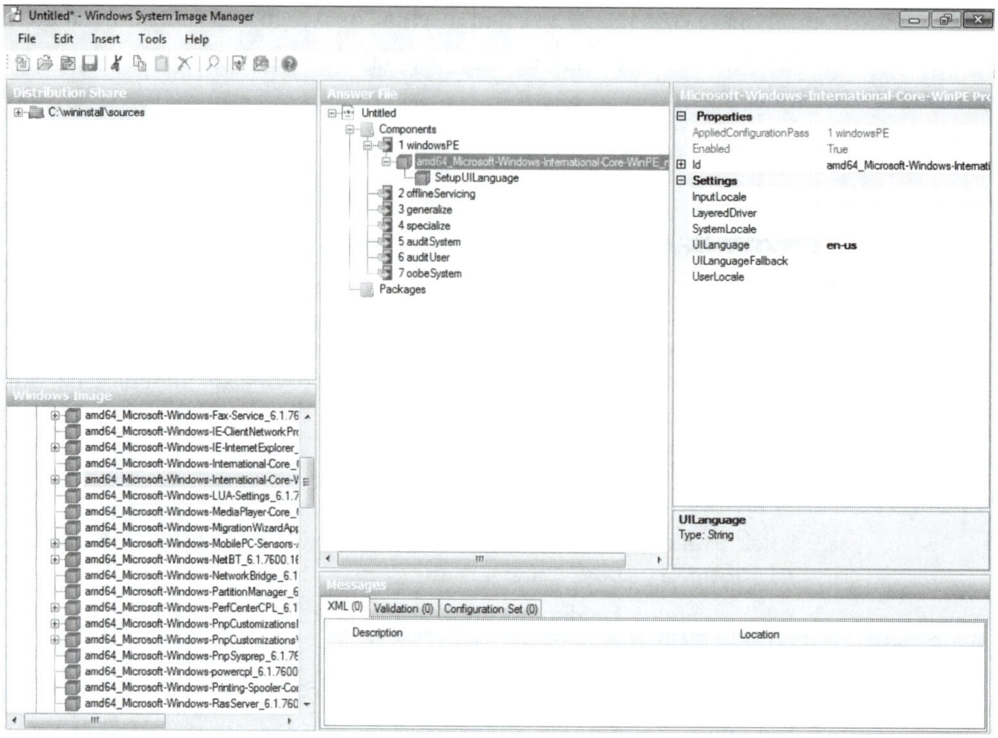

Figure 2-5   Windows System Image Manager
© Cengage Learning 2012

6. Add commands to wipe the hard disk and create new partitions, as detailed in the following steps:

    a. In the Windows Image pane, expand **DiskConfiguration**, right-click **Disk**, and click **Add Setting to Pass 1 windowsPE**.

    b. In the right pane, next to DiskID, type **0**.

    c. In the right pane, next to WillWipeDisk, select **true**.

    d. In the Answer File pane, expand **Disk**, right-click **CreatePartition**, and click **Insert New CreatePartition**. This will be the system partition.

    e. In the right pane, next to Order, type **1**.

    f. In the right pane, next to Size, type **200**.

    g. In the right pane, next to Type, select **Primary**.

    h. In the Answer File pane, right-click **CreatePartition**, and click **Insert New CreatePartition**. This will be the Windows partition.

    i. In the right pane, next to Extend, select **true**.

    j. In the right pane, next to Order, type **2**.

    k. In the right pane, next to Type, select **Primary**.

7. Format the new partitions, as detailed in the following steps:

    a. In the Answer File pane, right-click **ModifyPartitions** and click **Insert New ModifyPartition**. This will prepare the system partition.

    b. In the right pane, next to Active, select **true**.

    c. In the right pane, next to Format, select **NTFS**.

    d. In the right pane, next to Label, type **System**.

    e. In the right pane, next to Letter, select **S**.

    f. In the right pane, next to Order, select **1**.

    g. In the right pane, next to PartitionID, type **1**.

    h. In the Answer File pane, right-click **ModifyPartitions** and click **Insert New ModifyPartition**. This will prepare the Windows partition.

    i. In the right pane, next to Format, select **NTFS**.

    j. In the right pane, next to Label, type **Windows**.

    k. In the right pane, next to Letter, select **C**.

    l. In the right pane, next to Order, select **2**.

   m. In the right pane, next to PartitionID, type **2**.

8. Add required specialize settings to the answer file, as detailed in the following steps:

    a. In the Windows Image pane, right-click **arch_Microsoft-Windows-Shell-Setup_version_neutral**, and click **Add Setting to Pass 4 specialize**.

    b. In the right pane, next to ProductKey, type your product key.

    c. In the right pane, next to ComputerName, type *****.

9. Add required oobeSystem settings to the answer file, as detailed in the following steps:

    a. In the Windows Image pane, right-click **arch_Microsoft-Windows-International-Core_version_neutral**, and click **Add Setting to Pass 7 oobeSystem**.

    b. In the right pane, next to InputLocale, type **en-us**.

    c. In the right pane, next to SystemLocale, type **en-us**.

    d. In the right pane, next to UILanguage, type **en-us**.

    e. In the right pane, next to UserLocale, type **en-us**.

    f. In the Windows Image pane, right-click **arch_Microsoft-Windows-Shell-Setup_version_neutral**, and click **Add Setting to Pass 7 oobeSystem**.

    g. In the right pane, next to TimeZone, type your time zone, for example, Central Standard Time. You can view a complete list of available time zones by running tzutil /l at a command prompt.

    h. In the Answer File pane, expand **arch_Microsoft-Windows-Shell-Setup_version_neutral** and click **OOBE**.

    i. In the right pane, next to HideEULAPage, select **true**.

    j. In the right pane, next to NetworkLocation, select **Home**.

    k. In the right pane, next to ProtectYourPC, type **1**.

    l. In the Answer File pane, click expand **UserAccounts** and click **AdministratorPassword**.

   m. In the right pane, next to Value, type **password**.

    n. In the Answer File pane, right-click **LocalAccounts** and click **Insert New LocalAccount**.

    o. In the right-pane, next to DisplayName, type **DefaultUser**.

    p. In the right pane, next to Group, type **Administrators**.

    q. In the right pane, next to Name, type **DefaultUser**.

    r. In the Answer File pane, expand **LocalAccount[Name="DefaultUser"]** and click **Password**.

    s. In the right pane, next to Value, type **password**.

10. Save the answer file to removable storage, as detailed in the following steps:

    a. Click **File** and then click **Save Answer file As**.

    b. Browse to removable storage that you can move to the computer where you will be performing the unattended installation of Windows 7. If you are using a physical computer for the unattended installation, use a USB drive. If you are using a virtual machine for the unattended installation, use a virtual floppy disk.

    c. In the File name box, type **autounattend** and then click **Save**.

11. Perform an unattended installation on the spare computer, as detailed in the following steps:

    a. On the spare computer or virtual machine, insert the removable storage with the autounattend.xml file.

    b. Insert the Windows 7 Installation DVD.

    c. Boot the computer from DVD.

    d. If prompted, **Press any key to boot from CD or DVD**. You will only be prompted if a bootable partition already exists on the hard drive.

    e. Wait for the installation to complete. This can take up to 30 minutes.

    f. When the installation completes, log in as **LocalAdmin** with a password of **password**.

Certification Objectives

Objectives for MCTS Exam #70-680: Windows 7, Configuring:

• Installing, Upgrading, and Migrating to Windows 7: Perform a clean installation

Review Questions

1. Is it necessary to create new partitions when performing an unattended installation on a new PC?

2. Which program is used to create an answer file for an unattended installation?

3. When booting from the Windows 7 installation DVD, where does the setup program look for autounattend.xml?

4. The specialize and oobeSystem configuration passes read their unattended settings from unattend.xml rather than from autounattend.xml. How did the settings you configured in autounattend.xml get passed to the specialize and oobeSystem configuration passes?

5. Why should you use the * to specify a random computer name in your answer file?

CHAPTER THREE

USING THE SYSTEM UTILITIES

Labs included in this chapter:

- Lab 3.1 Modifying Display Settings
- Lab 3.2 Adding, Repairing, and Removing Programs
- Lab 3.3 Creating a Scheduled Task
- Lab 3.4 Creating a Custom MMC Console

Microsoft MCTS Exam #70-680 Objectives

Objective	Lab
Configure devices	3.1
Configure application compatibility	3.2
Monitor systems	3.3, 3.4

Lab 3.1: Modifying Display Settings

Objectives

The object of this activity is to modify the display setting for Windows 7.

Materials Required

This lab requires the following:

- A physical computer or virtual machine running Windows 7 that is configured as User*x*-PC or as specified by your instructor

Estimated completion time: **15 minutes**

Activity Background

Display settings are an integral part of the user experience in Windows 7. Many users attempt to modify the display settings on their computer and a technician needs to understand what the options are to resolve any problems that may occur. The best picture quality for an LCD monitor is obtained when the display resolution used by Windows 7 matches the native display resolution of the monitor. In some cases, performance issues can be resolved by lowering the image quality of the display.

Activity

1. Log on to User*x*-PC.

2. Modify the screen resolution, as detailed in the following steps:

   a. On the Desktop, right-click an open area and click **Screen resolution**. Your screen should resemble Figure 3-1.

   b. Take note of the current setting in the Resolution box: _____

   c. In the Resolution box, select **800 x 600** and then click **Apply**.

   d. In the Display Settings window, click **Keep changes**.

   e. Take a few moments to notice how the display has changed.

   f. In the Resolution box, select the resolution noted in Step 2b and then click **Apply**.

3. In the upper-right corner of the Screen Resolution window, click **Identify**.

4. Enlarge text without changing the screen resolution, as detailed in the following steps:

   a. In the Screen Resolution window, click the **Make text and other items larger or smaller** link.

   b. Take note of the current setting and click **Larger - 150%** and click **Apply**.

   c. In the Microsoft Windows window, click **Log off now**.

   d. Log on to User*x*-PC.

   e. Take a few moments to notice how the display has changed.

5. Fine-tune display settings for reading text, as detailed in the following steps:

   a. On the Desktop, right-click an open area and click **Screen resolution**.

   b. In the Screen Resolution window, click the **Make text and other items larger or smaller** link.

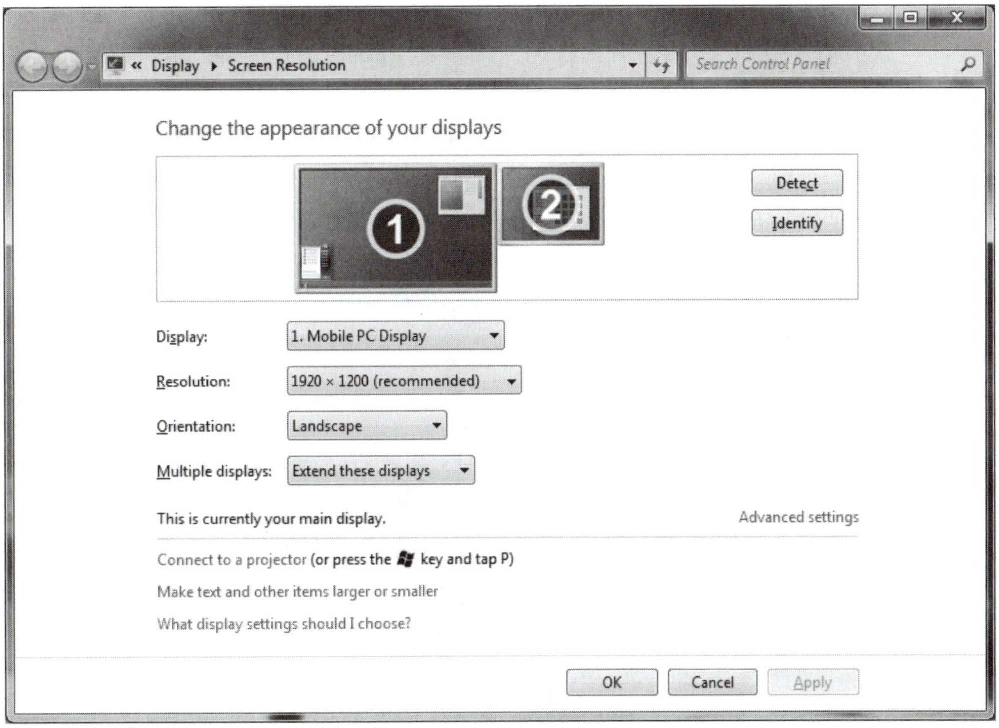

Figure 3-1 Changing screen resolution
© Cengage Learning 2012

    c. In the Display window, click **Adjust ClearType** text.

    d. In the ClearType Text Tuner window, clear the **Turn on ClearType** check box. Notice how the text appearance changes.

    e. Click **Next** and the resolution of your monitor is verified as being native resolution.

    f. Click **Next** and, on each of the next four screens, select the text sample that looks best and click **Next**.

    g. Click **Finish**.

6. Return the text size to the original settings, as detailed in the following steps:

    a. In the Display window, click the original text size and click **Apply**.

    b. In the Microsoft Windows window, click **Log off now**.

    c. Log on to User*x*-PC.

7. Modify the desktop theme, as detailed in the following steps:

    a. On the Desktop, right-click an open area and click **Personalize**. Your screen should resemble Figure 3-2.

    b. Scroll through the list of available themes, and then click **Characters**.

    c. Take note of the changed settings for Desktop Background, Sounds.

8. Modify the screen saver, as detailed in the following steps:

    a. In the Personalization window, click **Screen Saver**.

    b. In the Screen saver area, select **Bubbles**.

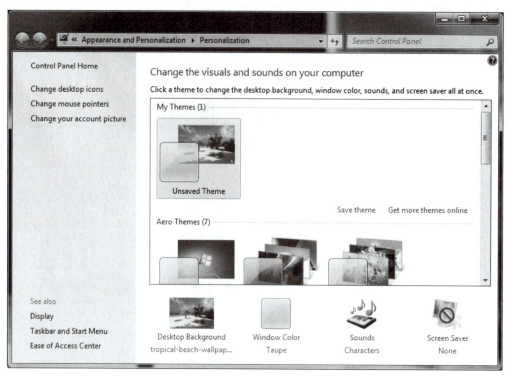

Figure 3-2   Personalizing Windows 7 display settings
© Cengage Learning 2012

   c. In the Wait box, type **2**.

   d. Select the **On resume, display logon screen** check box and click **OK**.

   e. Wait two minutes for the screensaver to start.

   f. After the screen saver starts, press any key to stop the screen saver.

   g. Log on to User*x*-PC.

   h. Take note of any desktop changes that have occurred.

   i. In the Personalization window, click **Screen Saver**.

   j. In the Screen saver area, select **(None)**, clear the **On resume, display logon screen** check box, and click **OK**.

9. Customize the background, as detailed in the following steps:

   a. In the Personalization windows, click **Desktop Background**.

   b. Copy a picture file to the Pictures library. If necessary, you can use Internet Explorer and search Google for **free wallpaper** to find an appropriate picture.

   c. In the Desktop Background window, click **Browse**, expand **Libraries**, click **Pictures**, and click **OK**.

   d. Click the picture you downloaded and saved to the Pictures library, and click **Save changes**.

   e. Close the Personalization window.

Certification Objectives

Objectives for MCTS Exam #70-680: Windows 7, Configuring:

• Configuring Hardware and Applications: Configure devices

Review Questions

1. Why would you choose to use a screen saver?

2. Why would you force the logon screen to be displayed after a certain number of minutes?

3. When a display is configured to use less than its native resolution, how does text appear?

4. When a display is configured to use a larger font size, how is the display affected?

5. Why would you want to identify the monitors attached to your computer?

Lab 3.2: Adding, Repairing, and Removing Programs

Objectives

The objective of this activity is add, repair, and remove a program.

Materials Required

This lab requires the following:

- A physical computer or virtual machine running Windows 7 that is configured as User*x*-PC or as specified by your instructor

- Connectivity to the Internet

Estimated completion time: **15 minutes**

Activity Background

A common task for desktop support personnel is adding, repairing, and removing programs. Even though large organizations often have automated methods for performing new installations of applications, when troubleshooting is required, a technician is often required to install, repair, and remove applications manually. One commonly used application is Adobe Reader, which is used for viewing PDF files. In this lab, you will install, repair, and remove Adobe Reader.

Activity

1. Log on to User*x*-PC.

2. Download and install Adobe Reader, as detailed in the following steps:

   a. On the taskbar, click **Internet Explorer**.

   b. In the address bar, type **http://www.adobe.com** and press **Enter**.

   c. Scroll down, and under Download, click **Adobe Reader**.

   d. On the Adobe Reader download page, uncheck the **Include in your download** check box. This prevents Google Toolbar for IE from being installed.

   e. Scroll down and click **Download now**.

   f. Click the **yellow information bar** at the top of the Web page, and then click **Install This Add-on for All Users on This Computer**. This allows the Adobe Download Manager to be installed and continue the installation process.

   g. In the User Account Control window, click **Yes** to allow the installation of Adobe Download Manager.

   h. Wait while Adobe Download Manager installs Acrobat Reader.

   i. When the installation of Acrobat Reader is complete, click **Close Download Manager**.

   j. Close Internet Explorer.

3. View a PDF document, as detailed in the following steps:

   a. Click **Start** and click **Computer**.

   b. Browse to **C:\Program Files (x86)\Adobe\Reader 9.0\Resource** and double-click **ENUtxt.pdf**.

   c. In the Adobe Reader – License Agreement window, click **Accept**.

   d. A single-page document is displayed with text only in the lower-left corner.

   e. Close Adobe Reader.

   f. Leave Windows Explorer open.

4. You now will break the file association for PDF from Adobe Reader to simulate breaking the application. File associations are sometimes lost because of malware or when conflicting applications are removed.

   a. Click **Start** and click **Default Programs**.

   b. In the Default Programs window, click **Associate a file type or protocol with a program**.

   c. In the Set Associations window, scroll down, click **.pdf**, and click **Change program**.

   d. In the Open with window, click **Browse**.

   e. In the File name box, type **C:\Windows\Notepad.exe** and click **Open**.

   f. In the Open with window, with Notepad selected, click **OK**.

   g. In the Set Associations window, click **Close**.

   h. Close the Default Programs window.

   i. In Windows Explorer, notice that the icon for ENUtxt.pdf has changed.

   j. Double-click **ENUtxt.pdf**.

   k. Notice that the content is not displayed correctly by Notepad.

   l. Close Notepad.

5. Repair Adobe Reader by using the installation files cached on your hard drive, as detailed in the following steps:

   a. Click **Start** and click **Control Panel**.

   b. Under Programs, click **Uninstall a program**. Your screen should resemble Figure 3-3.

   c. In the list of programs, right-click **Adobe Reader *versionnumber*** and click **Change**.

   d. In the Adobe Reader Setup window, click **Next**.

   e. On the Program Maintenance page, confirm that **Repair** is selected, and then click **Next**.

   f. On the Ready to Repair the Program page, click **Install**.

   g. When the repair is complete, click **Finish**.

   h. Close the Programs and Features window.

6. Test whether the file association is fixed, as detailed in the following steps:

   a. In Windows Explorer, notice that the icon for ENUtxt.pdf has changed.

   b. Double-click **ENUtxt.pdf**.

   c. Notice that the content is still displayed in Notepad. In many cases, a repair will fix file association problems, but not this in this instance. The repair performed would have fixed any missing program files.

   d. Close Notepad.

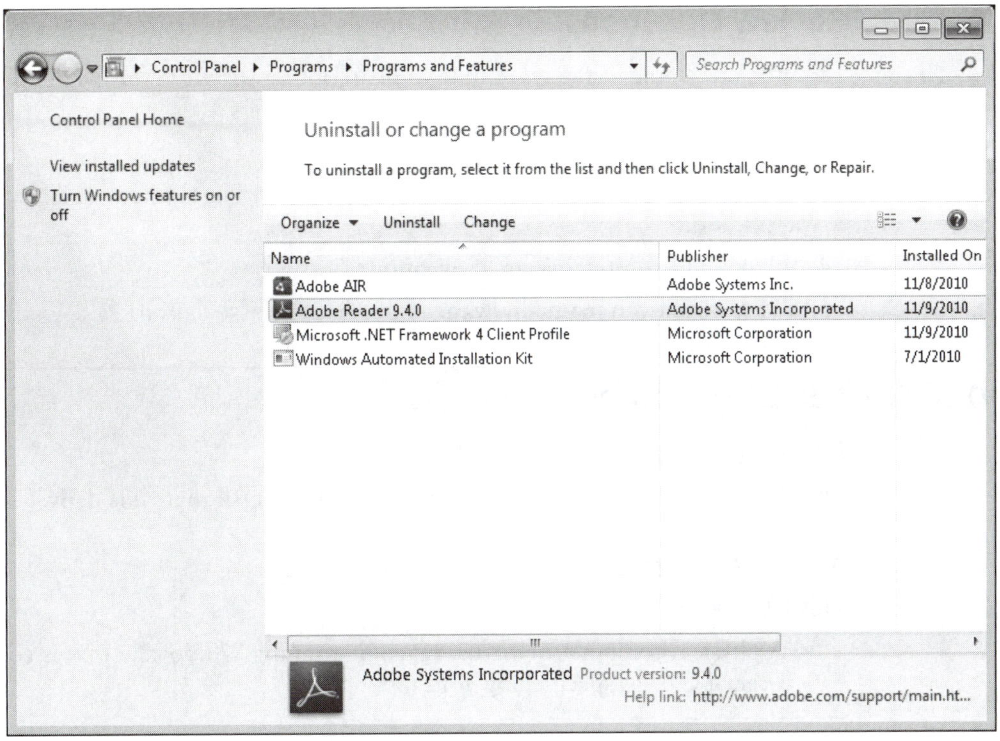

Figure 3-3   Uninstall or change a program
© *Cengage Learning 2012*

7. Reconfigure the file association for PDF files, as detailed in the following steps:

   a. Right-click **ENUtxt.pdf**, point to **Open with**, and click **Choose default program**.

   b. Under Recommended Programs, click **Adobe Reader *versionnumber***, verify that the **Always use the selected program to open this kind of file** check box is selected, and then click **OK**.

   c. The PDF file now opens properly in Adobe Reader.

   d. Close all open windows.

8. Remove Adobe Reader, as detailed in the following steps:

   a. Click **Start** and click **Control Panel**.

   b. Under Programs, click **Uninstall a program**.

   c. In the list of programs, right-click **Adobe Reader *versionnumber*** and click **Uninstall**.

   d. Click **Yes** to confirm that you want to remove Adobe Reader.

   e. In the User Account Control window, click **Yes**.

   f. Wait for Adobe Reader to be uninstalled.

   g. Click **Yes** to restart your computer.

Certification Objectives

Objectives for MCTS Exam #70-680: Windows 7, Configuring:

• Configuring Hardware and Applications: Configure application compatibility

Review Questions

1. What are some of the ways that you can obtain software for installation in a corporate environment?

2. Why might you need to repair an application?

3. Why do you not need a copy of the application installation media when repairing an application?

4. Why would you remove an application?

5. When would you manually want to define a file association?

Lab 3.3: Creating a Scheduled Task

Objectives

The objective of this activity is to create a scheduled task that runs daily.

Materials Required

This lab requires the following:

- A physical computer or virtual machine running Windows 7 that is configured as User*x*-PC or as specified by your instructor

Estimated completion time: **60 minutes**

Activity Background

Windows 7 uses scheduled tasks to perform a number of system maintenance tasks and operations on a regular basis. You also have the option to create scheduled tasks to perform system maintenance at regular intervals. One of the common causes of system instability is a Windows computer not being rebooted for extended periods of time. In this lab, you will create a scheduled task that ensures the computer is rebooted at least once per week.

Activity

1. Log on to User*x*-PC.
2. Click **Start** and click **Control Panel**.
3. Click **System and Security** and click **Administrative Tools**.
4. Double-click **Task Scheduler**.
5. Click **Task Scheduler Library**. This is the list of tasks you have created. None are listed.
6. Expand **Task Scheduler Library**, expand **Microsoft**, expand **Windows**, and click **Defrag**.
7. Notice that there is a task used by Windows to defragment the hard drive every Wednesday at 1 a.m.
8. In the left pane, click **CertificateServicesClient**.
9. Notice that several tasks are defined related to the Certificate Services Client.
10. In the left pane, click **Shell**.
11. Notice that two tasks are listed.

12. Click the **View** menu and click **Show Hidden Tasks**. This option was enabled by default because you are logged on as an administrative user. You have now disabled it.

13. Notice that the tasks in the Shell folder are no longer visible.

14. Click the **View** menu and click **Show Hidden Tasks** to make the hidden tasks visible again.

15. In the left pane, click **Task Scheduler Library**.

16. In the Actions pane, click **Create Task**.

17. In the Name box, type **Weekly Reboot**.

18. Click **Change User or Group**, type **SYSTEM**, click **Check Names**, and click **OK**. Notice the dimmed options, as shown in Figure 3-4.

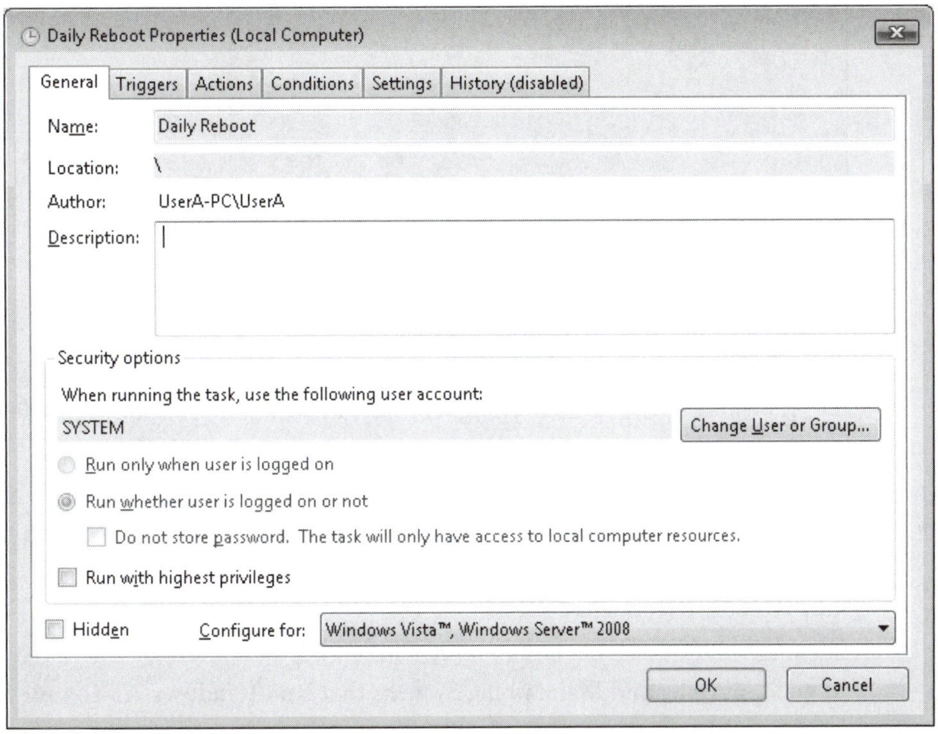

Figure 3-4   General tab of a scheduled task
© *Cengage Learning 2012*

19. Click the **Triggers** tab and click **New**.

20. In the Settings area, click **Weekly**.

21. Select the **Sunday** check box.

22. Set the Start time as **11:00:00 PM** and click **OK**.

23. Click the **Actions** tab and click **New**.

24. In the Program/Script box, type **C:\Windows\System32\shutdown.exe**.

25. In the Add Arguments box, type **-r -t 30**, as shown in Figure 3-5, and click **OK**.

26. Click the **Conditions** tab.

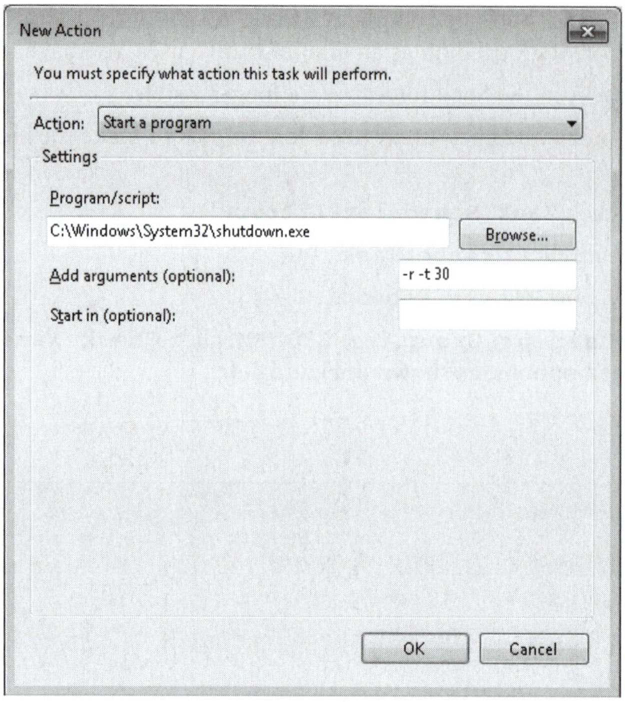

Figure 3-5 Adding an action to a scheduled task
© *Cengage Learning 2012*

27. Select the **Start the task only if the computer is idle for** check box. Take note of the default settings for how the computer responds to idle time.

28. Click the **Settings** tab, review the available settings, and click **OK**.

29. To test the task configuration, right-click **Weekly Reboot** and click **Run**.

30. Wait for the computer to restart in 30 seconds.

Certification Objectives

Objectives for MCTS Exam #70-680: Windows 7, Configuring:

• Monitoring and Maintaining Systems that Run Windows 7: Monitor Systems

Review Questions

1. In addition to scheduling a task weekly, what other options are available when beginning a task on a schedule?

2. In addition to beginning a task on a schedule, what other options are available to trigger a task?

3. This lab ran a specific executable file to perform a specific task. How would you complete a more complex task by using a scheduled task?

4. For the task configured in this lab, why is it important that the task starts only when the computer is idle?

5. Why were the options related to user logon dimmed when SYSTEM was selected as the user account to run the scheduled task? When is it appropriate to use this account?

Lab 3.4: Creating a Custom MMC Console

Objectives

The objective of this activity is to create a custom MMC console that includes snap-ins commonly used by an administrator.

Materials Required

This lab requires the following:

- A physical computer or virtual machine running Windows 7 that is configured as User*x*-PC or as specified by your instructor

Estimated completion time: **60 minutes**

Activity Background

In Control Panel, you have access to administrative tools. Most of the administrative tools are MMC consoles with a single snap-in. Each snap-in provides specific functionality. For example, the Event Viewer snap-in provides the ability to look at the contents of the event logs. The Event Viewer snap-in is included in the Event Viewer administrative tool and the Computer Management administrative tool. You can create custom MMC consoles that include the snap-ins you most commonly use. One of the commonly used snap-ins that is not available in any of the administrative tools is the Certificates snap-in. In this lab, you will create a custom MMC console that includes the Certificates snap-in and explores some of the folders in the certificates snap-in.

Activity

1. Log on to User*x*-PC.

2. Create a custom MMC console named Security Console, as detailed in the following steps:

   a. Click **Start**, type **mmc** in the Search Programs and Files box, and press **Enter**.

   b. In the User Account Control window, click **Yes**.

   c. In the Console1 window, click the **File** menu and click **Save As**.

   d. Take note of the default save location, in the File name box, type **Security Console.msc**, and then click **Save**.

   e. Close the Security Console window.

3. Add snap-ins to the Security Console, as detailed in the following steps:

   a. Click **Start**, type **Security** in the Search Programs and Files box, and then click **Security Console.msc**.

   b. In the User Account Control window, click **Yes**.

   c. In the Security Console window, click the **File** menu and click **Add/Remove Snap-in**.

   d. In the Available snap-ins list, double-click **Group Policy Object Editor**, and click **Finish** to accept the default Local Computer Group Policy Object.

   e. In the Available snap-ins list, double-click **Local Users and Groups**, and click **Finish** to accept the default of managing the local computer.

   f. In the Available snap-ins list, double-click **Windows Firewall with Advanced Security**, and click **Finish** to accept the default of managing the local computer.

g. In the Add or Remove Snap-ins window, click **OK**.

h. Notice that all three snap-ins are available for use in this console, as shown in Figure 3-6.

i. Close the Security Console window, and click **Yes** to save the console settings.

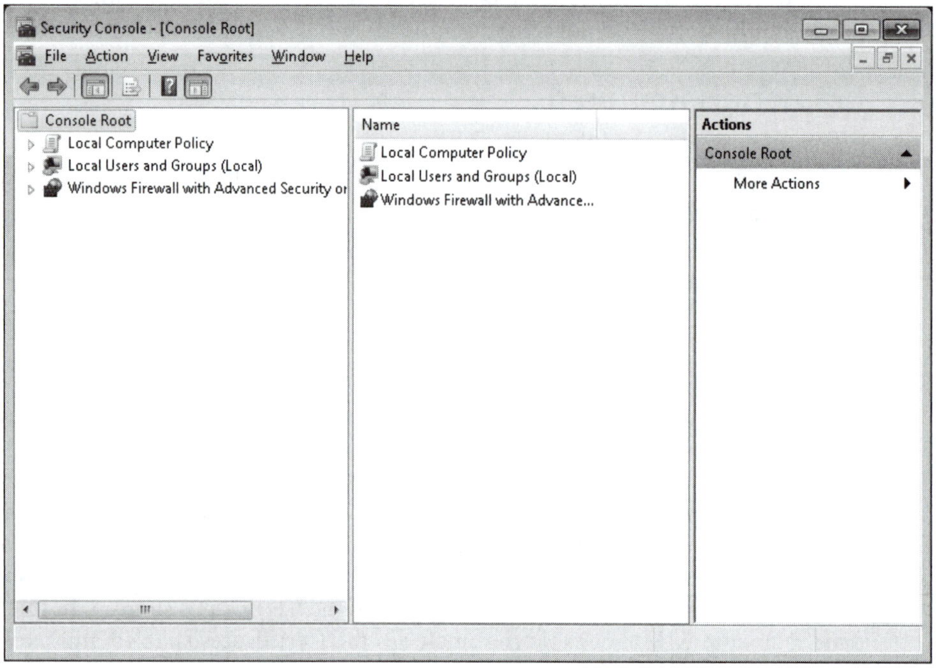

Figure 3-6 Custom MMC console
© Cengage Learning 2012

4. Add the Certificates snap-in to the Security Console, as detailed in the following steps:

a. Click **Start**, type **Security** in the Search Programs and Files box, and then click **Security Console.msc**.

b. In the User Account Control window, click **Yes**.

c. In the Security Console window, click the **File** menu and click **Add/Remove Snap-in**.

d. In the Available snap-ins list, double-click **Certificates**, and click **Finish** to accept the default of managing certificates for My user account.

e. In the Available snap-ins list, double-click **Certificates**, click **Computer account**, and click **Next**.

f. Click **Finish** to accept the default of managing certificates for the local computer.

g. In the Add or Remove Snap-ins window, click **OK**.

5. Explore the Certificates snap-in, as detailed in the following steps:

a. In the left pane, expand **Certificates - Current User** and click **Personal**. This is where certificates associated with the user are stored.

b. In the left pane, expand **Trusted Root Certification Authorities** and click **Certificates**. This is the list of certification authorities from which your computer will trust certificates.

c. In the left pane, expand **Untrusted Certificates** and click **Certificates**. This is a list of certificates that are not trusted by your computer even if they appear to be valid.

6. Change the console mode to prevent modification, as detailed in the following steps:

   a. In the Security Console window, click the **File** menu and click **Options**.

   b. In the Options window, in the Console mode box, select each available option and read the description.

   c. In the Console mode box, select **User mode - full access** and click **OK**.

   d. In the Security Console window, click the **File** menu and click **Save**.

   e. Close the Security Console and click **No** when prompted to save settings.

   f. Click **Start**, type **Security**, and then click **Security Console.msc**.

   g. In the User Account Control window, click **Yes**.

   h. In the Security Console window, click the **File** menu and review the available options. Notice that the option to add or remove a snap-in is not available.

   i. Close the Security Console.

Certification Objectives

Objectives for MCTS Exam #70-680: Windows 7, Configuring:

- Monitoring and Maintaining Systems that Run Windows 7: Monitor systems

Review Questions

1. Why would you want to create a custom MMC console?
2. Where are custom MMC consoles stored by default?
3. How can you make a custom MMC console available to multiple users?
4. What console modes are available in the options of an MMC console?
5. How can you ensure that a shared custom MMC console is not modified?

CHAPTER FOUR

MANAGING DISKS

Labs included in this chapter:

- Lab 4.1 Cleaning Disk Space with Advanced Disk-Cleaning Options
- Lab 4.2 Converting a Disk from MBR to GPT Partition Styles
- Lab 4.3 Compacting Virtual Hard Disks

Microsoft MCTS Exam #70-680 Objectives

Objective	Lab
Configure a VHD	4.2, 4.3
Manage disks	4.1, 4.2, 4.3

Lab 4.1: Cleaning Disk Space with Advanced Disk-Cleaning Options

Objectives

The object of this activity is to use advanced disk-cleaning options to recover disk space from past restore points without deleting the most recent restore point.

Materials Required

This lab requires the following:

- A physical computer or virtual machine running Windows 7 that is configured as User*x*-PC or as specified by your instructor

Estimated completion time: **15 minutes**

Activity Background

Windows 7 includes the Disk Cleanup function to help users remove unwanted and unused files from their computers. This is useful when a computer has a small hard drive and is low on disk space. Having less data on a disk can also help prevent drive fragmentation.

Activity

1. Log on to User*x*-PC.

2. Click **Start**, and then click **Computer** to open a computer browser window.

3. Right-click **(C:)** and select **Properties** from the pop-up menu. Click the **General** tab to select it if it is not selected by default.

4. Click the **Disk Cleanup** button, as seen in Figure 4-1. Your computer will examine areas of the disk from which it might be able to recover disk space. This may take a minute or so.

5. Note how much disk space can be recovered from each of the following file categories:
   - Downloaded Program Files _____
   - Temporary Internet Files _____
   - Recycle Bin _____
   - System error memory dump files (if listed) _____
   - Temporary files _____
   - Thumbnails _____

6. Note which of the following file categories are automatically selected for file deletion:
   - Downloaded Program Files Yes / No
   - Temporary Internet Files Yes / No
   - Recycle Bin Yes / No
   - System error memory dump files (if listed) Yes / No
   - Temporary files Yes / No
   - Thumbnails Yes / No

7. On the Disk Cleanup tab, click the **Clean up system files** button. Note that the Disk Cleanup window will close and the program will recalculate the amount of disk

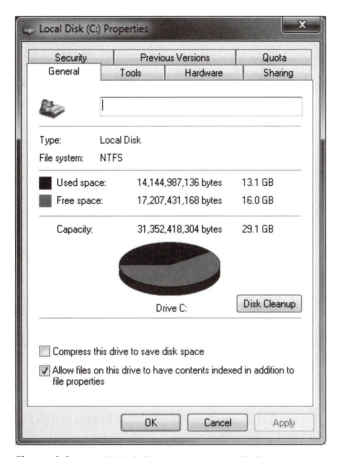

Figure 4-1   Local Disk (C:) Properties, General tab
© *Cengage Learning 2012*

space that can be freed with additional options active. When the Disk Cleanup window reappears, the **More Options** tab will be available.

8. Click the **More Options** tab.

9. In the System Restore and Shadow Copies area, read the text to learn which restore point will not be deleted if this option is selected.

10. In the System Restore and Shadow Copies area, click the **Clean up** button.

11. In the Disk Cleanup window that opens, click the **Delete** button.

12. Click the **OK** button to close the Disk Cleanup window.

13. Disk Cleanup will prompt you to confirm that you want to permanently delete the file categories that are selected on the Disk Cleanup tab. These categories of files were selected by default. Click the **Delete Files** button. Disk Cleanup will proceed to delete the files from each selected category.

14. Close all open windows.

15. Log off the computer.

Certification Objectives

Objectives for MCTS Exam #70-680: Windows 7, Configuring:

- Monitoring and Maintaining Systems that Run Windows 7: Manage disks

Review Questions

1. Which disk properties tab allows you to free disk space by removing programs you do not use?

   a. Previous Versions

   b. Quota

   c. Programs

   d. General

2. Before a category of files is deleted, the _____ button will show a preview list of the related content.

   a. Clean up system files

   b. Disk Cleanup

   c. View Files

   d. Advanced system settings

3. Which Disk Cleanup category of files should you select to delete cached images of pictures, video, and documents displayed when a user is browsing folders?

   a. Temporary files

   b. Temporary Internet Files

   c. Recycle Bin

   d. Thumbnails

4. What is the difference between the Downloaded Program Files category in Disk Cleanup and the Programs and Features option in Control Panel to uninstall programs?

5. How can you undo the cleanup operation performed through the Disk Cleanup utility if you require access to an older restore point after a cleanup has been performed?

   a. Restore from the Recycle Bin

   b. C: properties, Previous Versions tab

   c. Disk Cleanup, System Restore and Shadow Copies, Undo button

   d. There is no undo option in the Disk Cleanup Wizard.

Lab 4.2: Converting a Disk from MBR to GPT Partition Styles

Objectives

The objective of this activity is to identify differences that exist when partitions/volumes are created on disks formatted by using the MBR and GPT partition styles.

Materials Required

This lab requires the following:

- A physical computer or virtual machine running Windows 7 that is configured as User*x*-PC or as specified by your instructor
- A minimum of 1 GB of free space on drive C: of User*x*-PC

Estimated completion time: **30 minutes**

Activity Background

Windows 7 allows you to select between MBR and GPT partition styles when a new disk is added to a computer. The MBR partition style is limited to four partitions, one of which can be an extended partition containing multiple logical drives. The GPT partition style is not restricted to four partitions, which increases the flexibility in how partitions are used on a drive using the GPT partition style. However, the main benefit of the GPT partition style is support for partitions of 18 exabytes. MBR partitions are limited to 2 GB. Generally speaking, GPT is not suitable for bootable disks.

In this activity, you create partitions on disks using both the MBR and GPT partition styles. Virtual hard disks are used to simply the process for students with limited access to hardware.

Activity

1. Log on to User*x*-PC.

2. Click **Start**, right-click **Computer**, and then click **Manage**.

3. In the left pane of the Computer Management window that opens, click **Disk Management** below Storage to select it. Wait approximately 5 to 10 seconds while the utility scans for disks and their configuration information.

4. Click the **Action** menu to display a list of related disk management actions. Click **Create VHD** in the menu.

5. In the Create and Attach Virtual Hard Disk window that opens, in the **Location** text, type **C:\VDSKLAB42.VHD**.

6. In the **Virtual hard disk size** text field, type **1024**. Confirm that the unit drop-down next to that field displays **MB**.

7. Click the **Fixed size (Recommended)** option in the Virtual hard disk format section if it is not selected by default.

8. Click **OK** to begin the creation of the virtual disk. The process may take a minute or two to complete. After the successful creation of the disk, the virtual disk will be listed in the list of disks visible in the bottom-middle pane of the Computer Management window.

9. Confirm the following details for the new virtual disk:

    • Disk icon color _____

    • Disk number _____

    • Disk type (below disk number) _____

    • Disk size _____

    • Status _____

    • Partitions or volumes that currently exist on the disk _____

10. Right-click the new virtual disk's icon in the bottom-middle pane, and select **Initialize Disk** from the pop-up menu.

11. In the Initialize Disk window that opens, confirm that the disk number identified in Step 9 is selected and that the default partition style **MBR (Master Boot Record)** is selected. Click **OK** to initialize the disk.

12. Note the following changed details for the virtual disk after it is initialized:

    • Disk type (below disk number) _____

    • Status _____

    • Partitions or volumes that currently exist on the disk _____

4

13. Right-click the **Unallocated** space of the virtual disk drive. Select **New Simple Volume** from the pop-up menu.

14. In the New Simple Volume Wizard window that opens, click **Next** to pass the welcome screen, type **300** in the **Simple volume size in MB** box, and click the **Next** button to set the new volume size.

15. Note the displayed drive letter that will be assigned to the new simple volume, and click **Next** to keep that drive letter assignment.

16. In the Format Partition screen, confirm that the volume format will use the NTFS file system with a default allocation unit size. In the **Volume label** box, type **LAB42VOL1**. Select the **Perform a quick format** check box, if necessary, and click **Next**.

17. Review the summary screen and click **Finish** to create the volume. If an AutoPlay window opens for the volume, close it.

18. Note the partition type of the newly created partition: _____

19. Repeat Steps 13 to 17 to create a **100 MB** volume, using a volume label of **LAB42VOL2** in Step 16.

20. Repeat Steps 13 to 17 to create a **100 MB** volume, using a volume label of **LAB42VOL3** in Step 16.

21. Repeat Steps 13 to 17 to create a **50 MB** volume, using a volume label of **LAB42VOL4** in Step 16.

22. Note the partition type of the partition created in Step 21: _____

23. Right-click the new virtual disk's icon in the bottom-middle pane, and note that Convert to GPT disk is dimmed in the pop-up menu. Click outside the pop-up menu on the Computer Management window to avoid selecting anything from the menu and to close it.

24. Right-click the new **LAB42VOL4** partition and select **Delete Volume** from the pop-up menu. When prompted to continue with the deletion, click the **Yes** button. Repeat the process for all volumes remaining on the virtual disk until it no longer contains any partitions.

25. Right-click the new virtual disk's icon in the bottom-middle pane; note that Convert to Dynamic Disk is dimmed, but the menu option Convert to GPT Disk is now available.

26. Click **Convert to GPT Disk** in the menu. Identify the following details for the virtual disk as displayed in the bottom-middle pane:
    - Disk type (below disk number) _____
    - Status _____

27. To confirm that the conversion is completed, right-click the new virtual disk's icon in the bottom-middle pane, and click to select **Properties** from the pop-up menu.

28. In the Virtual Disk Device Properties window, select the **Volumes** tab. Note the current Partition style, which should be GUID Partition Table (GPT).

29. Click **OK** to close the Virtual Disk Drive Properties window.

30. Right-click the **Unallocated** space of the virtual disk drive. Select **New Simple Volume** from the pop-up menu.

31. In the New Simple Volume Wizard window that opens, click **Next** to pass the welcome screen, then type **50** in the **Simple volume size in MB** box, and click the **Next** button to set the new volume size.

32. Note the displayed drive letter that will be assigned to the new simple volume, and click **Next** to keep that drive letter assignment.

33. In the format partition screen, confirm that the volume format will use the NTFS file system with a default allocation unit size. Change the Volume label from New Volume to **LAB42VOL1**. Select the **Perform a quick format** check box, if necessary, and click **Next**.

34. Review the new simple volume summary screen, and click **Finish** to create the volume. If an AutoPlay window opens for the volume, close it.

35. Repeat Steps 30 to 34 to create a **50 MB** volume, using a volume label of **LAB42VOL2** in Step 33.

36. Repeat Steps 30 to 34 to create a **50 MB** volume, using a volume label of **LAB42VOL3** in Step 33.

37. Repeat Steps 30 to 34 to create a **50 MB** volume, using a volume label of **LAB42VOL4** in Step 33.

38. Repeat Steps 30 to 34 to create a **50 MB** volume, using a volume label of **LAB42VOL5** in Step 33.

39. Note the partition type of the newly created LAB42VOL5 partition: _____

40. Right-click the virtual disk icon in the bottom-middle pane, and then select **Detach VHD** from the pop-up menu.

41. Read the warning in the Detach Virtual Hard Disk window, and click **OK** to acknowledge the warning and proceed with the detach process. Note that the virtual disk and the drive letters belonging to its partitions are no longer visible to the operating system.

42. Close all open windows. Log off the computer.

Certification Objectives

Objectives for MCTS Exam #70-680: Windows 7, Configuring:

- Deploying Windows 7: Configure a VHD
- Monitoring and Maintaining Systems that Run Windows 7: Manage disks

Review Questions

1. In the Disk Management utility, a virtual disk icon or an icon representing volumes contained on the attached virtual disk are _____.

   a. gray

   b. dark blue

   c. black

   d. light blue

2. The default partition style for a new virtual disk is _____.

   a. GPT

   b. Online

   c. MBR

   d. IBM

3. When a virtual disk is detached, any volumes it contains _____ in the operating system.

   a. are deleted

   b. become unavailable

   c. appear as read-only

   d. remain available

4. What is the only type of partition that can be created on a disk using the GPT partition style?

   a. Primary partition

   b. Extended partition

   c. Logical drive

   d. MBR

5. The virtual disk in the activity could not be converted to a dynamic disk regardless of the number of volumes present on the disk and regardless of whether it was initialized with the GPT or MBR partition style. Why would the operating system prevent the conversion of the virtual disk to a dynamic disk?

Lab 4.3: Compacting Virtual Hard Disks

Objectives

The objective of this activity is to review the methods that can be applied to shrink the physical size of a virtual hard disk file.

Materials Required

This lab requires the following:

- A physical computer or virtual machine running Windows 7 that is configured as User*x*-PC or as specified by your instructor
- A minimum of 900 MB of free space on drive C: of User*x*-PC

Estimated completion time: **45 minutes**

Activity Background

Windows 7 includes support for mounting virtual hard disks (VHDs). VHDs are most commonly associated with Microsoft virtualization technologies such as Hyper-V or Virtual PC. You could use the VHD support in Windows 7 to mount, access, and modify the contents of a VHD taken from a virtual machine. You can also use VHD files to distribute content much as ISO files are used to distribute CD and DVD images. VHD files also allow you to create additional drive letters on your local disk without repartitioning the drive.

In this activity, you create, mount, and modify VHD files.

Activity

1. Log on to User*x*-PC.

2. Click **Start**, right-click **Computer**, and then click **Manage** to select it from the pop-up menu.

3. In the left pane of the Computer Management window, click **Disk Management** below Storage to select it.

4. Create and prepare a virtual disk, as detailed in the following steps:

   a. Click the **Action** menu and click **Create VHD**.

   b. In the Create and Attach Virtual Hard Disk window that opens, in the **Location** box, type **C:\VDSKLAB43.VHD**.

   c. In the Virtual hard disk size box, type **500**.

   d. Confirm that the unit drop-down next to that field displays **MB**.

e. Confirm that the **Fixed size (Recommended)** option is selected in the Virtual hard disk format section.

f. Click **OK** to begin create the virtual disk. Wait up to 15 or 30 seconds for the virtual disk to be created in the host file system. After the successful creation of the disk, the virtual disk will be listed and visible in the bottom-middle pane of the Computer Management window.

g. Right-click the icon for the new virtual disk in the bottom-middle pane, and select **Initialize Disk** from the pop-up menu.

h. In the Initialize Disk window that opens, confirm that the disk number for the virtual disk is selected, confirm that the default selection of **MBR (Master Boot Record)** is selected, and click **OK**.

i. Confirm the following details for the virtual disk:

- Disk icon color _____
- Disk type (below disk number) _____
- Status _____

5. Create and format a volume on the virtual disk, as detailed in the following steps:

a. Right-click the **Unallocated** space of the virtual disk drive and select **New Simple Volume** from the pop-up menu.

b. In the New Simple Volume Wizard window that opens, click **Next** to pass the welcome screen.

c. In the Simple volume size in MB box, type **400** and click the **Next** button to set the new volume size.

d. Note the displayed drive letter that will be assigned to the new simple volume, and click **Next** to keep that drive letter assignment.

e. In the format partition screen, confirm that the volume format will use the NTFS file system with a default allocation unit size.

f. In the Volume label box, type **LAB43VOL1**, select the **Perform a quick format** check box, if necessary, and click **Next**.

g. Review the summary screen and click **Finish** to create the volume.

6. Add content to the LAB43VOL1 volume, as detailed in the following steps:

a. If the AutoPlay window opens, click the **Open folder to view files** option and continue to the next step. If the AutoPlay window does not open, right-click the newly created **LAB43VOL1** volume in the bottom-middle pane of the Computer Management window and select **Explore** from the pop-up menu.

b. Note that there are no files currently in the newly created partition. In the open computer browser window, navigate to **C:\Windows\Help**, and press **Ctrl+A** to select all items displayed in that folder.

c. Right-click the selected content and click **Copy** from the pop-up menu.

d. Navigate to the drive letter assigned to the new LAB43VOL1 volume, right-click the empty space in the computer browser's right pane, and click **Paste** from the pop-up menu.

e. Repeat Steps 6a to 6d to copy all file content from **C:\Windows\IME** to the LAB43VOL1 volume.

7. Review the properties of the volume and virtual disk file, as detailed in the following steps:

a. Right-click the LAB43VOL1 volume's drive letter in the computer browser window and select **Properties** from the pop-up menu.

    b. Click to select the **General** properties tab if it is not selected by default. Note the following attributes:

       • Used space (MB)_____

       • Free space (MB) _____

    c. Close the LAB43VOL1 volume's properties window.

    d. In the computer browser window, navigate to the root folder of **C:** (i.e., C:\) and locate the VDSKLAB43.VHD file. Right-click the **VDSKLAB43.VHD** file and click **Properties** from the pop-up menu.

    e. Click the **General** properties tab if it is not selected by default. Note the following attributes:

       • Size (MB) _____

       • Size on disk (MB) _____

    f. Close the VDSKLAB43.VHD properties window.

    g. Close the computer browser window and the Computer Management window.

8. Use DiskPart to expand a virtual disk, as detailed in the following steps:

    a. Click **Start**, and then in the *Search programs and files* field, enter the text **CMD**, but do not press Enter.

    b. Right-click the **CMD** program displayed at the top of the Start menu, and select **Run as administrator** from the pop-up menu, as shown in Figure 4-2.

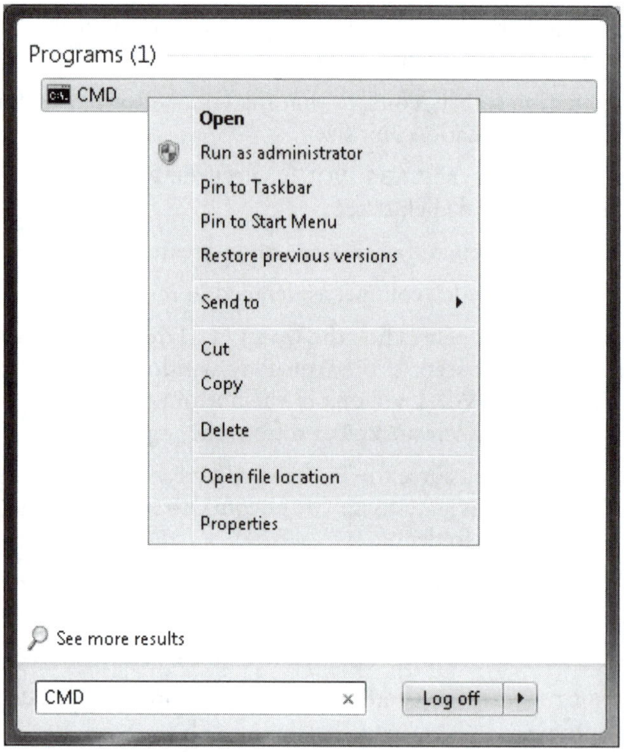

Figure 4-2 Starting the command prompt utility, CMD, with Administrator privileges
© *Cengage Learning 2012*

c. If User Account Control prompts you for permission to allow this operation, click **Yes** to continue.

d. In the command window that opens, type **DISKPART** at the command prompt and press **Enter**. This activates an interactive mode of the text-based disk partitioning utility.

e. Wait until the **DISKPART>** command prompt is displayed, as shown in Figure 4-3. Type the command **LIST VDISK** and press **Enter**. This lists the state of any active virtual disks. Note the following settings for the new VDSKLAB43.VHD virtual disk:

- VDisk # _____
- Disk # _____
- State _____
- Type _____

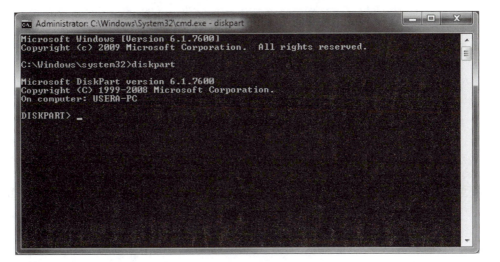

Figure 4-3   DISKPART prompt in a command window

© *Cengage Learning 2012*

f. Type the command **SELECT VDISK FILE=C:\VDSKLAB43.VHD** and press **Enter**. This focuses the DiskPart utility on that specific virtual disk file for the following commands.

g. Type the command **EXPAND VDISK MAXIMUM=600** and press **Enter**. Read the error message.

h. Enter the command **DETACH VDISK** and press **Enter**.

i. To enlarge the virtual disk file to a new size of 600 MB, enter the command **EXPAND VDISK MAXIMUM=600** and press **Enter**. Note that the DiskPart utility is still focused on the virtual disk file even though it is no longer attached to the operating system.

j. Once the expansion is completed, enter the command **ATTACH VDISK** and press **Enter** to attach the now larger virtual disk file. If an AutoPlay window opens, close it.

k. Enter the command **LIST VDISK** and press **Enter** to confirm the virtual disk's Disk number.

l. Enter the command **LIST DISK** and press **Enter** to display a list of known disks and their properties. Note the size and free space for the disk number matching that of the virtual disk.

9. Expand the volume on the virtual disk, as detailed in the following steps:

   a. Enter the command **LIST VOLUME** and press **Enter**. This command displays a list of volumes on the virtual disk, as shown in Figure 4-4. Identify the drive letter associated with LAB43VOL1 in the **Ltr** column.

Volume ###	Ltr	Label	Fs	Type	Size	Status	Info
Volume 0	D	LAB43VOL1	NTFS	Partition	575 MB	Healthy	
Volume 1		System Rese	NTFS	Partition	100 MB	Healthy	System
Volume 2	C		NTFS	Partition	297 GB	Healthy	Boot

Figure 4-4 DiskPart LIST VOLUME command results
© Cengage Learning 2012

   b. Enter the command **SELECT VOLUME=y,** where y is the drive letter of the volume LAB43VOL1, and press **Enter**. For example, enter the command *select volume=H* if the volume on the virtual disk has the drive letter H assigned. Confirm that the selected volume number reported by the command result matches the expected volume number.

   c. Enter the command **EXTEND SIZE=175** and press **Enter** to increase the size of the volume by 175 MB.

   d. Enter the command **LIST VOLUME** and press **Enter** to confirm that the selected volume size had grown by 175 MB. Note that the selected volume has an asterisk next to it.

   e. Enter the command **LIST DISK** and press **Enter** to confirm that the virtual disk's size has remained constant and that the free space on the virtual disk has been reduced.

   f. Enter the command **DETAIL VDISK** and press **Enter**. Note the virtual size and physical size reported by the command's results are identical because this is a fixed-size VHD.

10. Attempt to compact the VHD file to reduce physical disk utilization, as detailed in the following steps:

   a. Enter the command **DETACH VDISK** and press **Enter**. This will make the VHD file and its volumes unavailable to the operating system.

   b. Enter the command **ATTACH VDISK READONLY** and press **Enter** to open the VHD and its contents in a read-only mode.

   c. Enter the command **COMPACT VDISK** and press **Enter**. Note the error message that this operation is not supported on a virtual disk of this type (i.e., fixed size).

11. Create and prepare a new dynamic VHD, as detailed in the following steps:

   a. Enter the command **CREATE VDISK FILE=C:\TEMPVDSK.VHD MAXIMUM=600 TYPE=EXPANDABLE** and press **Enter**.

   b. Enter the command **DETAIL VDISK** and press **Enter**. Note the virtual size and physical size reported are not the same because this is a dynamically expanding virtual disk. The reported virtual size represents the maximum size allowed for the VHD file, and the physical size is the VHD file's current size in the host file system.

   c. Enter the command **ATTACH VDISK** and press **Enter**.

   d. Enter the command **LIST VDISK** and press **Enter**. Note the disk number assigned to C:\TEMPVDSK.VHD and the virtual disk's type.

   e. Enter the command **SELECT DISK=z**, where *z* is the disk number of the C:\TEMPVDSK.VHD virtual disk, and press **Enter**. For example, enter the command *SELECT DISK=2* if the disk number of the virtual disk is 2. The disk number is dynamically assigned depending on what other disks are present and active when the virtual disk was attached. Do not assume that a specific disk number will always be associated with the new virtual disk.

   f. Enter the command **CREATE PARTITION PRIMARY** and press **Enter**. This creates a primary partition on the selected disk that uses all available space on the disk for the new partition.

   g. Enter the command **LIST VOLUME** and press **Enter**. The new partition is selected with an asterisk to the left of its row in the results, as shown in Figure 4-5. Notice that no files system or drive letter are associated with new partition because it is unformatted.

```
DISKPART> list volume

  Volume ###  Ltr  Label        Fs     Type       Size    Status    Info
  ----------  ---  -----------  -----  ---------  ------  --------  -------
  Volume 0    D    LAB43VOL1    NTFS   Partition  575 MB  Healthy
  Volume 1         System Rese  NTFS   Partition  100 MB  Healthy   System
  Volume 2    C                 NTFS   Partition  297 GB  Healthy   Boot
* Volume 3                      RAW    Partition  598 MB  Healthy
```

Figure 4-5   Unformatted partition
© *Cengage Learning 2012*

   h. Enter the command **FORMAT FS=NTFS LABEL="LAB43VOLT" QUICK** and press **Enter**. This will quick-format the new partition with the NTFS file system and a volume label of LAB43VOLT.

   i. Enter the command **ASSIGN LETTER=P** and press **Enter**. This will assign the drive letter P: to the partition. Close the AutoPlay window if it opens.

   j. Enter the command **LIST VOLUME** and press **Enter**. Identify the drive letters assigned to LAB43VOL1 and LAB43VOLT, respectively.

12. Copy data from LAB43VOL1 to LAB43VOLT, as detailed in the following steps:

   a. Click **Start**, click **Computer**, and then double-click the **LAB43VOL1** volume.

   b. Press **Ctrl+A** to select all the content of that drive. Right-click the selection and then click **Copy** from the pop-up menu.

   c. Click the **Back** button in the computer browser window, and then double-click the **LAB43VOLT** volume.

   d. Right-click any empty space in the right pane of the computer browser window and select **Paste** from the pop-up menu. This will copy the contents of the fixed size virtual disk to the dynamically expanding virtual disk.

   e. In the command window running diskpart, enter the command **DETAIL VDISK** and press **Enter**. Note the reported physical size of the dynamically expanding disk has changed.

13. Replace the fixed virtual disk with the dynamic virtual disk, as detailed in the following steps:

   a. Enter the command **DETACH VDISK**. This will close the computer browser window as well as detach the virtual disk from the operating system.

   b. Enter the command **SELECT VDISK FILE="C:\VDSKLAB43.VHD"** and press **Enter**.

   c. Enter the command **DETACH VDISK** and press **Enter** to detach that virtual disk as well.

   d. Both virtual disks are now detached; as such, they can be manipulated as regular files in the host file system. The fixed size virtual disk file can now be replaced with the dynamically growing virtual disk file. Enter the command **EXIT** and press **Enter** to exit DiskPart and return to the regular command prompt.

e. In the command prompt window, enter the command **COPY C:\TEMPVDSK.VHD C:\VDSKLAB43.VHD** and press **Enter** to begin the copy process. When you are prompted for permission to overwrite C:\VDSKLAB43.VHD, press **Y** and then press **Enter** to answer yes.

f. Enter the command **DEL C:\TEMPVDSK.VHD** and press **Enter** to delete the original dynamically expanding virtual disk file.

g. Enter the command **DISKPART** and press **Enter** to start DiskPart.

h. Enter the command **SELECT VDISK FILE="C:\VDSKLAB43.VHD"** and press **Enter**.

i. Enter the command **DETAIL VDISK** and press **Enter**. Note that the virtual disk file has the same name and location as the original fixed size file; however, the reported virtual and physical disk sizes are no longer identical.

j. Enter the command **ATTACH VDISK** and press **Enter**. If an AutoPlay window opens, close it.

k. The virtual drive has the same filename, but the partition label is still the temporary label assigned earlier. Click **Start**, click **Computer**, and then right-click the **LAB43VOLT** volume.

l. Click to select **Rename** from the pop-up menu, then change the text LAB43VOLT to **LAB43VOL** and press **Enter** to complete the change. Note the free space reported for that volume. From the user's perspective, this virtual disk contains the same data and free space as the original fixed size virtual disk.

14. Remove data and shrink the virtual disk, as detailed in the following steps:

a. To simulate a large number of deleted files in the virtual disk file where space can be recovered, you will now delete all file content in the volume. In the computer browser window, open the **LAB43VOL** volume. Press **Ctrl+A** to select all files and folders in the volume. Press **Shift+Delete**; when prompted to permanently delete this content, click **Yes**.

b. In the command window running diskpart, enter the command **DETAIL VDISK** and press **Enter**. Note the physical size of the disk has not changed even though data contained in the virtual disk has been deleted. When new data is written to the virtual disk, the dynamically expanding virtual disk will reuse the deleted space in the virtual disk first and then free space from the host file system second, if necessary. The virtual disk can increase in size up to the limit specified by the virtual size property or until there is no free space on the host file system.

c. To recover the free space in the dynamically expanding virtual disk, the file must be opened in read-only mode. Enter the command **DETACH VDISK** and press **Enter**.

d. The virtual disk file is still selected. Enter the command **ATTACH VDISK READONLY** and press **Enter**. If the AutoPlay window opens, close it.

e. Enter the command **COMPACT VDISK** and press **Enter**. The diskpart utility will report percent completion, up to 100 percent.

f. Enter the command **DETAIL VDISK** and press **Enter**. Note that the reported physical size has reduced.

15. Enter the command **DETACH VDISK** and press **Enter**.

16. Enter the command **EXIT** and press **Enter** to exit the diskpart utility.

17. Close the command prompt window.

18. Log off the computer.

Certification Objectives

Objectives for MCTS Exam #70-680: Windows 7, Configuring:

- Deploying Windows 7: Configure a VHD
- Monitoring and Maintaining Systems that Run Windows 7: Manage disks

Review Questions

1. Which diskpart command will display the drive letters assigned to all volumes mounted in the local operating system?

   a. LIST VOLUME

   b. LIST DISK

   c. LIST PARTITION

   d. LIST VDISK

2. A dynamically expanding virtual disk file called Q2VDSK.VHD has its virtual size currently set to 400 MB. When you issue the command EXPAND VDISK MAXIMUM=900, you receive the error "Virtual Disk Service error. The requested operation cannot be performed while the virtual disk is attached." What command should you issue next to allow the virtual size to be increased?

   a. ATTACH VDISK READONLY

   b. DETAIL VDISK FILE=Q2VDSK.VHD MAXIMUM=900

   c. SELECT VDISK FILE=Q2VDSK.VHD MAXIMUM=900

   d. DETACH VDISK

3. What advantages does compacting a virtual hard disk file present to an administrator? What disadvantages does it present?

4. Which command will allow you to later compact a virtual disk file called Q4VDSK.VHD?

   a. SELECT VDISK FILE="C:\Q4VDSK.VHD" MAXIMUM=600 READONLY

   b. CREATE VDISK FILE=C:\Q4VDSK.VHD MAXIMUM=600 TYPE=EXPANDABLE

   c. ATTACH VDISK FILE=C:\Q4VDSK.VHD MAXIMUM=120 READONLY

   d. CREATE VDISK FILE=C:\Q4VDSK.VHD MAXIMUM=600 TYPE=FIXED

5. After you compact a virtual disk, can it immediately be used to store additional files? If not, what is required to make it ready?

4

CHAPTER FIVE

MANAGING FILE SYSTEMS

Labs included in this chapter:

- Lab 5.1 Working with Links in the File System
- Lab 5.2 Working with Attributes on Files, Folders, and Links
- Lab 5.3 Creating a Basic NTFS Security Structure for Files and Folders
- Lab 5.4 Determining Effective NTFS Permissions and Restricting Access

Microsoft MCTS Exam #70-680 Objectives

Objective	Lab
Configure file and folder access	5.1, 5.2, 5.3, 5.4

Lab 5.1: Working with Links in the File System

Objectives

The object of this activity is to create hard links and symbolic links. You then will configure them for accessing content between different folders or volumes where possible.

Materials Required

This lab requires the following:

- A physical computer or virtual machine running Windows 7 that is configured as User*x*-PC or as specified by your instructor
- A minimum of 600 MB of free space on drive C: of User*x*-PC

Estimated completion time: **30 minutes**

Activity Background

File and folders are typically found in all volumes; however, NTFS also supports the use of special hard link and symbolic link entries to point to content or other files and folders, respectively. You will investigate their creation and use to access information stored in different locations.

Activity

1. Log on to User*x*-PC.
2. A virtual disk will be created to host two NTFS volumes labeled drives M: and N:; in addition, one FAT-formatted volume labeled as drive O: will be created, as detailed in the following steps:

   a. Click **Start**, right-click **Computer**, and then click **Manage** to select it from the pop-up menu.

   b. In the left pane of the Computer Management window that opens, click **Disk Management** below Storage to select it. Wait approximately 5 to 10 seconds while the utility scans for disks and their configuration information.

   c. Click the **Action** menu to display a list of related disk management actions. Click **Create VHD** in the menu to select it.

   d. In the Create and Attach Virtual Hard Disk window that opens, click the **Location** text box to focus the cursor in that text field. Enter the text **C:\VDSKLAB51.VHD** in the Location field.

   e. Click to focus the cursor in the **Virtual hard disk size** text field. Enter the value **600** in that field. Confirm that the unit drop-down next to that field displays **MB**.

   f. If it is not selected by default, click to select the **Fixed size (Recommended)** option in the Virtual hard disk format section.

   g. Click **OK** to begin the creation of the virtual disk. The process may take a minute or two to complete. After the successful creation of the disk, the virtual disk will be listed in the list of disks visible in the bottom-middle pane of the Computer Management window.

   h. Right-click the new virtual disk's icon in the bottom-middle pane, and select **Initialize Disk** from the pop-up menu.

   i. In the Initialize Disk window that opens, confirm that the correct disk number is selected and that the default partition style **MBR (Master Boot Record)** is selected. Click **OK** to initialize the disk.

j. Right-click the **Unallocated** space of the newly initialized virtual disk drive. Select **New Simple Volume** from the pop-up menu.

k. In the New Simple Volume Wizard window that opens, click **Next** to pass the welcome screen, type **200** as the Simple volume size in MB, and click the **Next** button to set the new volume size.

l. Click the **Assign the following drive letter** drop-down arrow, select **M**, and then click **Next** to assign that drive letter.

m. In the format partition screen, confirm that the volume format will use the **NTFS** file system with a default allocation unit size. Change the Volume label from New Volume to **LAB5VOL1**. Confirm that **Perform a quick format** is selected, and click **Next**.

n. Review the new simple volume summary screen, and click **Finish** to create the volume. If an AutoPlay window opens for the volume, close it.

o. Repeat Steps 2.j to 2.n to create another new **200 MB** volume; however, change the drive letter to assign in Step 2.l to **N**, and use a volume label of **LAB5VOL2** in Step 2.m.

p. Repeat Steps 2.j to 2.n to create a volume that uses up the remaining space on the virtual drive; however, change the drive letter to assign in Step 2.l to **O**, as well as a file system format of **FAT** and a volume label of **LAB5VOL3** in Step 2.m.

3. Create sample files and folders required for the remainder of this activity, as detailed in the following steps:

a. Click **Start**, and then in the *Search programs and files* field, enter the text **CMD**, and then press **Enter**.

b. In the command window that opens, type **M:** at the command prompt and press **Enter**.

c. In the command window, type **MD LEVEL1** and press **Enter**.

d. In the command window, type **MD LEVEL1\LEVEL2** and press **Enter**.

e. In the command window, type **ECHO This is one line of text for a work file. > LEVEL1\FILE1.TXT** and press **Enter**.

f. In the command window, type **COPY LEVEL1\FILE1.TXT LEVEL1\FILE2.TXT** and press **Enter**.

g. In the command window, type **CD LEVEL1** and press **Enter**.

h. In the command window, type **DIR** and press **Enter**. Note that two data files are now present, FILE1.TXT and FILE2.TXT, plus one subdirectory, LEVEL2, that is currently empty.

4. Examine the behavior of hard links, as detailed in the following steps:

a. In the command window, type **MKLINK /H HLNKFILE1.TXT FILE1.TXT** and press **Enter**. This will create a hard link from the file content to both filenames, HLNKFILE1.TXT and FILE1.TXT.

b. To confirm that the content linked to each filename is the same, enter the command **TYPE HLNKFILE1.TXT** and press **Enter**. To confirm the second file's content, enter the command **TYPE FILE1.TXT** and press **Enter**. Note that the text shown after each command is the same.

c. Modify the original FILE1.TXT file by typing the command **ECHO This is a second line of text. >> FILE1.TXT** and then press **Enter**.

d. To confirm that the content linked to both filenames is still the same after the change to one file, type the command **TYPE HLNKFILE1.TXT** and press **Enter**. Type the command **TYPE FILE1.TXT** and press **Enter**. Note that the text shown after each command is still the same for both files and includes the new text.

5

e. Move the HLNKFILE1.TXT directory entry to a different folder by typing the command **MOVE HLNKFILE1.TXT LEVEL2** and press **Enter**.

f. Modify the original FILE1.TXT file by typing the command **ECHO This is a third line of text. >> FILE1.TXT** and press **Enter**.

g. Confirm the hard-linked file is updated as expected by displaying the contents of the file. Type the command **TYPE LEVEL2\HLNKFILE1.TXT** and press **Enter**. Note the change in content of the hard-linked file, even though the change was made to FILE1.TXT in a different folder.

h. Delete the original file, FILE1.TXT, by entering the command **DEL FILE1.TXT** and then press **Enter**.

i. Confirm the hard-linked file's contents by entering the command **TYPE LEVEL2\ HLNKFILE1.TXT** and press **Enter**. Note the content that is displayed.

5. Observe the behavior of symbolic links, as detailed in the following steps:

a. Symbolic links are pointers to directory entries, while hard links are pointers to content. Create a symbolic link from FILE2.TXT to a new filename. In the command window, type **MKLINK SLNKFILE2.TXT FILE2.TXT** and press **Enter**. Note that you are presented with an error message because the ability to create symbolic links requires Administrator permissions by default.

b. Close the command window.

c. Click **Start**, and then in the *Search programs and files* field, enter the text **CMD**, but do not press Enter.

d. Right-click the CMD program displayed at the top of the Start menu and select **Run as administrator** from the pop-up menu. If User Account Control prompts you for permission to continue, click **Yes**.

e. In the command window, change the current directory to M:\LEVEL1 by typing **M:** and pressing **Enter**; then type **CD LEVEL1** and press **Enter**.

f. Create a symbolic link from FILE2.TXT to a new filename. In the command window, type **MKLINK SLNKFILE2.TXT FILE2.TXT** and press **Enter**. Note that the command now completes successfully.

g. Symbolic links are pointers to other directory items, not the content of a specific file. Windows will report a symbolic link as a symbolic link in a directory listing. In the command window, type **DIR** and press **Enter**. Note the directory entry for SLNKFILE2.TXT and the additional detail reported by the DIR command. Note that the target is listed inside square brackets without a fully specified path; therefore, the target is relative to the location of the symbolic link itself.

h. Now you will modify the content of SLNKFILE2.TXT. Enter the command **ECHO This is a second line of text. >> SLNKFILE2.TXT** and then press **Enter**.

i. Now you will confirm the change to the linked file. Enter the command **TYPE FILE2.TXT** and press **Enter**. Note that the change made to SLNKFILE2.TXT in the previous step has updated FILE2.TXT.

j. Move FILE2.TXT to the subfolder LEVEL2 by typing the command **MOVE FILE2.TXT LEVEL2** and pressing **Enter**.

k. Confirm that the symbolic link is still present by typing the command **DIR** and pressing **Enter**. Note that SLNKFILE2.TXT still exists in the folder LEVEL1.

l. Now you will confirm the data that is reported by the symbolic link when its target is missing. Type the command **TYPE SLNKFILE2.TXT** and press **Enter**. Note the error message.

m. Create a new FILE2.TXT file in the folder LEVEL1 by entering the command **ECHO This is the first line of the new FILE2.TXT > FILE2.TXT** and pressing **Enter**.

n. Now you will confirm the data that is reported by the symbolic link. Type the command **TYPE SLNKFILE2.TXT** and press **Enter**. Note the reported content.

o. Confirm the data that is reported by the moved FILE2.TXT data file by typing the command **TYPE LEVEL2\FILE2.TXT** and pressing **Enter**. Note the difference to the content reported by the previous step.

6. Symbolic links to items can be absolute pointers instead of relative to the location of the symbolic link itself. Create an absolute symbolic link that spans volumes, as detailed in the following steps:

a. Now you will change the command prompt focus to a different volume. Enter the command **N:** and press **Enter**.

b. Next, you will create a symbolic link from FILE2.TXT on M: to a new filename on N:. In the command window, type **MKLINK SLNKFILE2.TXT M:\LEVEL1\FILE2.TXT** and press **Enter**.

c. Confirm the data that is reported by programs accessing content through the new symbolic link by typing the command **TYPE SLNKFILE2.TXT** and pressing **Enter**

d. Confirm how the symbolic link is presented in a directory listing by typing the command **DIR** and pressing **Enter**. Note that SLNKFILE2.TXT specifies an exact target path to FILE2.TXT. This is an absolute symbolic link and not a relative one because the full path to the target is specified.

7. Symbolic links can point to content in different volumes, but hard links cannot. Attempt to create a hard link from FILE1.TXT on M: to a new filename on N:. In the command window, type **MKLINK /H HLNKFILE1.TXT M:\LEVEL1\FILE2.TXT** and press **Enter**. Note the error message.

8. Create a symbolic link from an NTFS-formatted volume to a FAT-formatted volume, as detailed in the following steps:

a. Change the focus to a different volume by entering the command **O:** and pressing **Enter**.

b. Now you will attempt to create a symbolic link from FILE2.TXT on M: to a new filename on O:. In the command window, type **MKLINK SLNKFILE2.TXT M:\ LEVEL1\FILE2.TXT** and press **Enter**. Note the error message.

c. You now will confirm the file systems in use for each volume through the diskpart utility by entering the command **DISKPART** and pressing **Enter**.

d. When the *DISKPART*> prompt appears, enter the command **LIST VOLUME** and press **Enter**. Note the Fs (i.e., file system) column in the command's results and identify the volume type for the volumes M, N, and O.

e. Exit diskpart by typing the command **EXIT** and pressing **Enter**.

9. Examine how free space is reported when a symbolic link is created from one NTFS volume to a folder in a different NTFS volume, as detailed in the following steps:

a. New data folders must be created on N: for the rest of this activity. Change the focus to a volume N: by entering the command **N:** and pressing **Enter**.

b. In the command window, type **MD LEVELA** and press **Enter**.

5

    c. In the command window, type **MD LEVELA\LEVELB** and press **Enter**.

    d. Change the focus to a different volume. Enter the command **M:** and press **Enter**.

    e. Now you will create a symbolic link to a directory, instead of a file, that links the folder N:\LEVELA\LEVELB to a folder in M: called DLNK. In the command window, type **MKLINK /D DLNK N:\LEVELA\LEVELB** and press **Enter**.

    f. Confirm how the symbolic link is presented in a directory listing by typing the command **DIR** and pressing **Enter**. Note the differences between the SLNKFILE2.TXT and DLNK symbolic links in the command's results.

    g. Copy data into the DLNK folder by entering the command **XCOPY C:\WINDOWS\ IME*.* DLNK /S** and then pressing **Enter**.

    h. Enter the command **DIR DLNK** and press **Enter**. Write down the bytes free for M:\ LEVEL1\DLNK: _____.

    i. Enter the command **DIR** and press **Enter**. Write down the bytes free for M:\LEVEL1: _____.

    j. Enter the command **DIR N:\LEVELA\LEVELB** and press **Enter**. Write down the bytes free for N:\LEVELA\LEVELB: _____. Compare those to the values for free space returned in Steps h and i.

    k. Enter the command **CD DLNK** and press **Enter** to change directories to M:\LEVEL1\ DLNK. Note that this is actually the folder N:\FOLDERA\FOLDERB that is being accessed through a directory symbolic link.

    l. Enter the command **CD ..** and press **Enter**. This command changes the current directory to the parent folder of the current folder. Note which folder becomes the new current folder.

10. Close all windows and log out.

Certification Objectives

Objectives for MCTS Exam #70-680: Windows 7, Configuring:

- Configuring Access to Resources: Configure file and folder access

Review Questions

1. Which of the following commands will create a hard link called FILE3.TXT that is linked to the content of an original file called FILE1.TXT?

    a. MKLINK /H FILE1.TXT FILE3.TXT

    b. MKLINK /H FILE3.TXT FILE1.TXT

    c. MKLINK FILE1.TXT FILE3.TXT

    d. MKLINK FILE3.TXT FILE1.TXT

2. Creating a symbolic link to a file requires _____ and _____.

    a. FAT file system

    b. User permissions

    c. Administrative permissions

    d. NTFS file system

3. When a user tries to open a symbolic link in a data folder, the user receives an error message that the content cannot be found. What is the most likely reason the user received this error?

4. A workstation used for application testing has a large number of data files installed on a NTFS C: volume. The application is written to access data files on C: only. Currently, the data files are using slightly more than 20 GB of disk space. It has been decided that the workstation will have its operating system reinstalled multiple times to test new application installation routines. You can restore the data files from backup, but you would like to minimize the time required to do this. How could you leverage either symbolic or hard links to minimize the time between tests?

5. Creating a hard link to a file requires _____ and
_____.

   a. FAT file system

   b. User permissions

   c. Administrative permissions

   d. NTFS file system

Lab 5.2: Working with Attributes on Files, Folders, and Links

Objectives

The objective of this activity is to confirm the behavior of file and folder attributes for NTFS and FAT volumes. Attributes on symbolic and hard links are also investigated.

Materials Required

This lab requires the following:

- A physical computer or virtual machine running Windows 7 that is configured as Userx-PC or as specified by your instructor

- Completion of Lab 5.1.

Estimated completion time: **30 minutes**

Activity Background

Windows 7 computers commonly have multiple NTFS- and FAT-formatted volumes to store data files. Attributes can be used as part of an access control strategy for files and folders; however, there are limits to how effective they will function. This activity will apply and test attributes on regular files and folders, as well as hard links and symbolic links. Changes to attributes and testing will include command-line and graphical utilities.

Activity

1. Log on to Userx-PC.

2. Click **Start**, click **Computer**, and confirm that drive letters M:, N:, and O: are present. If they are not, attach the VHD file created in Lab 5.1.

3. Create sample files and folders used for the remainder of this activity, as detailed in the following steps:

   a. Click **Start**, and then in the **Search programs and files** field, enter the text **CMD**, but do not press Enter.

   b. Right-click the CMD program displayed at the top of the Start menu and select **Run as administrator** from the pop-up menu. If User Account Control prompts you for permission to continue, click **Yes**.

5

 c. In the command window that opens, type **M:** at the command prompt and press **Enter**.

 d. In the command window, type **MD LAB52** and press **Enter**.

 e. In the command window, type **MD LAB52\TERRY** and press **Enter**.

 f. In the command window, type **MD LAB52\TYLER** and press **Enter**.

 g. In the command window, type **MD LAB52\TERRY\PRIVATE** and press **Enter**.

 h. Change the command prompt focus to the folder M:\LAB52\TERRY\PRIVATE by entering the command **CD LAB52\TERRY\PRIVATE** and press **Enter**.

 i. In the command window, type **ECHO President, Terry: Bonus this year will be $51,000. > TERRYBNS.TXT** and press **Enter**.

 j. In the command window, type **ECHO VP, Tyler: Bonus this year will be $25,000. > TYLERBNS.TXT** and press **Enter**.

 k. In the command window, type **ECHO Staff: Bonus this year will be $500. > STAFFBNS.TXT** and press **Enter**.

 l. The staff bonus file will also be accessed through a hard link called HLNKSBNS.TXT. In the command window, type **MKLINK /H HLNKSBNS.TXT STAFFBNS.TXT** and press **Enter**.

 m. The staff bonus file will also be accessed through an absolute symbolic link called SLNKSBNS.TXT. In the command window, type **MKLINK SLNKSBNS.TXT M:\LAB52\TERRY\PRIVATE\STAFFBNS.TXT** and press **Enter**.

 n. Confirm that the files do not have any special file attributes set by entering the command **ATTRIB** and pressing **Enter**. Note that the only attribute set for each file is the archive attribute (i.e., the *A* attribute). The archive attribute is used by some applications to indicate that the content of a file is new or has changed since the last archive (i.e., backup) operation. Note the attributes for the symbolic linked and hard-linked filenames.

4. To limit undesirable changes to these files, the files can be marked as read-only at the command line. Type the command **ATTRIB +R *.TXT** and press **Enter**.

5. To confirm the attributes on the files, type the command **ATTRIB** and press **Enter**. Note which files are marked with the read-only attribute (i.e., the *R* attribute).

6. You decide to modify the STAFFBNS.TXT file. Before you can do so, you must reverse the read-only attribute on the file. Type the command **ATTRIB -R STAFFBNS.TXT** and press **Enter**.

7. To confirm the attribute change, type the command **ATTRIB** and press **Enter**. Note which files are no longer marked with the read-only attribute (i.e., the *R* attribute). Note the difference between the hard-linked and symbolically linked files pointing to STAFFBNS.TXT.

8. Key NTFS attributes are stored as part of the file content and do not immediately update the directory listing until the content is accessed. Now you will update the content of STAFFBNS.TXT through the hard link filename. Type the command **ECHO Plus 1.5% profit sharing. >> HLNKSBNS.TXT** and press **Enter**. Note any resulting error messages.

9. Confirm that STAFFBNS.TXT has been updated by typing the command **TYPE STAFFBNS.TXT** and pressing **Enter**.

10. To confirm all file attributes, type the command **ATTRIB** and press **Enter**. Note which files are no longer marked with the read-only attribute (i.e., the *R* attribute). Note the change for the hard-linked file.

11. Symbolic links are pointers, and the pointer has its own attributes separate from the content to which it points. Manage attributes for symbolic links, as detailed in the following steps:

a. Symbolic links are pointers to targets identified by a path that is part of the symbolic link. Attributes of the symbolic link are separate from the target. Type the command **ATTRIB +R SLNKSBNS.TXT /L** and press **Enter**.

b. Now you will confirm that the read-only attribute on the symbolic link file is in effect by trying to delete it. Type the command **DEL SLNKSBNS.TXT** and press **Enter**. Note the command's results.

c. To see the symbolic linked file's attributes, type the command **ATTRIB /L** and press **Enter**.

d. To confirm all file attributes, type the command **ATTRIB** and press **Enter**. Note that the attributes reported for the symbolic link when the /L parameter is not specified are those of the link's target.

12. Examine the effect on attributes when symbolic link pointers and the content to which they point are copied to a different location on the same NTFS volume, as detailed in the following steps:

a. Copy TYLERBNS.TXT to a folder on the same volume by typing the command **COPY TYLERBNS.TXT M:\LAB52\TYLER** and then press **Enter**.

b. Copy SLNKSBNS.TXT to a folder on the same volume by typing the command **COPY SLNKSBNS.TXT M:\LAB52\TYLER** and then press **Enter**.

c. Confirm the attributes on the copied file and symbolic link in M:\LAB52\TYLER by typing the command **ATTRIB M:\LAB52\TYLER*.* /L** and then press **Enter**. Note the reported attributes on the copied items.

13. Examine the effect on attributes when symbolic link pointers and the content to which they point are moved to a different location on the same NTFS volume, as detailed in the following steps:

a. Delete the items in M:\LAB52\TYLER by typing the command **DEL M:\LAB52\TYLER*.* /Q** and then press **Enter**.

b. Move TYLERBNS.TXT to a folder on the same volume by typing the command **MOVE TYLERBNS.TXT M:\LAB52\TYLER** and then press **Enter**.

c. Move SLNKSBNS.TXT to a folder on the same volume by typing the command **MOVE SLNKSBNS.TXT M:\LAB52\TYLER** and then press **Enter**.

d. Change the focus of the command prompt by typing **CD M:\LAB52\TYLER** and then press **Enter**.

e. Confirm the attributes on the moved file and symbolic link in M:\LAB52\TYLER by typing the command **ATTRIB *.* /L** and then press **Enter**. Note the reported attributes on the moved items.

14. Examine the effect on attributes when symbolic link pointers and the content to which they point are copied to a different location on a different NTFS volume, as detailed in the following steps:

a. Create a destination folder on drive N: by typing the command **MD N:\LAB52** and then press **Enter**.

b. Copy TYLERBNS.TXT to a folder on a different NTFS volume by typing the command **COPY TYLERBNS.TXT N:\LAB52** and then press **Enter**.

c. Copy SLNKSBNS.TXT to a folder on a different NTFS volume by typing the command **COPY SLNKSBNS.TXT N:\LAB52** and then press **Enter**.

d. Confirm the attributes on the copied file and symbolic link in N:\LAB52 by typing the command **ATTRIB N:\LAB52*.* /L** and then press **Enter**. Note the reported attributes on the copied items.

5

15. Examine the effect on attributes when symbolic link pointers and the content to which they point are copied to a FAT-formatted volume, as detailed in the following steps:

    a. Create a destination folder on drive O: by typing the command **MD O:\LAB52** and then press **Enter**.

    b. Copy TYLERBNS.TXT to a folder on a FAT volume by typing the command **COPY TYLERBNS.TXT O:\LAB52** and then press **Enter**.

    c. Copy SLNKSBNS.TXT to a folder on a FAT volume by typing the command **COPY SLNKSBNS.TXT O:\LAB52** and then press **Enter**.

    d. Confirm the attributes on the copied file and symbolic link in O:\LAB52 by typing the command **ATTRIB O:\LAB52*.* /L** and then press **Enter**. Note the reported attributes on the copied items.

    e. Type the command **DIR O:\LAB52** and then press **Enter**. Note that the symbolic link's target, and not the symbolic link itself, is copied to the FAT volume. This volume does not support symbolic link entries.

16. Delete the items in N:\LAB52 by typing the command **DEL N:\LAB52*.* /Q** and then press **Enter**.

17. Delete the items in O:\LAB52 by typing the command **DEL O:\LAB52*.* /Q** and then press **Enter**.

18. Examine the effect on attributes when symbolic link pointers and the content to which they point are moved to a different NTFS-formatted volume, as detailed in the following steps:

    a. Move TYLERBNS.TXT to a folder on a different NTFS volume by typing the command **MOVE TYLERBNS.TXT N:\LAB52** and then press **Enter**.

    b. Move SLNKSBNS.TXT to a folder on a different NTFS volume by typing the command **MOVE SLNKSBNS.TXT N:\LAB52** and then press **Enter**.

    c. Change the focus of the command prompt to the target volume by typing **N:** and then press **Enter**. Complete the change of focus by typing the command **CD N:\LAB52** and then press **Enter**.

    d. Confirm the attributes on the moved file and symbolic link in N:\LAB52 by typing the command **ATTRIB *.* /L** and then press **Enter**. Note the reported attributes on the moved items. Note that the file retained its original attributes, but the symbolic link itself did not.

    e. Confirm that the symbolic link SLNKSBNS.TXT is still a symbolic link after the move by typing the command **DIR** and then press **Enter**. Confirm that the link is functional by typing the command **TYPE SLNKSBNS.TXT** and then press **Enter**. Note the displayed text.

    f. Make the symbolic link's target read-only by typing the command **ATTRIB +R M:\ LAB52\TERRY\PRIVATE\STAFFBNS.TXT** and then press **Enter**.

    g. To confirm the attributes reported in the current directory, type the command **ATTRIB** and then press **Enter**. Note which files are now flagged as read-only.

19. Examine the effect on attributes when symbolic link pointers and the content to which they point are moved to a FAT-formatted volume, as detailed in the following steps:

    a. Move TYLERBNS.TXT to a folder on a FAT volume by typing the command **MOVE TYLERBNS.TXT O:\LAB52** and then press **Enter**.

    b. Attempt to move SLNKSBNS.TXT to a folder on a FAT volume by typing the command **MOVE SLNKSBNS.TXT O:\LAB52** and then press **Enter**. Note that the move command will not substitute the symbolic link's target when the destination is formatted with the FAT file system.

    c. Change the focus of the command prompt to the target volume by typing **O:** and then press **Enter**. Complete the change of focus by typing the command **CD O:\LAB52** and then press **Enter**.

    d. Confirm the attributes on the moved file in O:\LAB52 by typing the command **ATTRIB *.*** and then press **Enter**. Note that the file retained its original attributes.

20. Folders can be marked as read-only using command-line tools, but the attribute is interpreted differently by graphical tools such as Windows Explorer. Examine this read-only feature on a sample folder, as detailed in the following steps:

    a. To create a folder in the current directory that will hold temporary content, type the command **MD DISPOSE** and press **Enter**.

    b. To use the ATTRIB command to configure the folder as read-only, type the command **ATTRIB +R DISPOSE** and press **Enter**.

    c. To confirm that the folder is protected by attempting to delete it, type the command **RD DISPOSE** and press **Enter**. Note the command's results.

    d. To confirm the folder's attributes, type the command **ATTRIB O:\LAB52\DISPOSE** and then press **Enter**. Note that the folder is flagged as read-only.

    e. In the computer browser window, double-click the icon for drive **O:** in the right pane.

    f. Double-click the **LAB52** folder in the right pane to expand that folder.

    g. Right-click the **DISPOSE** folder and select **Properties** from the pop-up menu.

    h. If the **General** tab is not selected by default, click it to select it. Note that the read-only attribute is blocked out, and note the comment that the read-only setting applies only to files in the folder, as shown in Figure 5-1.

    i. Click the **Cancel** button to close the DISPOSE folder's properties.

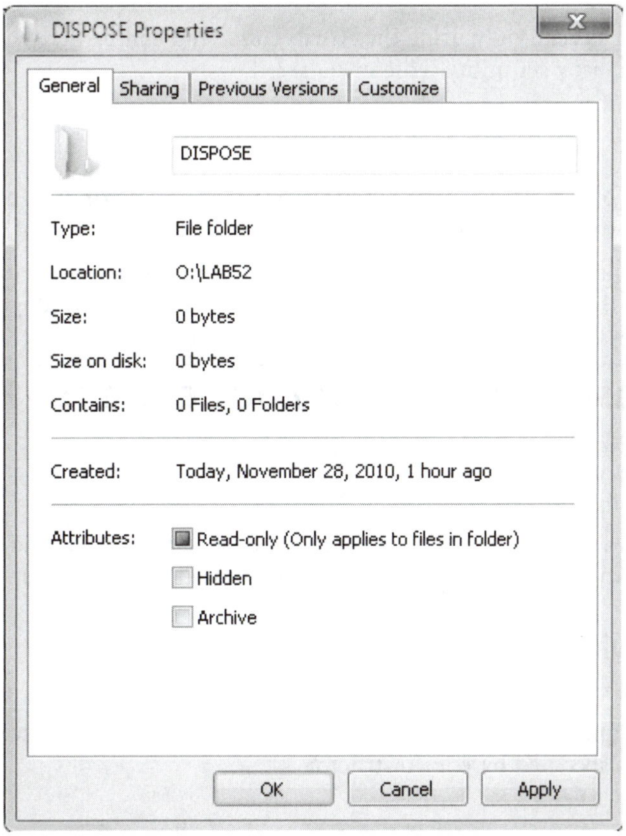

5

Figure 5-1 Folder attributes when viewed through Windows Explorer

© *Cengage Learning 2012*

j. Right-click the DISPOSE folder and select **Delete** from the pop-up menu.

k. When you are prompted to confirm the folder deletion, click the **Yes** button to proceed. Note that the read-only attribute on the folder does not prevent folder deletion in this case.

21. Close all open windows. Log off the computer.

Certification Objectives

Objectives for MCTS Exam #70-680: Windows 7, Configuring:

- Configuring Access to Resources: Configure file and folder access

Review Questions

1. When you try to move a symbolic link to a FAT-formatted volume, the operation will _____.

   a. Create a hard link

   b. Create a copy of the symbolic link's target

   c. Copy the symbolic link

   d. Fail

2. A folder marked as read-only using the Attrib command can be deleted with the Remove Directory (RD) command-line utility. True or False?

   a. True

   b. False

3. A folder marked as read-only using the Attrib command can be deleted with the graphical computer file browser utility. True or False?

   a. True

   b. False

4. When files and folders are accessed by different programs, attributes might not be interpreted by each program as expected. What might explain this behavior?

5. Individual hard links pointing to the same content do not have unique attributes for each hard link. From the user's perspective, how might this be a disadvantage?

Lab 5.3: Creating a Basic NTFS Security Structure for Files and Folders

Objectives

The objective of this activity is to create a simple folder structure, users, and groups, and then manage NTFS security for that folder structure using those users and groups.

Materials Required

This lab requires the following:

- A physical computer or virtual machine running Windows 7 that is configured as User*x*-PC or as specified by your instructor
- Completion of Lab 5.1

Estimated completion time: **45 minutes**

Activity Background

Windows 7 provides the ability to configure a shared folder structure that allows multiple users to access data that is secured with NTFS permissions. A folder structure will be created, along with users and groups to control access to different folders. NTFS permission inheritance will be blocked at different levels and specific permission assignments will be made to groups and individual accounts.

Activity

1. Log on to User*x*-PC.

2. Click **Start**, right-click **Computer**, and then click **Manage** to select it from the pop-up menu.

3. In the left pane of the Computer Management window, click **Local Users and Groups** below System Tools to select it. Several groups will be created through Steps 4 to 10, and will later be used in this activity to manage access to folders containing company files.

4. Double-click the **Groups** folder in the right pane to select it.

5. Click the **Action** menu to display a list of related group-management actions. Click **New Group** in the menu to select it.

6. After the New Group window opens, in the *Group name* field, enter the text **BOSS**. In the *Description* field, enter the text **Full access to all business files**. Click the **Create** button to create the new group.

7. The New Group window will stay open as a convenience in case you want to create more groups. In the *Group name* field, enter the text **STAFF**. In the *Description* field, enter the text **Staff level access to general business files**. Click the **Create** button to create the new group.

8. In the *Group name* field, enter the text **PRIVATE**. In the *Description* field, enter the text **Restricted access to private files**. Click the **Create** button to create the new group.

9. In the *Group name* field, enter the text **DENIED**. In the *Description* field, enter the text **No access to specific business files**. Click the **Create** button to create the new group.

10. Click the **Close** button to close the New Group window. Note that the list of groups in the Computer Management window's right pane has updated to include the list of groups just created.

11. In the left pane of the Computer Management window, click **Users** below Local Users and Groups to select it. Several users will be created in Steps 12 to 18, and the users will be used later in this activity to manage access to folders and files.

12. Click the **Action** menu to display a list of related user-management actions. Click **New User** in the menu to select it.

13. In the New User window, create a new user, as detailed in the following steps:

    a. In the *User name* field, enter the text **TERRY**.

    b. In the *Description* field, enter the text **President**.

    c. In the *Password* field, enter the text **P@ssw0rd**.

    d. In the *Confirm password* field, enter the text **P@ssw0rd**.

    e. Uncheck the **User must change password at next logon** check box.

    f. Click the **Create** button to create the new user.

5

14. Using Steps 13.a to 13.f, create a new user, with the only differences being the username is **TYLER** and the description is **Vice-President**.

15. Using Steps 13.a to 13.f, create a new user, with the only differences being the username is **JEN** and the description is **Confidential Secretary**.

16. Using Steps 13.a to 13.f, create a new user, with the only differences being the username is **ASHLEY** and the description is **Office Clerk**.

17. Using Steps 13.a to 13.f, create a new user, with the only differences being the username is **BOBBIE** and the description is **Office Manager**.

18. In the New User window, click the **Close** button. Note that the list of users in the Computer Management window's right pane has been updated to include the list of users just created.

19. Click **Start,** click **Computer,** and then double-click the icon for drive **M:** in the right-hand pane of the computer browser window that opens.

20. Click the **New folder** toolbar menu item in the computer's browser window to create a new folder on drive **M:**. Change the new folder's name from *New folder* to **LAB53** and press **Enter**.

21. Double-click the **LAB53** folder to drill down one level in the computer's file browser window. Use the **New folder** toolbar menu item to create the following folders in the LAB53 folder, one at a time:

    a. **PRESIDENT**

    b. **VP**

    c. **STAFF**

22. Double-click the **STAFF** folder to drill down one level in the computer's file browser window. Use the **New folder** toolbar menu item to create the following folders in the STAFF folder, one at a time:

    a. **BULLETINS**

    b. **WORKING FILES**

23. Click the back arrow to refocus the computer's file browser window up one folder level. Double-click the **VP** folder to drill down one level in the computer's file browser window. Use the **New folder** toolbar menu item to create the following folders in the VP folder, one at a time:

    a. **NEW POSITIONS**

    b. **STAFF PROFILES**

24. Click the back arrow to refocus the computer file browser window up one folder level. Double-click the **PRESIDENT** folder to drill down one level in the computer's file browser window. Use the **New folder** toolbar menu item to create the following folders in the PRESIDENT folder, one at a time:

    a. **EXPANSION PLANS**

    b. **FINAL BUDGET**

25. Double-click the **FINAL BUDGET** folder to drill down one level. Use the **New folder** toolbar menu item to create a folder named **DRAFTS** in the FINAL BUDGET folder.

26. Refocus the computer's browser window up three folder levels to M:\LAB53.

27. Groups can be used to assign permissions to local resources, such as files and folders. Assign the BOSS group and your user account to the PRESIDENT folder and its subfolders, as detailed in the following steps:

    a. Right-click the **PRESIDENT** folder and select **Properties** from the pop-up menu.

    b. In the PRESIDENT folder's properties window, click the **Security** tab to select it.

c. Click the **Advanced** button. This will open an *Advanced Security Settings for PRESIDENT* window that displays current permissions and additional security settings using a more detailed view.

d. In the Advanced Security Settings window, click the **Change Permissions** button. This will open an advanced permissions window that allows for updates to the permissions listed in the previous window.

e. Deselect the **Include inheritable permissions from this object's parent** option. This action will immediately open a Windows Security dialog box. Click the **Add** button to copy the parent folder's permissions to this folder and automatically close the window.

f. In the Advanced Security Settings window with only the Permissions tab displayed, click the **OK** button to close the window.

g. In the Advanced Security Settings window, click the **OK** button to close the window.

h. In the PRESIDENT Properties window with the Security tab displayed, click the **Edit** button to change folder permissions using a simpler permissions view than that displayed by the Advanced button.

i. In the Permissions for PRESIDENT window that opens, click the **Add** button to add a new NTFS permission to the folder.

j. In the Select Users or Groups window that opens, type the name **BOSS** under the heading *Enter the object names to select* and then click **OK** to save the change.

k. Notice that the BOSS group's name is now listed on the Permissions window in the list of Group or user names. Click the **BOSS** group's name in the list to select it.

l. In the Permissions window, in the section titled *Permissions for BOSS*, click the **Allow** check box on the same line as **Modify**, as shown in Figure 5-2.

m. Click the **Add** button to add a new NTFS permission to the folder.

n. In the Select Users or Groups window that opens, type your username under the heading **Enter the object names to select** and then click **OK** to save the change.

o. Notice that your username is now listed on the Permissions window in the list of Group or user names. Click your username in the list to select it.

p. Click the **Allow** check box on the same line as **Full Control** and then click **OK** to save the change.

q. In the folder's properties window, in the list of Group or user names, click **Authenticated Users** to select it, and then click the **Remove** button.

r. In the list of Group or user names, click **SYSTEM** to select it, and then click the **Remove** button.

s. In the list of Group or user names, click **Users** to select it, and then click the **Remove** button.

t. In the list of Group or user names, click **Administrators** to select it, and notice that in the section Permissions for Administrators, all permissions are marked as Allow.

u. Click the **OK** button to save the permission changes and close the Properties window.

v. Click the **OK** button to close the PRESIDENT Properties window.

28. Repeat Steps 27.a to 27.v to assign the **PRIVATE** group **Modify** permissions to the **VP** folder instead of the PRESIDENT folder.

29. Repeat Steps 27.a to 27.v to assign the **STAFF** group **Modify** permissions to the **STAFF** folder instead of the PRESIDENT folder.

5

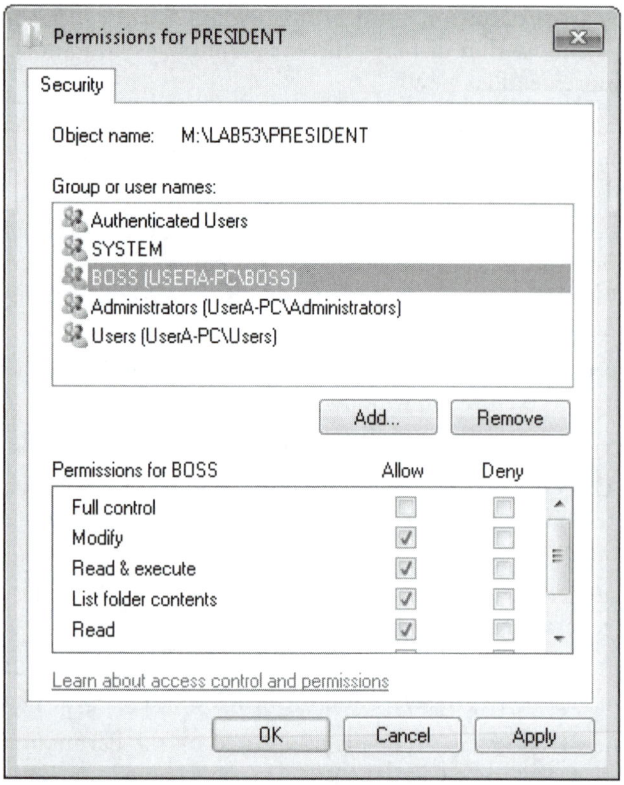

Figure 5-2 Granting the Modify, Allow permission for a folder
© Cengage Learning 2012

30. For a user to be granted a group's NTFS permissions, the user must be a member of the group. When a user is made a member of a group, the next time the user logs in, the user's security token for that session will be created with that group's identity included. The security token includes a list of groups to which the user belongs, but the list in the token is only updated when the token is created. For Terry and Tyler to receive Modify rights to the VP folder, their user accounts can be added as members of the PRIVATE group, as detailed in the following steps:

   a. In the Computer Management window, click to select the **Groups** tool below Local Users and Groups in the left pane.

   b. In the right pane, right-click the **PRIVATE** group and select **Add to Group** from the pop-up menu.

   c. In the group's properties window that opens, click the **Add** button.

   d. In the Select Users window that opens, type the username **TERRY** under the heading *Enter the object names to select* and then click **OK** to save the change.

   e. Repeat Steps 30.a to 30.d to add another user; however, type the username **TYLER** instead of TERRY.

   f. Click the **OK** button to save the changes and close the group's properties window.

31. Repeat Steps 30.a to 30.f to configure the users **JEN**, **ASHLEY**, and **BOBBIE** as members of the **STAFF** group instead of the PRIVATE group.

32. Repeat Steps 30.a to 30.f to configure the user **TERRY** as a member of the **BOSS** group instead of the PRIVATE group.

33. Groups are a convenient tool to organize users with the same security requirements, but are not the only way to assign security rights to users. Individual users can be assigned NTFS permissions to files and folders directly. A company policy to manage file and folder access through groups does not stop another permission-assignment method from being used. Consider the situation in which someone has permission to assign permissions to other users, but is unaware of company policy. If that person decides to assign permissions to a user account directly, the system will not prevent it. Assume you are a junior IT administrator and you act on a request from JEN to get access to the PRESIDENT folder. Being unaware of the company's requirement to use groups for permission assignment, you act to grant it through permissions applied directly to her user account, as detailed in the following steps:

    a. Right-click the **PRESIDENT** folder in the computer file browser window and select **Properties** from the pop-up menu.

    b. Click to select the **Security** tab.

    c. Click the **Edit** button to change permissions on the folder.

    d. Click the **Add** button in the Permissions window that opens.

    e. In the Select Users or Groups window that opens, type the username **JEN** under the heading *Enter the object names to select*, and then click **OK** to save the change.

    f. Notice that JEN's username is now listed in the Permissions window in the list of Group or user names. Click the username **JEN** in the list to select it.

    g. In the Permissions window, in the section titled *Permissions for JEN*, click the **Allow** check box next to **Full Control**.

    h. Click **OK** to save the permission change and close the window.

    i. Click **OK** to close the PRESIDENT folder's properties window.

34. Without a periodic review or audit of file and folder permission assignments, a permission assigned outside company policy may be difficult to detect. A user may operate with undesirable permissions for some time and make unapproved changes, which may be directly against company policy, even if the user does not intend to do so. Jen continues to work with good intentions, and decides to create a file in the PRESIDENT folder, as detailed in the following steps:

    a. Log out as the current user and log in as the user JEN, using the password defined in Step 13.c.

    b. Click **Start** and in the *Search Programs and files* box, type **M:\LAB53\PRESIDENT\ EXPANSION PLANS**, and then press **Enter**.

    c. Right-click anywhere on the right pane of the computer browser window that opens and select **New**; then select **Text Document** from the pop-up menus.

    d. Change the name of the new document from **New Text Document.txt** to **Jen's Expanding.txt** and press **Enter** to save the change.

    e. Double-click the **Jen's Expanding.txt** file to open it in Notepad. Enter the text **Jen's notes for assisting with company expansion** and then save the file and close Notepad. Note if the file was successfully saved.

35. Log off the computer.

Certification Objectives

Objectives for MCTS Exam #70-680: Windows 7, Configuring:

- Configuring Access to Resources: Configure file and folder access

Review Questions

1. What is the most permissive NTFS permission automatically allowed when a new permission entry is added to a file?

   a. Full Control

   b. Modify

   c. Read and Execute

   d. Write

2. When the Full Control Allow permission is selected, what other permissions are automatically assigned? (Select two.)

   a. Modify

   b. Read

   c. Write

   d. Special permissions

3. When the Full Control Allow permission is deselected, what is the most permissive permission that still applies?

   a. Modify

   b. Read

   c. Write

   d. Special permissions

4. Some businesses want high-level managers to have full visibility for all files in the corporate environment. To ensure that the BOSS group has full access to all files and folders below M:\LAB53, at what level, or levels, should the permission assignment be made?

5. A user has been made a member of a group that grants the user access to a preexisting folder structure. The user calls you to inform you that he cannot access the folder structure. When the user attempts to open it, he receives an access-denied message. Other members of the group are not reporting any problems. What should you ask the user to do as an initial troubleshooting step?

Lab 5.4: Determining Effective NTFS Permissions and Restricting Access

Objectives

The objective of this activity is to inspect effective permissions to NTFS resources and then restrict access to resources using a Deny permission.

Materials Required

This lab requires the following:

- A physical computer or virtual machine running Windows 7 that is configured as User*x*-PC or as specified by your instructor
- Completion of Lab 5.3

Estimated completion time: **15 minutes**

Activity Background

NTFS permissions can be allowed or denied. A user can have both allow and deny permissions applied to a file or folder at the same time. This activity examines what happens when allow and deny permissions are combined. A file called "Jen's Expanding.txt" will be created in the folder M:\LAB53\PRESIDENT\EXPANSION PLANS. You will check effective NTFS permissions on the file for a userid, JEN. A deny permission will be applied to that file to remove access to that file for JEN. The userid JEN will attempt to access the file to confirm if the combined allow and deny permission will allow the operation to complete.

Activity

1. Log on to User*x*-PC as User*x*.

2. Determine Jen's effective NTFS permissions to the file M:\LAB53\PRESIDENT\ EXPANSION PLANS\Jen's Expanding.txt, as detailed in the following steps:

    a. Click **Start**, and then click **Computer** to open a computer file browser window.

    b. Navigate to the folder **M:\LAB53\PRESIDENT\EXPANSION PLANS**.

    c. Right-click **Jen's Expanding.txt** and then select **Properties**.

    d. Click the **Security** tab to select it.

    e. Click the **Advanced** button.

    f. In the Advanced Security Settings window that opens, click the **Effective Permissions** tab to select it.

    g. Next to the Group or user name box, click the **Select** button.

    h. In the Select User or Group window that opens, type the name of the suspect user, **JEN**, and click **OK** to save the selection. Review the list of effective permissions with a check mark next to them, indicating what permissions the selected user has to that NTFS item.

    i. Click **OK** to close the Advanced Security Settings window.

    j. Click **OK** to close the Jen's Expanding.txt Properties window.

3. Configure restricted access on the file Jen's Expanding.txt by assigning the DENIED group an NTFS permission that denies access to the file, as detailed in the following steps:

    a. Right-click **Jen's Expanding.txt** and then select **Properties**.

    b. Click the **Security** tab to select it.

    c. Click the **Edit** button to open the Permissions window for Jen's Expanding.txt.

    d. Click the **Add** button to open the Select Users or Groups window.

    e. In the Enter the object names to select field, type the group name **DENIED** and click **OK** to save the selection.

    f. The DENIED group is already highlighted in the list of Group and user names. Click the **Deny** check box on the same line as **Full Control** in the *Permissions for DENIED* list, as seen in Figure 5-3. Note which other permissions for the group are automatically changed.

    g. Note the Windows Security message that opens, and then click **Yes** to continue.

    h. Click **OK** to close the Properties window.

4. Assign the user Jen to the DENIED group to restrict her access to the file M:\LAB53\ PRESIDENT\EXPANSION PLANS\Jen's Expanding.txt, as detailed in the following steps:

    a. Right-click **Computer** in the left-pane of the computer file browser window.

    b. Select **Manage** from the pop-up menu.

Figure 5-3 Assigning the Full Control, Deny permission for a folder
© *Cengage Learning 2012*

    c. If you are prompted by User Account Control to continue, click **Yes**.

    d. In the left pane of the Computer Management window, click **Local Users and Groups** below System Tools to select it.

    e. Double-click the **Groups** folder in the right pane to select it.

    f. Double-click the group **DENIED** to open the group's properties.

    g. Click the **Add** button.

    h. In the Select Users window that opens, type the username **JEN** and click **OK** to save the selection.

    i. Click **OK** to close the group's properties window.

5. Log off and then log in as the user **JEN**, using the password defined in Lab 5.3, Step 13.c.

6. When you are logged in as JEN, the security token for that session will include the DENIED group as a group to which the user JEN belongs. Attempt to open the file M:\LAB53\PRESIDENT\EXPANSION PLANS\Jen's Expanding.txt, as detailed in the following steps:

    a. Click **Start**, and then click **Computer** to open a computer file browser window.

    b. Navigate to the folder **M:\LAB53\PRESIDENT\EXPANSION PLANS**.

    c. Double-click **Jen's Expanding.txt** and note the error message. Click **OK** to continue.

    d. Close **Notepad**.

7. Attempt to create a new file in the folder M:\LAB53\PRESIDENT\EXPANSION PLANS, as detailed in the following steps:

   a. Right-click anywhere on the right pane of the computer browser window that opens and select **New**; then select **Text Document** from the pop-up menu.

   b. Change the name of the new document from New Text Document.txt to **Jen's Revised Plans.txt** and press **Enter** to save the change.

   c. Double-click the file **Jen's Revised Plans.txt** to open the file in Notepad. Enter the text **Jen's notes for assisting with company expansion**, save the file, and then close Notepad. Note if the file was successfully saved without an error message being displayed.

8. Log off the computer.

Certification Objectives

Objectives for MCTS Exam #70-680: Windows 7, Configuring:

- Configuring Access to Resources: Configure file and folder access

Review Questions

1. A group currently has the NTFS Read and Modify permission allowed for a file. When the group is assigned the Full Control Deny permission, what, if any, permissions are denied as well?

   a. All allowed permissions

   b. FULL ACCESS

   c. MODIFY

   d. None

2. Effective permission can be determined for _____.

   a. Only files that the user has created

   b. Files only

   c. Any NTFS file or folder

   d. Folders only

3. In Step 7 of the lab, if the user JEN should not have been able to save files to the folder, what allowed the user JEN to save files to that folder even after the Deny permission was in place?

4. Effective NTFS permissions viewed in the Advanced Security Settings window for a file or folder can be exported to the _____ format.

   a. XML

   b. CSV

   c. HTML

   d. None of the above

5. What would be the best method to achieve the goal of restricting the user's ability to save and create files in a folder? If the administrator decides to move the file with Deny permissions to a different folder, a folder where the user has Full Control and is on the same NTFS volume, will the Deny permission be removed?

5

CHAPTER SIX

USER MANAGEMENT

Labs included in this chapter:

- Lab 6.1 Creating Users
- Lab 6.2 Identifying Differences Between User Types
- Lab 6.3 Applying Permissions by Using Groups
- Lab 6.4 Managing User Passwords
- Lab 6.5 Managing User Profiles

Microsoft MCTS Exam #70-680 Objectives

Objective	Lab
Configure authentication and authorization	6.1, 6.2, 6.3, 6.4, 6.5
Configure user account control	6.2

Lab 6.1: Creating Users

Objectives

The object of this activity is to create user accounts by using Control Panel and Computer Management.

Materials Required

This lab requires the following:

- A physical computer or virtual machine running Windows 7 that is configured as User*x*-PC or as specified by your instructor

Estimated completion time: **10 minutes**

Activity Background

User accounts are the primary mechanism used to control access to Windows 7. To allow users to have access to a computer, you must create user accounts. In small peer-to-peer networks, the user accounts are created locally in Windows 7. Larger corporate networks typically store user accounts in a central Active Directory database on a server. A commonly used option is to force users to change their password on first logon. This ensures that only the user knows the new password.

Activity

1. Log on to User*x*-PC.

2. Create a new user account by using Control Panel, as detailed in the following steps:

    a. Click **Start** and click **Control Panel**.

    b. In the Control Panel window, under User Accounts and Family Safety, click **Add or remove user accounts**.

    c. In the Manage Accounts window, click **What is a user account**.

    d. Read the content in the Windows Help and Support window and then close the window.

    e. In the Manage Accounts window, click **Create a new account**.

    f. In the New account name box, type **Standard1**, as shown in Figure 6-1.

    g. Verify that **Standard user** is selected, and then click **Create Account**.

    h. Close the Manage Accounts window.

3. Create a new user account by using Computer Management, as detailed in the following steps:

    a. Click **Start**, right-click **Computer**, and click **Manage**.

    b. In Computer Management, expand **Local Users and Groups** and click **Users**. Notice that the user Standard1 appears here.

    c. Right-click **Users** and click **New User**.

    d. In the New User window, in the User name box, type **Standard2**, as shown in Figure 6-2.

    e. Clear the **User must change password at next logon** check box, and then click **Create**.

    f. Click **Close**.

    g. Close Computer Management.

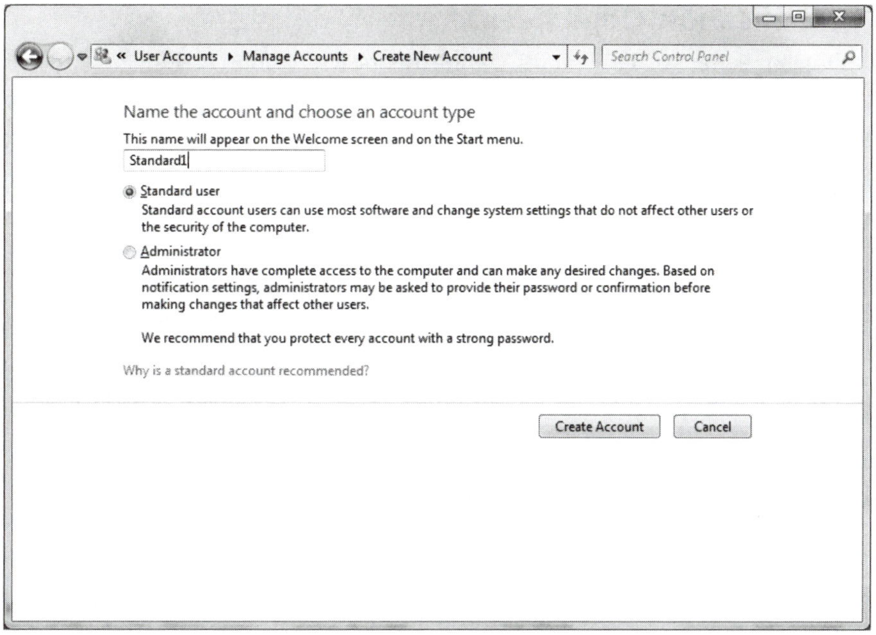

Figure 6-1 Creating a user account by using Control Panel
© *Cengage Learning 2012*

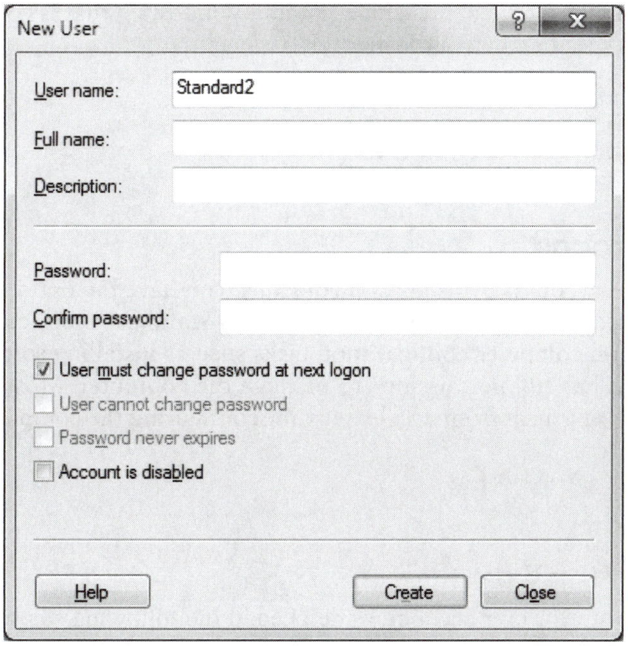

Figure 6-2 Creating a user account by using Computer Management
© *Cengage Learning 2012*

4. Log off. Notice that both Standard1 and Standard2 appear on the logon screen.

5. Click **Standard1** to log on as the Standard1 user. It will take a few moments to log on because a new profile is created.

6. Log off.

Certification Objectives

Objectives for MCTS Exam #70-680: Windows 7, Configuring:

- Configuring Access to Resources: Configure authentication and authorization

Review Questions

1. Which two graphical utilities can be used to create user accounts?
2. Does the utility that you select for creating user accounts affect the user experience?
3. Why would you select one utility over the other when creating user accounts?
4. Why is the first logon for an account slower than subsequent logons?
5. If two people are sharing a computer, should they share a single account?

Lab 6.2: Identifying Differences Between User Types

Objectives

The objective of this activity is to identify differences between standard users and administrative users.

Materials Required

This lab requires the following:

- A physical computer or virtual machine running Windows 7 that is configured as User*x*-PC or as specified by your instructor
- Completion of Lab 6.1

Estimated completion time: **10 minutes**

Activity Background

When you create user accounts by using Control Panel, you have the option to create a standard user account or an administrator user account. A standard user account has limited permissions to perform computer configuration tasks such as installing software. An administrator user account has full permissions to manage the computer. Most users should be standard users to prevent them from accidentally misconfiguring the computer and installing unauthorized software.

Activity

1. Log on to User*x*-PC as User*x*.
2. Create an administrator user account, as detailed in the following steps:
   a. Click **Start** and click **Control Panel**.
   b. Under User Accounts and Family Safety, click **Add or remove user accounts**.
   c. In the Manage Accounts window, click **Create a new account**.
   d. In the Create New Account window, click **Why is a standard account recommended**.
   e. In the Windows Help and Support Window, read the content.
   f. Click the green **standard account** to view and read the definition.

    g. Click the green **administrator account** to view and read the definition.

    h. Close the Windows Help and Support window.

    i. In the Create New Account window, in the New account name box, type **Administrator1**.

    j. Click **Administrator** and click **Create Account**.

    k. Close the Manage accounts window.

3. Verify administrative capabilities of Administrator1, as detailed in the following steps:

    a. Switch user to **Administrator1**.

    b. Click **Start** and click **Control Panel**.

    c. In Control Panel, click **System and Security**.

    d. In the System and Security window, read the available options. The options with a shield beside them, as shown in Figure 6-3, require administrative privileges to perform.

    e. Under Action Center, click **Change User Account Control settings**.

    f. In the User Account Control Settings window, move the slider to **Notify me only when programs try to make changes to my computer (do not dim my desktop)** and click **OK**.

    g. In the User Account Control window, click **Yes**.

    h. In the System and Security window, under System, click **Device Manager**.

    i. After Device Manager successfully starts, close Device Manager.

    j. Close the System and Security window.

    k. Log off

6

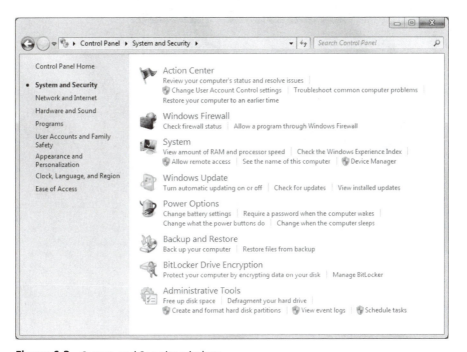

Figure 6-3 System and Security window

© Cengage Learning 2012

4. Test the administrative capabilities of Standard1, as detailed in the following steps:

   a. Log on as **Standard1**.

   b. Click **Start** and click **Control Panel**.

   c. In Control Panel, click **System and Security**.

   d. In the System and Security window, read the available options. The options are the same as for Administrator1.

   e. Under Action Center, click **Change User Account Control settings**. A standard user is unable to perform this action and is prompted for Administrator credentials, as shown in Figure 6-4.

   f. In the User Account Control window, click **Administrator1** and then click **Yes**.

   g. In the User Account Control Settings window, move the slider to **Notify me only when programs try to make changes to my computer (do not dim my desktop)**. Notice that a standard user cannot change this setting because the OK button is dimmed.

   h. Close the User Account Control Settings window.

   i. In the System and Security window, under System, click **Device Manager**.

   j. Read the warning message and then click **OK** to close the warning window.

   k. Close Device Manager.

   l. Close the System and Security window.

5. Log off.

Figure 6-4 User Account Control window
© Cengage Learning 2012

Certification Objectives

Objectives for MCTS Exam #70-680: Windows 7, Configuring:

- Configuring Access to Resources: Configure authentication and authorization
- Configuring Access to Resources: Configure user account control

Review Questions

1. In the adjective graphical interface, how can you tell which actions require administrative privileges?
2. What is the difference between a standard user and an administrator user?
3. Why should most user accounts be configured as standard user accounts?
4. What happens when a standard user tries to perform a task that requires administrative permissions?
5. Do standard users and administrator users see different content in Control Panel?

Lab 6.3: Applying Permissions by Using Groups

Objectives

The objective of this activity is to identify the default groups available in Windows 7 and how groups are used to assign permissions.

Materials Required

This lab requires the following:

- A physical computer or virtual machine running Windows 7 that is configured as User*x*-PC or as specified by your instructor
- Completion of Lab 6.2

Estimated completion time: **10 minutes**

Activity Background

In Windows 7, groups are a way to assign permissions to multiple users at the same time. A user who is a member of a group is given the ability to perform all of the tasks that have been assigned to the group.

Several default groups in Windows 7 are assigned specific permissions, such as the Administrators group. In many cases, the default groups are sufficient for assigning users access to the necessary resources. However, you can also create groups.

Activity

1. Log on to User*x*-PC as User*x*.
2. View the default groups created in Windows 7, as detailed in the following steps:
   a. Click **Start**, right-click **Computer**, and click **Manage**.
   b. In the left pane of Computer Management, expand **Local Users and Groups**, and click **Groups**.
   c. Read the list of default groups.
   d. Move your mouse pointer over the description of each group to display the full description. Read each description.

3. Modify group membership, as detailed in the following steps:

    a. In Computer Management, right-click **Administrators** and click **Properties**.

    b. In the Administrators Properties window, read the list of group members. Notice that Administrator1 is a member of the Administrators group and that Standard1 is not a member.

    c. Click the **Add** button.

    d. In the Select Users window, type **Standard1** and click **OK**.

    e. In the Administrator Properties window, click **OK**.

4. View the user type for Standard1, as detailed in the following steps:

    a. Click **Start** and click **Control Panel**.

    b. In the Control Panel window, under User Accounts and Family Safety, click **Add or remove user accounts**.

    c. In the Manage Accounts window, read the description of Standard1. Notice that the account type has changed to Administrator.

5. View group membership for user accounts, as detailed in the following steps:

    a. In Computer Management, in the left pane, click **Users**.

    b. Right-click **Standard2** and click **Properties**.

    c. In the Standard2 Properties window, on the Member Of tab, read the list of groups of which this user is a member. This is the group membership for a standard user.

    d. Click **Cancel**.

    e. Right-click **Administrator1** and click **Properties**.

    f. In the Administrator1 Properties window, on the Member Of tab, read the list of groups of which this user is a member. This is the group membership for an administrator user.

    g. Read the note at the bottom of the windows about when membership changes take effect.

    h. Click **Cancel**.

6. Create a group for project files, as detailed in the following steps:

    a. In Computer Management, in the left pane, click **Groups**.

    b. Right-click **Groups** and click **New Group**.

    c. In the New Group window, in the Group name box, type **Projects**.

    d. In the Description box, type **Members have access to project files on the local computer**.

    e. Click the **Add** button.

    f. In the Select Users window, type **Standard1;Standard2** and then click **OK**.

    g. In the New Group window, click **Create** and then click **Close**.

    h. Close Computer Management.

7. Give the Projects group access to a Projects folder, as detailed in the following steps:

    a. Click **Start** and click **Computer**.

    b. In Windows Explorer, click **Local Disk (C:)** and then click **New folder**.

    c. Type **Projects** and press **Enter** to rename the new folder.

    d. Right-click **Projects** and click **Properties**.

    e. In the Projects Properties window, on the Security tab, click **Edit**.

    f. In the Permissions for Projects window, click **Add**.

g. In the Select Users or Groups window, type `Projects` and click `OK`.

h. In the Permission for Projects window, click `Projects (Userx-PC\Projects)`, select the `Allow Full control` check box, and click `OK`.

i. In the Projects Properties window, click `OK`.

j. Close Windows Explorer.

Certification Objectives

Objectives for MCTS Exam #70-680: Windows 7, Configuring:

- Configuring Access to Resources: Configure authentication and authorization

Review Questions

1. Standard users are members of which group?

2. Administrator users are members of which group or groups?

3. Which default group can use Remote Desktop to remotely access a Windows 7 computer?

4. How does using groups simplify the application of permissions?

5. Which graphical management tool must you use to create and manage groups in Windows 7?

Lab 6.4: Managing User Passwords

Objectives

The objective of this activity is to manage user authentication by configuring passwords.

Materials Required

This lab requires the following:

- A physical computer or virtual machine running Windows 7 that is configured as Userx-PC or as specified by your instructor
- A formatted USB flash drive or floppy disk
- Completion of Lab 6.3

Estimated completion time: **15 minutes**

Activity Background

By default, Windows 7 does not force user accounts to have a password. However, it is a best practice that all user accounts have passwords. In many organizations, a simple password is configured initially and then the user is forced to change the password at first logon.

Almost all users forget passwords at some time or another. Windows 7 provides several methods to help users recover their passwords.

Activity

1. Log on to Userx-PC as Userx.

2. Set a password for a user account, as detailed in the following steps:

   a. Click `Start`, right-click `Computer`, and click `Manage`.

   b. In Computer Management, expand `Local Users and Groups` and click `Users`.

6

c. Right-click **Standard1** and click **Set Password**.

d. Read the warning message that appears. The data loss mentioned in the warning message is relevant for files encrypted by EFS. Users do not typically lose access to any data.

e. Click **Proceed**.

f. In the Set Password for Standard2 window, in the New password and Confirm password boxes, type **password**, and click **OK**.

g. Click **OK** to clear the message about the password being set.

3. Require a user account to have a password, as detailed in the following steps:

a. In Computer Management, right-click **Standard1** and click **Properties**.

b. In the Standard1 Properties window, on the General tab, clear all check boxes, as shown in Figure 6-5, and read the available options.

c. Select the **User must change password at next logon** check box, and click **OK**.

d. Close Computer Management.

4. Test the password change for Standard1, as detailed in the following steps:

a. Switch user to **Standard1** and log on with the password of **password**.

b. Read the message that appears about changing the password, and then click **OK**.

c. In the New password and Confirm password boxes, type **newpassword** and then press **Enter**.

d. Read the message that appears about changing the password, and then click **OK**.

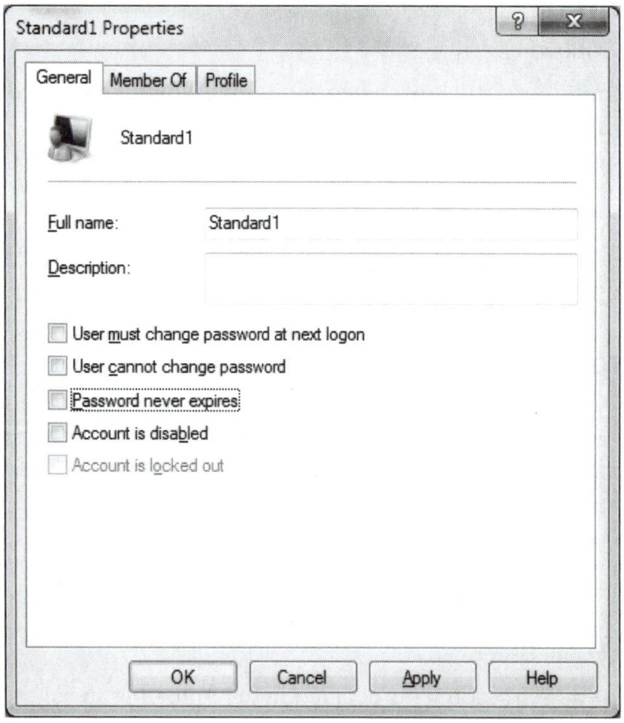

Figure 6-5 Properties of user account, General tab
© Cengage Learning 2012

5. Connect a USB flash drive to your computer. If you are using a virtualized version of Windows, you can use a virtual floppy disk for this activity. In both cases, the drive must be formatted.

6. Back up the user password, as detailed in the following steps:

   a. Click **Start** and click **Control Panel**.

   b. In Control Panel, click **User Accounts and Family Safety** and click **User Accounts**.

   c. In the User Accounts window, in the left pane, click **Create a password reset disk**.

   d. In the Forgotten Password Wizard window, read the information presented and then click **Next**.

   e. On the Create a Password Reset Disk page, select the removable storage that will be your password reset disk and click **Next**. This is the USB drive or floppy disk that you will use for recovery.

   f. On the Current User Account Password page, in the Current user account password box, type **newpassword** and click **Next**.

   g. On the Creating Password Reset Disk page, when progress has reached 100%, click **Next**.

   h. On the Completing the Forgotten Password Wizard page, click **Finish**.

   i. Close the User Accounts Window and log off.

7. Use the password reset disk, as detailed in the following steps:

   a. Log on as **Standard1**, but enter an incorrect password of **qwerty**.

   b. When the message about the incorrect password appears, click **OK**.

   c. Notice that a Reset password link is visible now.

   d. Click **Reset password**.

   e. In the Password Reset Wizard window, click **Next**.

   f. On the Insert the Password Reset Disk page, select the removable media with your password reset information and then click **Next**.

   g. On the Reset the User Account Password page, in the Type a new password and Type the password again to confirm boxes, type **PasswordRst**.

   h. In the New password hint box, type **Password is reset** and then click **Next**.

   i. On the Completing the Password Reset Wizard page, read the message and click **Finish**.

   j. Log on as Standard1 with a password of **PasswordRst**.

   k. Log off.

8. View a password hint, as detailed in the following steps:

   a. Log on as **Standard1**, but enter an incorrect password of **qwerty**.

   b. When the message about the incorrect password appears, click **OK**.

   c. Log on as Standard1 with an incorrect password again.

   d. Notice that the password hint is shown now.

Certification Objectives

Objectives for MCTS Exam #70-680: Windows 7, Configuring:

- Configuring Access to Resources: Configure authentication and authorization

Review Questions

1. Why should all users have a password?

2. Why is it a good idea to force users to change a password on the next logon after you reset their password?

3. What is the difference between the user account options User cannot change password and Password never expires?

4. Do you need to create a new password reset disk after you change your password?

5. Is there any risk associated with configuring password hints?

Lab 6.5: Managing User Profiles

Objectives

The objective of this activity is to manage user profiles.

Materials Required

This lab requires the following:

- A physical computer or virtual machine running Windows 7 that is configured as User*x*-PC or as specified by your instructor

- Completion of Lab 6.4

Estimated completion time: **15 minutes**

Activity Background

Each user who logs on to a Windows 7 computer has a user profile that is stored on the computer. The first time a user logs on, the profile is created based on the default profile. A user profile contains private information such as the Documents folder, user-specific registry settings, user certificates, and Favorites. In rare cases, a user profile can be corrupted. In such a case, the user profile is removed or renamed to allow the creation of a new profile based on the default profile.

You can modify the default profile to ensure that all new users get a specific configuration. You can also configure the public profile with information that is merged into the profile of each user.

Activity

1. Log on to User*x*-PC as **Standard1** with a password of **PasswordRst**.

2. View the content in a user profile, as detailed in the following steps:

   a. Click **Start** and click **Computer**.

   b. In Windows Explorer, browse to **C:\Users\Standard1** and read the list of folders.

   c. Press **Alt** to display the menu bar.

   d. Click the **Tools** menu and click **Folder** options.

   e. In the Folder Options window, on the View tab, click **Show hidden files, folders, and drives**.

   f. Clear the **Hide protected operating system files (recommended)** check box.

g. Read the contents of the Warning window and click **Yes**.

h. Click **OK**.

i. Read the list of folders, as shown in Figure 6-6. The faded-out folders are system folders that were hidden before you changed the view. The folders that look like shortcuts are links to other folders and are included for backward compatibility with older applications.

j. Scroll down and read the files that are listed. NTUSER.DAT contains the user-specific registry settings for Standard1.

3. Configure the Public profile, as detailed in the following steps:

a. In Computer Management, browse to **C:\Users** and read the list of profiles.

b. Double-click **Public** and read the list of folders. Notice that this list of folders is a subset of those in a user profile.

c. In the left pane, click **Documents**.

d. In the right pane, right-click an open area, point to **New**, and click **Shortcut**.

e. In the Create Shortcut window, in the Type the location of the item box, type **C:\Windows\System32\notepad.exe**, and click **Next**.

f. In the Type a name for this shortcut box, type **NotePad** and click **Finish**.

g. In Windows Explorer, right-click the **NotePad** shortcut and click **Cut**.

h. Browse to **C:\Users\Public\Public Desktop**, right-click an open area, and click **Paste**.

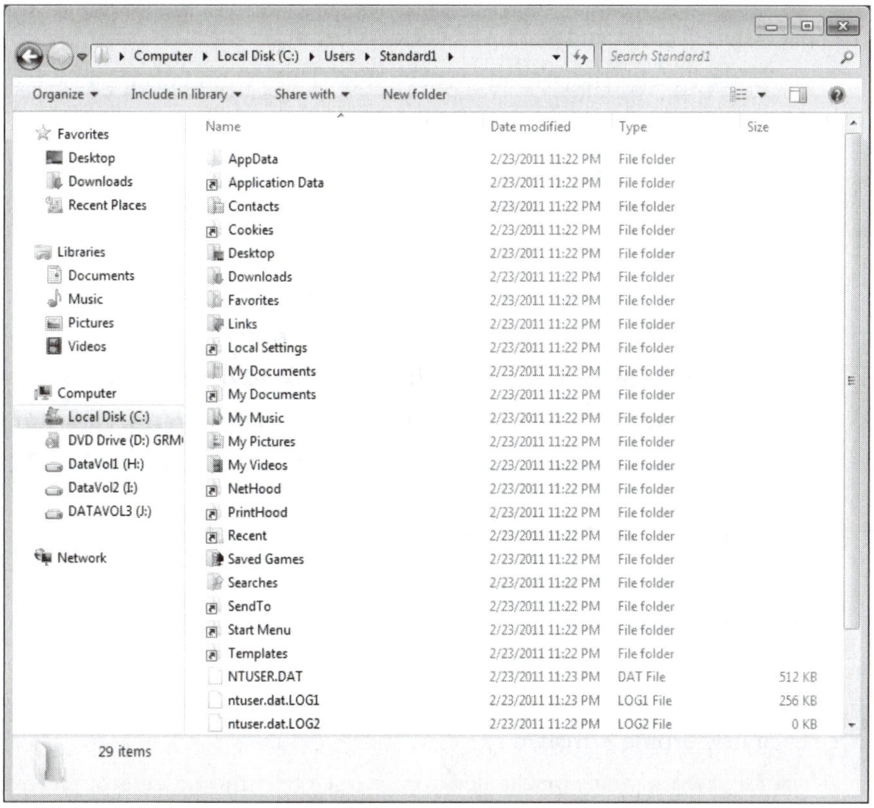

Figure 6-6 Folders in a user profile
© Cengage Learning 2012

    i. In the Destination Folder Access Denied windows, click **Continue**. Standard1 is configured as an administrator, but still needs to manually consent to pasting the file.

    j. Review the items on your desktop. Notice that the NotePad shortcut has been added.

4. Configure the Default profile, as detailed in the following steps:

    a. In Windows Explorer, browse to **C:\Users\Default**.

    b. Read the folders and files that are located in the Default profile. Notice that the content is the same as that in a user profile, including NTUSER.DAT.

    c. In the left pane, click **Documents**.

    d. In the right pane, right-click an open area, point to **New**, and click **Shortcut**.

    e. In the Create Shortcut window, in the Type the location of the item box, type **C:\Windows\System32\calc.exe**, and click **Next**.

    f. In the Type a name for this shortcut box, type **Calculator** and click **Finish**.

    g. In Windows Explorer, right-click the **Calculator** shortcut and click **Cut**.

    h. Browse to **C:\Users\Default\Desktop**, right-click an open area, and click **Paste**.

    i. In the Destination Folder Access Denied windows, click **Continue**. Standard1 is configured as an administrator, but still needs to manually consent to pasting the file.

    j. Review the items on the Desktop. Notice that the Calculator shortcut is not present.

5. Delete a user profile, as detailed in the following steps:

    a. In Windows Explorer, browse to **C:\Users**.

    b. Right-click **Standard1** and click **Delete**.

    c. In the Delete Folder window, click **Yes**. This action fails because the profile is in use.

    d. In the Folder In Use window, click **Cancel**.

    e. Log off.

    f. Log on as User*x*.

    g. Click **Start** and click **Control Panel**.

    h. In the Control Panel window, click **System and Security**.

    i. In the System and Security window, click **System**.

    j. In the System window, in the left pane, click **Advanced system settings**.

    k. In the System Properties window, in the User Profiles area, click **Settings**.

    l. In the User Profiles window, click **User*x*-PC\Standard1** and then click **Delete**.

    m. In the Confirm Delete window, click **Yes**.

    n. In the User Profiles window, click **OK**.

    o. In the System Properties window, click **OK**.

6. Create a new profile for Standard1, as detailed in the following steps:

    a. Log on as **Standard1** with the password **PasswordRst**. Notice that during logon, a new profile is created.

    b. Review the items on the desktop. Notice that the Calculator shortcut is included on the desktop.

    c. Log off.

Certification Objectives

Objectives for MCTS Exam #70-680: Windows 7, Configuring:

- Configuring Access to Resources: Configure authentication and authorization

Review Questions

1. What are the contents of a user profile?
2. What happens when you add content to the Public profile?
3. When is content from the Default profile used?
4. What does the file NTUSER.DAT contain?
5. Does the Public profile contain registry settings?

6

WINDOWS 7 SECURITY FEATURES

Labs included in this chapter:

- Lab 7.1 Configuring Account Policies
- Lab 7.2 Configuring User Rights Assignment
- Lab 7.3 Sharing EFS-Encrypted Files
- Lab 7.4 Implementing BitLocker To Go

Microsoft MCTS Exam #70-680 Objectives

Objective	Lab
Configure authentication and authorization	7.1, 7.2
Configure shared resources	7.3
Configure file and folder access	7.3
Configure BitLocker and BitLocker To Go	7.4

Lab 7.1: Configuring Account Policies

Objectives

The object of this activity is to configure account policies that control user password and account lockout.

Materials Required

This lab requires the following:

- A physical computer or virtual machine running Windows 7 that is configured as User*x*-PC or as specified by your instructor
- The user Standard1 created in Lab 6.1

Estimated completion time: **10 minutes**

Activity Background

Each Windows 7 computer has a wide range of policies that can be configured in the Local Security Policy. Some of the most commonly configured settings in the Local Security Policy relate to passwords and account lockout. Password settings are used to ensure that passwords are difficult for unauthorized users to guess. Account lockout settings prevent passwords from being guessed over time by locking accounts after a predetermined number of unsuccessful logon attempts. In a corporate environment, these settings are configured centrally in Active Directory as Group Policy objects rather than individually at each computer.

Activity

1. Log on to User*x*-PC as **User*x***.
2. Read about the password policy settings, as detailed in the following steps:
   a. Click **Start**, type **Local**, and then click **Local Security Policy**.
   b. In the Local Security Policy window, expand **Account Policies** and click **Password Policy**, as shown in Figure 7-1.
   c. Double-click **Enforce password history**.
   d. In the Enforce password history window, click the **Explain** tab and read the content.
   e. Click **Cancel**.
   f. Repeat Steps c through e for the remaining password policy settings.
3. Configure password policy settings, as detailed in the following steps:
   a. In the Local Security Policy window, double-click **Enforce password history**.
   b. In the Enforce password history Properties window, in the passwords remembered box, type **3**, and click **OK**.
   c. In the Local Security Policy window, double-click **Minimum password age**.
   d. In the Minimum password age Properties window, in the days box, type **1**, and click **OK**.
   e. In the Local Security Policy window, double-click **Minimum password length**.
   f. In the Minimum password length Properties window, in the characters box, type **5**, and click **OK**.
4. Change **Standard1**'s password, as detailed in the following steps:
   a. Log off as **User*x***.

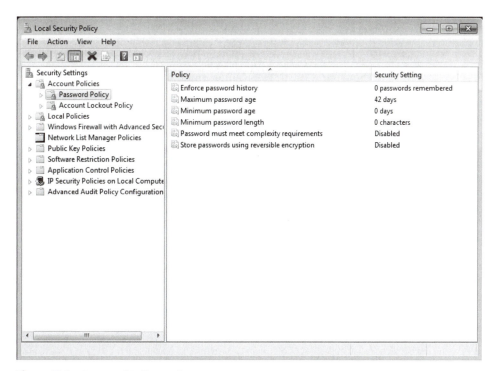

Figure 7-1   Password Policy settings
© *Cengage Learning 2012*

    b. Log on as **Standard1** using the password **PasswordRst**.

    c. Press **Ctrl+Alt+Del** and then click **Change a password**.

    d. In the Old password box, type **PasswordRst**.

    e. In the New Password and Confirm password boxes, type **FirstPW** and press **Enter**.

    f. After the password is changed, click **OK**.

5. Test enforcement of the minimum password age, as detailed in the following steps:

    a. Press **Ctrl+Alt+Del** and then click **Change a password**.

    b. In the Old password box, type **FirstPW**.

    c. In the New Password and Confirm password boxes, type **NextPW** and press **Enter**.

    d. Read the error message that is displayed and click **OK**.

    e. Click **Cancel** twice to go back to the Windows desktop.

6. Log off as **Standard1** and log on as **User*x***.

7. Read about the account lockout policy settings, as detailed in the following steps:

    a. Click **Start**, type **Local**, and then click **Local Security Policy**.

    b. In the Local Security Policy window, expand **Account Policies** and click **Account Lockout Policy**, as shown in Figure 7-2.

    c. Double-click **Account lockout duration**.

    d. In the Enforce password history window, click the **Explain** tab and read the content.

    e. Click **Cancel**.

    f. Repeat Steps c through e for the remaining account lockout policy settings.

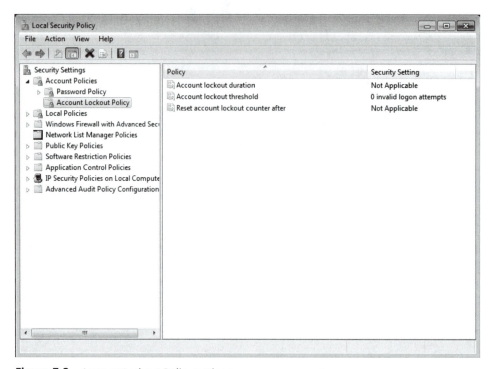

Figure 7-2 Account Lockout Policy settings
© *Cengage Learning 2012*

8. Configure account lockout policy settings, as detailed in the following steps:

   a. In the Local Security Policy window, double-click `Account lockout threshold`.

   b. In the Account lockout threshold Properties window, in the invalid logon attempts box, type **3**, and click **OK**.

   c. In the Suggested Value Changes window, read the proposed values, and click **OK**.

   d. In the Local Security Policy window, verify that the Account lockout duration and Reset account lockout count after settings have been updated to 30 minutes.

   e. Close Local Security Policy.

9. Test the account lockout policy, as detailed in the following steps:

   a. Log off as User*x*.

   b. Attempt to log on as **Standard1** by using the password **Pass1**.

   c. Click **OK** to clear the error about an incorrect username or password.

   d. Attempt to log on as **Standard1** by using the password **Pass2**.

   e. Click **OK** to clear the error about an incorrect username or password.

   f. Attempt to log on as **Standard1** by using the password **Pass3**.

   g. Click **OK** to clear the error about an incorrect username or password.

   h. Attempt to log on as **Standard1** by using the password **Pass4**.

   i. Click **OK** to clear the error about the account being locked.

   j. Attempt to log on as **Standard1** by using the password **FirstPW**.

   k. Click **OK** to clear the error about the account being locked.

10. Unlock the Standard1 account, as detailed in the following steps:

    a. Log on as User*x*.

    b. Click **Start**, right-click **Computer**, and click **Manage**.

    c. In Computer Management, under **System Tools**, expand **Local Users and Groups**, and click **Users**.

    d. Double-click **Standard1**.

    e. In the Standard1 Properties window, clear the **Account is locked** check box, and then click **OK**.

    f. Close Computer Management.

11. Return the account policy settings back to default values, as detailed in the following steps:

    a. Click **Start**, type **Local**, and then click **Local Security Policy**.

    b. In the Local Security Policy window, expand **Account Policies** and click **Password Policy**.

    c. Change all password policy settings to the default values shown in Figure 7-1.

    d. In the Local Security Policy window, click **Account Lockout Policy**.

    e. Change all account lockout policy settings to the default values shown in Figure 7-2.

    f. Close the Local Security Policy window.

Certification Objectives

Objectives for MCTS Exam #70-680: Windows 7, Configuring:

- Configuring Access to Resources: Configure authentication and authorization

Review Questions

1. Which password policy setting can you use to prevent users from reusing the same password when they are forced to change their password?

2. How does a minimum password age make passwords more secure?

3. How does setting an account lockout threshold make passwords more secure?

4. What is the difference between the Account lockout duration setting and the Reset account lockout counter after setting?

5. In a corporate environment with centralized administration, where are account policies configured?

7

Lab 7.2: Configuring User Rights Assignment

Objectives

The objective of this activity is to configure user rights assignments for a standard user.

Materials Required

This lab requires the following:

- A physical computer or virtual machine running Windows 7 that is configured as User*x*-PC or as specified by your instructor

- Completion of Lab 7.1

Estimated completion time: **10 minutes**

Activity Background

The simplest way to control the ability of users to perform system level operations in Windows 7 is by configuring user accounts as either a standard user or administrator user. Only administrator users have the ability to perform systemwide operations that could affect system stability. For example, only administrators can load new device drivers and change the networking configuration.

You can give standard users accounts additional permissions to manage Windows 7 by configuring user rights assignment. For example, giving a standard user the ability to load and unload device drivers ensures that the standard user can load device drivers for any USB device that is attached to the computer. You can also restrict standard user accounts by removing them from user rights assignment.

Activity

1. Log on to User*x*-PC as **User*x***.

2. Configure Standard1 as a standard user account, as detailed in the following steps:

   a. Click **Start**, right-click **Computer**, and click **Manage**.

   b. In the Computer Management window, expand **Local Users and Groups** and click **Users**.

   c. Double-click **Standard1**.

   d. In the Standard1 Properties windows, on the Member Of tab, click **Administrators** and then click **Remove**.

   e. Click **OK** to close the Standard1 Properties window.

   f. Close Computer Management.

3. Review Local Polices in Windows 7, as detailed in the following steps:

   a. Click **Start**, type **Local**, and click **Local Security Policy**.

   b. In the Local Security Policy window, expand **Local Policies** and click **Audit Policy**.

   c. Read the list of policies that are available for configuration.

   d. Click **User Rights Assignment**.

   e. Scroll down and read the list of policies that are available for configuration.

   f. Click **Security Options**.

   g. Scroll down and read the list of policies that are available for configuration.

4. Review the configuration of user rights assignment policies, as detailed in the following steps:

   a. In Local Security Policy, click **User Rights Assignment** and then double-click **Allow log on through Remote Desktop Services**.

   b. In the Allow log on through Remote Desktop Services Properties window, read the groups that are allowed, as shown in Figure 7-3.

   c. Click the **Explain** tab and read the explanation. Notice that this information includes a description, the default configuration, and the operating systems to which this configuration applies.

   d. Click **Cancel**.

   e. In the Local Security Policy window, double-click **Change the system time**.

   f. In the Change the system time Properties window, read the groups that are able to change the system time.

   g. Click **Cancel**.

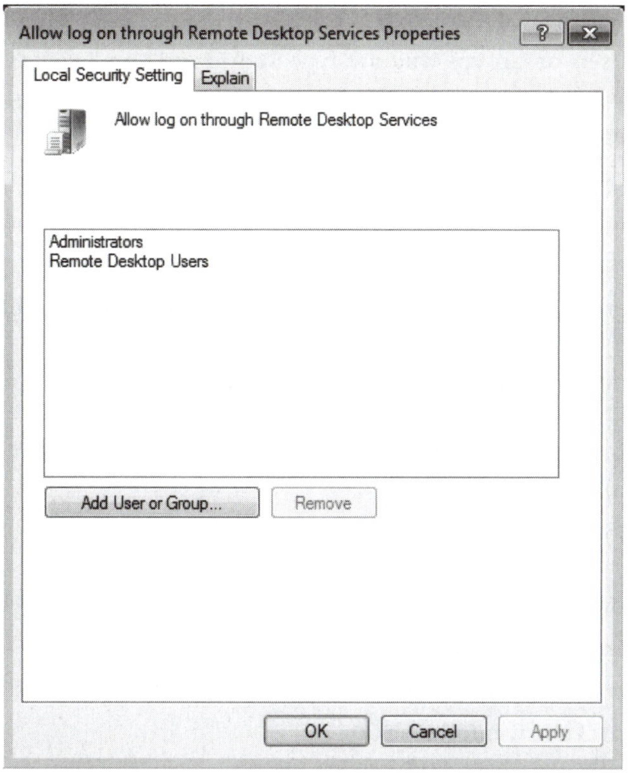

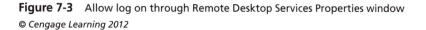

Figure 7-3 Allow log on through Remote Desktop Services Properties window
© Cengage Learning 2012

5. Verify that standard users cannot change the system time, as detailed in the following steps:

   a. Switch to **Standard1** by using the password **FirstPW**.

   b. In the lower-right corner of the screen, right-click the clock and click **Adjust date/time**.

   c. In the Date and Time window, notice that the **Change date and time** button has a shield symbol to indicate that performing this task requires administrative permissions.

   d. Click the **Change date and time** button. You are prompted for administrative credentials by User Account Control.

   e. In the User Account Control window, read the list of users that have administrator rights and then click **No**.

   f. In the Date and Time window, click **Cancel**.

   g. Log off as Standard1.

6. Grant additional rights to Standard1, as detailed in the following steps:

   a. Switch to **User***x*.

   b. In the Local Security Policy window, in the User Rights Assignment node, double-click **Change the system time**.

   c. In the Change the system time Properties window, click **Add User or Group**.

   d. In the Select Users or Groups window, type **Standard1** and click **OK**.

   e. In the Change the system time Properties window, click **OK**.

   f. In the Local Security Policy window, scroll down and double-click **Load and unload device drivers**.

g. In the Load and unload device drivers Properties window, click **Add User or Group**.

h. In the Select Users or Groups window, type **Standard1** and click **OK**.

i. In the Load and unload device drivers Properties window, on the **Explain** tab, read the description and then click **OK**.

j. Close the Local Security Policy window.

7. Verify that Standard1 can change the system time, as detailed in the following steps:

a. Switch to **Standard1**.

b. In the lower-right corner of the screen, right-click the clock and click **Adjust date/time**.

c. In the Date and Time window, notice that the **Change date and time** button has a shield symbol to indicate that performing this task requires administrative permissions.

d. Click the **Change date and time** button. You are not prompted for administrative credentials by User Account Control.

e. In the Date and Time Settings window, click a day at least one day in the future and then click **OK**.

f. Look in the lower-right corner and confirm that the date has changed.

g. Click the **Change date and time** button.

h. In the Date and Time Settings window, click today's date and then click **OK**.

i. In the Date and Time window, click **OK**.

j. Log off as Standard1.

Certification Objectives

Objectives for MCTS Exam #70-680: Windows 7, Configuring:

- Configuring Access to Resources: Configure authentication and authorization

Review Questions

1. Which Windows 7 administrative tool can you use to modify the rights assigned to users?

2. How do user rights differ from NTFS permissions?

3. Why would you assign user rights rather than configuring a user as an administrator?

4. What happens when standard users try to perform a task that they do not have the necessary user right to perform?

5. Why would you want to give standard users the ability to load and unload device drivers?

Lab 7.3: Sharing EFS-Encrypted Files

Objectives

The objective of this activity is to encrypt a file by using EFS and then share the encrypted file with another user.

Materials Required

This lab requires the following:

- A physical computer or virtual machine running Windows 7 that is configured as User*x*-PC or as specified by your instructor

- The completion of Lab 7.2
- The user account Standard2 created in Lab 6.1

Estimated completion time: **15 minutes**

Activity Background

In Windows 7, Encrypting File System (EFS) allows users to encrypt files stored on the local hard drive. This is often done to protect data on laptop computers. By default, EFS-encrypted files can be accessed only by the person who encrypted the files. When multiple users share a computer, it might be useful for them to also share files that are encrypted by EFS.

Large organizations can create and assign certificates to user accounts that are used for EFS. The certificates are issued by a certification authority. In smaller organizations, the certificates are typically generated automatically by Windows 7 when the first file is encrypted. The certificate for encryption is stored in the user profile.

Activity

1. Log on to User*x*-PC as **Standard1** with the password **FirstPW**.
2. Create a new text file, as detailed in the following steps:
   a. Click **Start** and click **Computer**.
   b. In Windows Explorer, under **Libraries**, double-click **Documents** to expand it.
   c. Click **Public Documents**.
   d. In the right-pane, right-click an open area, point to **New** and click **Text Document**.
   e. Type **NewFile** and press **Enter** to rename the document.
   f. Double-click **NewFile** to open the document.
   g. In Notepad, type **This is the encrypted document for Standard1**.
   h. Click the **File** menu and click **Save**.
   i. Close Notepad.
3. Encrypt NewFile, as detailed in the following steps:
   a. In Windows Explorer, right-click **NewFile** and click **Properties**.
   b. In the NewFile Properties window, on the **General** tab, click **Advanced**.
   c. In the Advanced Attributes window, select the **Encrypt contents to secure data** check box and then click **OK**.
   d. In the NewFile Properties window, click **OK**.
   e. In the Encryption Warning window, click **Encrypt the file only** and click **OK**. A notification balloon might appear prompting you to back up your encryption key.
   f. Review the filenames listed in Public Documents. Notice that NewFile is displayed in green to signify that it is encrypted.
4. View the users that can access NewFile, as detailed in the following steps:
   a. In Windows Explorer, right-click **NewFile** and click **Properties**.
   b. In the NewFile Properties window, on the **General** tab, click **Advanced**.
   c. In the Advanced Attributes window, click **Details**.
   d. Read the information displayed in the User Access to NewFile window. Notice that Standard1 is the only user with access to this file, as shown in Figure 7-4. Recovery certificates are used in organizations where computers are joined to a domain.

7

Figure 7-4 Users with access to NewFile

© Cengage Learning 2012

  e. Click **Add** and read the list of users to whom you are able to give access. This list includes any users with a certificate suitable for file encryption. Notice that Standard2 is not in the list.

  f. In the Windows Security window, click **Cancel**.

  g. In the User Access to NewFile window, click **Cancel**.

  h. In the Advanced Attributes window, click **Cancel**.

  i. In the NewFile Properties window, click **Cancel**.

5. Verify that Standard2 cannot open NewFile, as detailed in the following steps:

  a. Switch to **Standard2** with a password of **password**.

  b. If are prompted to change your password, change it to **password**. This is allowed because no password restrictions are in place.

  c. Click **Start** and click **Computer**.

  d. In Windows Explorer, under **Libraries**, double-click **Documents** to expand it.

  e. Click **Public Documents** and double-click **NewFile**.

  f. Click **OK** to clear the Access is denied message.

  g. Close Notepad.

6. Create a new certificate for Standard2, as detailed in the following steps:

  a. In Windows Explorer, in the right pane, right-click an open area, point to **New** and click **Text Document**.

  b. Type **NewFile2** and press **Enter** to rename the document.

  c. Double-click **NewFile2** to open the document.

    d. In Notepad, type **This is the encrypted document for Standard2.**

    e. Click the **File** menu and click **Save**.

    f. Close Notepad.

    g. In Windows Explorer, right-click **NewFile** and click **Properties**.

    h. In the NewFile Properties window, on the **General** tab, click **Advanced**.

    i. In the Advanced Attributes window, select the **Encrypt contents to secure data** check box and then click **OK**.

    j. In the NewFile Properties window, click **OK**.

    k. In the Encryption Warning window, click **Encrypt the file only** and click **OK**. A notification balloon might appear prompting you to back up your encryption key.

7. Give Standard1 access to NewFile2, as detailed in the following steps:

    a. In Windows Explorer, right-click **NewFile2** and click **Properties**.

    b. In the NewFile2 Properties window, on the **General** tab, click **Advanced**.

    c. In the Advanced Attributes window, click **Details**.

    d. Read the information displayed in the User Access to NewFile window. Notice that Standard2 is the only user with access to this file.

    e. Click **Add** and read the list of users to whom you are able to give access. This list includes any users with a certificate suitable for file encryption. Notice that Standard1 is in the list.

    f. In the Windows Security window, click **Standard1** and then click **OK**.

    g. In the User Access to NewFile2 window, click **OK**.

    h. In the Advanced Attributes window, click **OK**.

    i. In the NewFile2 Properties window, click **OK**.

    j. Log off as Standard2.

8. Verify that Standard1 can open NewFile2, as detailed in the following steps:

    a. Log on as **Standard1**.

    b. In Windows Explorer, double-click **NewFile2**.

    c. In Notepad, create a new line and type **Added by Standard1**.

    d. Click the **File** menu and click **Save**.

    e. Close Notepad.

    f. Log off as Standard1.

Certification Objectives

Objectives for MCTS Exam #70-680: Windows 7, Configuring:

- Configuring Access to Resources: Configure shared resources
- Configuring Access to Resources: Configure file and folder access

Review Questions

1. Why are EFS-encrypted files more secure than those protected only by NTFS permissions?

2. How can you recover access to EFS-encrypted files if your profile is corrupted and your certificate is lost?

3. Why did Standard2 not appear in the list of available certificates when NewFile was initially encrypted?

4. Can an EFS-encrypted file be shared with a group?

5. For EFS, is there any disadvantage to using a self-signed certificate generated by Windows 7?

Lab 7.4: Implementing BitLocker To Go

Objectives

The objective of this activity is to secure data on a USB drive by using BitLocker To Go.

Materials Required

This lab requires the following:

- A physical computer or virtual machine running Windows 7 that is configured as User*x*-PC or as specified by your instructor. This computer is referred to a User A-PC in this lab.

- A formatted USB flash drive and a computer or virtual machine that can connect to the USB flash drive. (*Note*: It is not possible to connect a USB flash drive to Hyper-V virtual machines.)

Estimated completion time: **15 minutes**

Activity Background

Unlike EFS, which is used to encrypt individual files and folders, BitLocker encrypts entire volumes. This ensures that all data on a volume is automatically protected and the complexity of user certificates is avoided. The encryption keys for BitLocker are stored in a Trusted Platform Module (TPM) or on a USB drive.

Windows 7 introduces a new feature called BitLocker To Go. BitLocker To Go protects data on USB drives. When the protected USB drive is moved to a new computer running Windows 7, you must enter a password to access the drive. Windows XP and Windows Vista clients can view files on a USB drive protected by BitLocker To Go, but not modify the files.

Activity

1. Log on to User*x*-PC as **User*x***.

2. Insert the USB flash drive into UserA-PC.

3. If necessary, close the AutoPlay window.

4. Verify that the edition of Windows 7 supports BitLocker To Go, as detailed in the following steps:

   a. Click **Start**, right-click **Computer**, and click **Properties**.

   b. Read the Windows edition that is installed on your computer.

   c. Close the System window.

   d. Open Internet Explorer.

   e. In Internet Explorer, in the address bar, type **http://windows.microsoft.com/ en-US/windows7/products/features/bitlocker** and press **Enter**.

f. In the upper-right corner of the page, read which editions of Windows 7 support BitLocker.

g. At the bottom of the page, click the `Help protect your files using BitLocker` link and read the contents of the page.

h. Close Internet Explorer.

5. Enable BitLocker To Go on the USB flash drive, as detailed in the following steps:

a. Click `Start` and click `Computer`.

b. In Windows Explorer, right-click the USB flash drive and click `Turn on BitLocker`.

c. In the BitLocker Drive Encryption window, select the `Use a password to unlock the drive` check box, as shown in Figure 7-5.

e. In the Type your password and Retype your password boxes, type `BitLocker` and then click `Next`.

f. On the How do you want to store your recovery key? page, click `Save the recovery key to a file`.

g. In the Save BitLocker Recovery Key as window, click `Save`. This saves the text file in the Documents folder of the current user.

h. On the How do you want to store your recovery key? page, click `Next`.

i. On the Are you ready to encrypt this drive? page, click `Start Encrypting`. Encryption of a 1 GB flash drive will take about two minutes. No data is lost.

j. When encryption is complete, click `Close`.

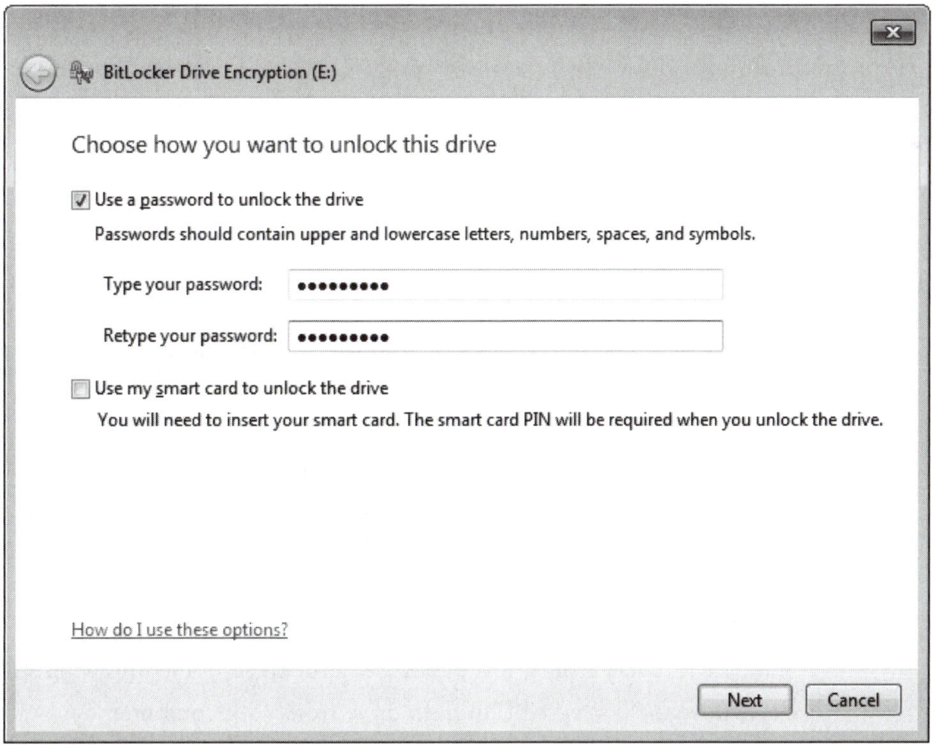

Figure 7-5   Enabling BitLocker To Go

6. Verify that BitLocker is enabled for the USB flash drive, as detailed in the following steps:

   a. Click **Start** and click **Computer**.

   b. Verify that the icon for the USB flash drive has a lock icon, as shown in Figure 7-6.

DOS (E:)
898 MB free of 989 MB

Figure 7-6 Encrypted USB flash drive
© *Cengage Learning 2012*

7. View the recovery key for the encrypted USB flash drive, as detailed in the following steps:

   a. In Windows Explorer, browse to Documents and double-click the file **BitLocker Recovery Key** *serial number***.txt**.

   b. Read the contents of the file, as shown in Figure 7-7.

   c. Close NotePad.

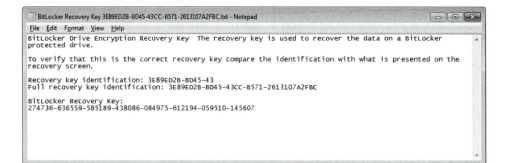

Figure 7-7 BitLocker Recovery Key file
© *Cengage Learning 2012*

8. Simulate moving the encrypted USB flash drive to another computer, as detailed in the following steps:

   a. Remove the encrypted USB flash drive from your computer.

   b. Insert the encrypted USB flash drive in your computer.

   c. On the This drive is protected by BitLocker Drive Encryption page, in the Type your password to unlock this drive box, type **BitLocker**, as shown in Figure 7-8.

   d. Click **Unlock**.

   e. If necessary, close the AutoPlay window.

9. Simulate recovery from a lost password, as detailed in the following steps:

   a. Remove the encrypted USB flash drive from your computer.

   b. Insert the encrypted USB flash drive in your computer.

   c. On the This drive is protected by BitLocker Drive Encryption page, click **I forgot my password**.

   d. On the Unlock the drive using your recovery key page, click **Type the recovery key**.

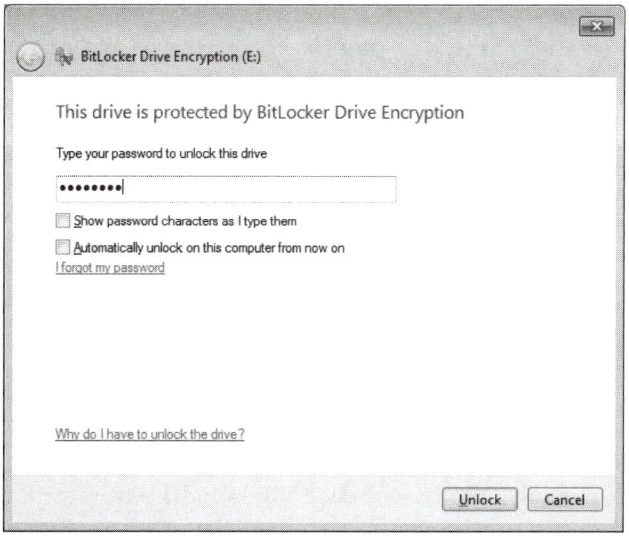

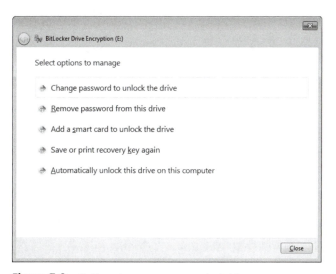

Figure 7-8   Unlock encrypted drive

e. In Windows Explorer, browse to Documents and double-click the file **BitLocker Recovery Key** *serial number*.**txt**.

f. On the Enter your recovery key page, click the down arrow next to **More information**.

g. Verify that the **Full BitLocker recovery key identification** matches the one listed in the BitLocker Recovery Key file.

h. Copy the BitLocker Recovery Key from Notepad to the type your BitLocker recovery key box and click **Next**.

i. On the You now have temporary access to this drive page, click **Manage BitLocker**.

j. On the Select options to manage page, shown in Figure 7-9, click **Change password to unlock the drive**.

7

Figure 7-9   Options to manage encrypted drive

    k. On the Create a password to unlock this drive page, in the Type your password and Retype you password boxes, type **password** and then click **Next**.

    l. Click **OK** to clear the message about the password being changed.

    m. Close all open windows.

10. Remove encryption from the USB drive, as detailed in the following steps:

    a. Click **Start** and click **Control Panel**.

    b. Click **System and Security** and click **BitLocker Drive Encryption**.

    c. In the BitLocker Drive Encryption – BitLocker To Go area, click **Turn Off BitLocker**, as shown in Figure 7-10.

    d. In the Turn Off BitLocker window, click **Decrypt Drive**. Decryption takes approximately the same amount of time as the encryption process did. No data is lost.

    e. Click **Close** when decryption is complete.

    f. Close all open windows and remove the USB flash drive from your computer.

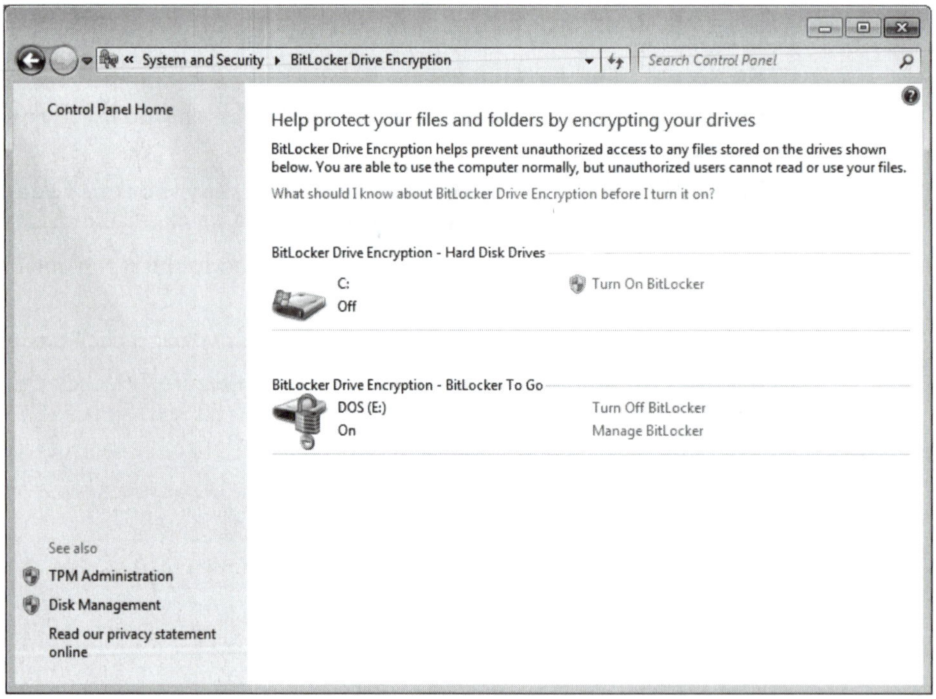

Figure 7-10 BitLocker management in Control Panel

© Cengage Learning 2012

Certification Objectives

Objectives for MCTS Exam #70-680: Windows 7, Configuring:

- Configuring Mobile Computing: Configure BitLocker and BitLocker To Go

Review Questions

1. What is the difference between BitLocker and BitLocker To Go?

2. How is BitLocker To Go useful if you are moving documents between a work computer and a home computer on a USB flash drive?

3. Which operating systems can encrypt a USB flash drive by using BitLocker To Go?

4. How to you obtain the BitLocker recovery key?

5. Do you lose data when you decrypt a drive that is BitLocker To Go?

7

NETWORKING

Labs included in this chapter:

- Lab 8.1 Network Configuration with netsh
- Lab 8.2 Working with Shared Folder Connections
- Lab 8.3 Using Windows Calculator with IPv4 Addresses
- Lab 8.4 Configuring Windows Remote Management in a Workgroup

Microsoft MCTS Exam #70-680 Objectives

Objective	Lab
Configure IPv4 network settings	8.1, 8.3
Configure network settings	8.2
Configure Windows Firewall	8.4
Configure remote management	8.4
Configure shared resources	8.2
Configure authentication and authorization	8.2

Lab 8.1: Network Configuration with netsh

Objectives

The objective of this activity is to observe the operation of the netsh configuration utility when it is used to update basic network interface settings.

Materials Required

This lab requires the following:

- A physical computer or virtual machine running Windows 7 that is configured as User*x*-PC or as specified by your instructor

Estimated completion time: **30 minutes**

Activity Background

Network settings are typically viewed and managed using graphical utilities in Windows 7. They can also be managed with the netsh command-line tool. Netsh is powerful because it has so many options and functions. For example, netsh has the ability to store network settings to a configuration file, update specific configuration settings, and configure settings from a configuration file. This activity will review these basic operations with netsh.

Activity

1. Log on to User*x*-PC.

2. Click **Start**, point to **All Programs**, click **Accessories**, and then right-click **Command Prompt**.

3. Select the option **Run as administrator** from the pop-up menu. Click **Yes** when User Account Control asks if you want to allow the program to make changes to the computer. Configuring IP address information with netsh requires administrative permission to the computer.

4. At the command prompt, type **netsh /?** to display a general help screen for the netsh utility. Note the comment at the bottom of the help screen that explains how to obtain detailed help for other netsh commands.

5. Display a list of network interfaces present on the computer by typing the command **netsh interface ipv4 show interface** and then pressing **Enter**. For the purposes of this activity, the name assigned to the primary network connection is expected to be **Local Area Connection**; the name may be different for your computer. In that case, substitute the name of your primary network connection for **Local Area Connection** where instructed in this activity.

6. Display the primary network connection interface settings by typing the command **netsh interface ipv4 show config name="Local Area Connection"** and press **Enter**. Note the current values for the following:

   a. DHCP enabled _____

   b. IP Address _____

   c. Subnet Prefix _____

   d. Default Gateway _____

   e. DNS servers configured through DHCP _____ (if displayed)

   f. Statically configured DNS servers _____ (if displayed)

7. Save the current configuration of your computer's network interfaces to a file on your desktop by typing the command **netsh -c interface dump > %USERPROFILE%\ DESKTOP\originalnet.txt** and then press **Enter**. Locate the file on the desktop and double-click it to open the file in Notepad. Review the format of the file's contents and then close Notepad.

8. At the command prompt, type **ping** *defaultgateway*, where *defaultgateway* is the default gateway recorded in Step 6.c. Press **Enter** and confirm that the default gateway responds to the ping command with four replies.

9. Display the help screen for the netsh command used to set a network interface's IPv4 parameters by typing the command **netsh interface ipv4 set address ?** and then pressing **Enter**. Note that the list of parameters does not include any options to configure the network adapter's IPv4 DNS settings.

10. Update the IPv4 settings for the primary network connection to assign a static IPv4 address by using the netsh command, as detailed in the following steps:

    a. To configure the interface with a static IPv4 address of 192.168.199.215, a subnet mask of 255.255.0.0 and a default gateway address of 192.168.0.1, type the command **netsh interface ipv4 set address "Local Area Connection" static 192.168.199.215 255.255.0.0 192.168.0.1** and press **Enter**. Note that if you are connected to a classroom network, your instructor may assign you a specific IP address to avoid IP address conflicts with other student machines. In that case, substitute the IP address given by the instructor in place of *192.168.199.215* in the preceding netsh command.

    b. Confirm that the changes have taken effect by typing the command **netsh interface ipv4 show config name="Local Area Connection"** and then pressing **Enter**. Verify that the displayed value for Statically configured DNS server is None.

    c. To configure the interface with a static IPv4 DNS server address of 192.168.10.1, type the command **netsh interface ipv4 set dns "Local Area Connection" static 192.168.10.1** and press **Enter**. Note that the command will take up to 15 seconds to complete and will generate an error. An error is generated because netsh checks the validity of the IP address you have configured for the DNS server and a DNS server does not exist at that IP address. In a real-life scenario, this error indicates that you may have typed the IP address of the DNS server incorrectly. In this case, you can ignore the error.

    d. Confirm that the changes have taken effect by typing the command **netsh interface ipv4 show config name="Local Area Connection"** and then pressing **Enter**. Note the displayed value for Statically configured DNS server has been updated with the static DNS server address.

11. Now that the primary network adapter's IPv4 address and its related settings have been changed, attempt to ping the default gateway by typing **ping** *defaultgateway*, where *defaultgateway* is the default gateway recorded in Step 6.c. Press **Enter** and confirm that the default gateway does not respond to the ping command.

12. Save the updated configuration of your computer's network interfaces to a file on your desktop and view it, as detailed in the following steps:

    a. Type the command **netsh interface ipv4 dump > %USERPROFILE%\ DESKTOP\newnet.txt** and then press **Enter**.

    b. Locate the file on the desktop and double-click it to open the file in Notepad. Note that the scope of information has been restricted to IPv4 address information, unlike the generic interface dump created in Step 7.

    c. Review the format of the file's contents and then close Notepad.

8

13. Update the IP address assigned in Step 10.a with a static IPv4 address of 10.10.10.100 by typing the command **netsh interface ipv4 set address "Local Area Connection" static 10.10.10.100** and then pressing **Enter**.

14. Confirm that the changes have taken effect by typing the command **netsh interface ipv4 show config name="Local Area Connection"** and then pressing **Enter**. Note the displayed value for **IP Address** has been updated with the new IP address.

15. In Step 12, the netsh dump command output was saved to the file newnet.txt. Restore the saved configuration in that file by typing the command **netsh exec %USERPROFILE%\ DESKTOP\newnet.txt** and pressing **Enter**. Note that the output of the command will appear similar to that seen in Figure 8-1, and it includes the instruction that the computer must be restarted to complete the change.

16. Restart the computer and log back in.

17. Open an elevated command prompt, as detailed in Steps 2 and 3 of this activity.

18. Confirm that the changes have taken effect by typing the command **netsh interface ipv4 show config name="Local Area Connection"** and then pressing **Enter**. Note the displayed value for the IP Address has changed from 10.10.10.100 to the value specified in the newnet.txt file.

19. A network interface can have its IPv4 DNS server setting configured to be obtained automatically via DHCP, even when the IPv4 address itself is statically configured. Update the DNS server setting last configured in Step 10.c by entering the command **netsh interface ipv4 set dns "Local Area Connection" dhcp** and then pressing **Enter**.

20. Confirm that the changes have taken effect by typing the command **netsh interface ipv4 show config name="Local Area Connection"** and then pressing **Enter**. Note the displayed value for Statically configured DNS server has been updated.

21. To configure Local Area Connection to use DHCP to obtain IP configuration, type the command **netsh interface ipv4 set address "Local Area Connection" dhcp** and then press **Enter**. If the name of the network connection is different, substitute its name for *Local Area Connection* in the netsh command.

Figure 8-1 Using netsh to execute networking changes from a script file
© Cengage Learning 2012

22. If you identified your computer as using a static IP address in Step 6.a, change the configuration of Local Area Connection back to the original settings recorded in Step 6. You can do this by using the graphical interface or netsh. If you choose to use netsh, use Steps 10.a and 10.c as examples for the correct syntax.

23. Close all windows and log out.

Certification Objectives

Objectives for MCTS Exam #70-680: Windows 7, Configuring:

- Configuring Network Connectivity: Configure IPv4 network settings

Review Questions

1. When a single netsh command is used at the command line to configure a static IPv4 address on an interface, what essential IPv4 configuration parameter cannot be set at the same time with that one command?

    a. Subnet mask

    b. DNS server address

    c. Default gateway

    d. None

2. Updating network configuration settings with netsh requires _____ permissions.

    a. Standard

    b. Power user

    c. Administrative

    d. NTFS

3. Using netsh to set a static IP address on a network interface forces the DNS server setting for that interface to be static as well. True or false?

4. Multiple netsh commands stored in a file can be executed at the same time by running the netsh utility with the _____ command-line parameter.

    a. Exec

    b. Batch

    c. MSI

    d. CMD

5. Which of the following netsh commands is a valid configuration command for a network interface called "Local Area Connection" that must be assigned the following static IPv4 settings: IPv4 address of 172.16.1.2, subnet mask of 255.255.0.0, default gateway address of 172.16.1.1, and DNS server address of 172.16.1.1?

    a. netsh interface ipv4 set dns "Local Area Connection" static 172.16.1.2 255.255.0.0 172.16.1.1

    b. netsh interface ipv4 set address "Local Area Connection" static 172.16.1.2 255.255.0.0 172.16.1.1

    c. netsh interface ipv4 set "Local Area Connection" static address 172.16.1.2 sm 255.255.0.0 gw 172.16.1.1 dns 172.16.1.1

    d. None of the above

8

Lab 8.2: Working with Shared Folder Connections

Objectives

The objectives of this activity are to connect to shared folders over the network and then manage optionally persistent settings such as drive letter associations and cached credentials.

Materials Required

This lab requires the following:

- A physical computer or virtual machine running Windows 7 that is configured as User*x*-PC or as specified by your instructor
- A lab partner with a physical computer or virtual machine running Windows 7 that is configured as User*x*-PC or as specified by your instructor

Estimated completion time: **30 minutes**

Activity Background

When users connect to a shared folder over the network, they can specify the location of the folder as a Universal Naming Convention (UNC) path. The UNC path identifies the computer hosting the shared folder and the shared folder. Because the UNC path can be long and users might make mistakes while they are typing it, users can optionally associate a drive letter with the shared folder.

The connection to a shared folder is restricted by the credentials (i.e., username and password) that are specified by the user. Those credentials must be recognized by the remote computer and that username must grant the user access. To avoid users having to type their credentials each time they access a shared folder, user credentials can be cached. Once the credentials are cached, they must be managed in case they need to change. The Credential Manager and Stored User Names and Passwords utilities are used to manage cached credentials.

Activity

1. Log on to User*x*-PC.

2. Create a new user account on your computer that will be used to restrict connectivity to shared folders, as detailed in the following steps:

   a. Click **Start**, click **Control Panel**, and then click **Add or remove user accounts** below the User Accounts and Family Safety heading.

   b. In the Manage Accounts window that appears, click the link **Create a new account**.

   c. Enter the name **lab82usr** as the new user account name. Confirm that the **Standard user** selection is already selected.

   d. Click the **Create Account** button to create the user.

   e. When the Manage Accounts windows reappears, click the **lab82usr** icon.

   f. When the Change an Account window appears, click the **Create a password** link.

   g. When the Create Password window appears, enter **workpass** in the *New password* field.

   h. Enter **workpass** in the *Confirm new password* field.

   i. Click the **Create password** button.

   j. Close the Change an Account window.

3. A folder will be created on your lab computer and shared for general access from other computers in the lab, as detailed in the following steps:

   a. Click **Start**, click **Computer**, and then double-click **Local Disk (C:)** in the Computer file browser window that opens.

   b. Click **New folder** in the menu bar and rename *New folder* to **LAB8-2** and press **Enter** to save the change.

   c. The new folder should already be highlighted. If not, click the **LAB8-2** folder once to select it.

   d. Click **Share with** in the menu bar, and select **Specific people** from the menu.

   e. In the File Sharing window that opens, type the name **lab82usr** in the field specifying the name of a person to share the folder with, as shown in Figure 8-2. Click the **Add** button to save the change. Note that the username lab82usr now shows up in the list of people that the folder is shared with.

   f. By default, the permission assigned to a new name in the list is Read. On the same line as the *lab82usr* in the list of names, click the down arrow next to the **Read** permission to open a menu of selectable permissions, as shown in Figure 8-3.

   g. Select **Read/Write** from the menu, and then click the **Share** button to complete the operation.

   h. When you are notified that the folder is shared, record the UNC path displayed below the folder name LAB8-2: _____.

   i. Click the **Done** button to close the File Sharing Wizard. In the computer browser window, note the folder LAB8-2 icon is not different from other folder icons displayed in the same window. Read the shared folder details displayed at the bottom of the computer browser window.

   j. Minimize the Computer file browser window.

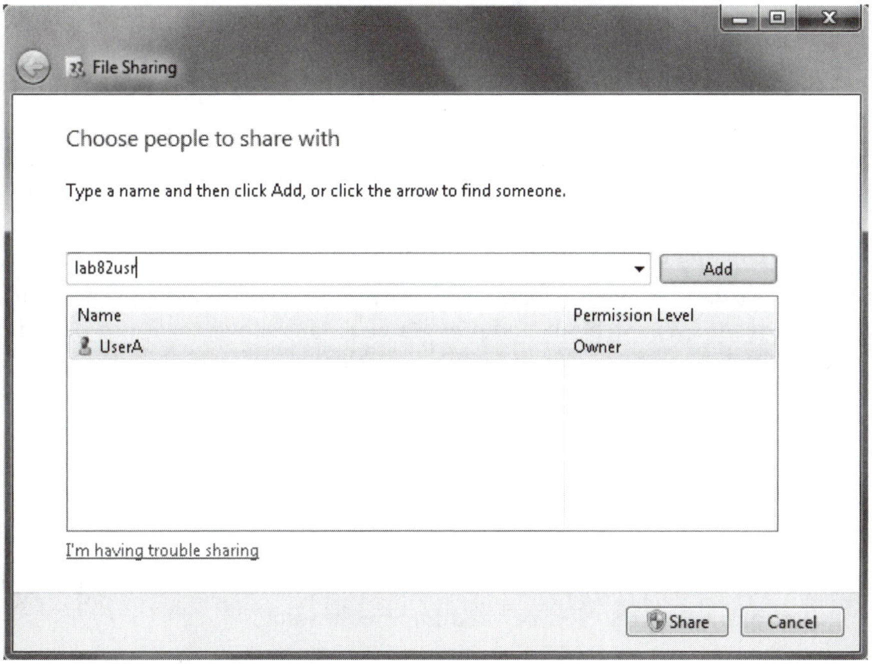

Figure 8-2   Selecting user accounts to share a folder with
© *Cengage Learning 2012*

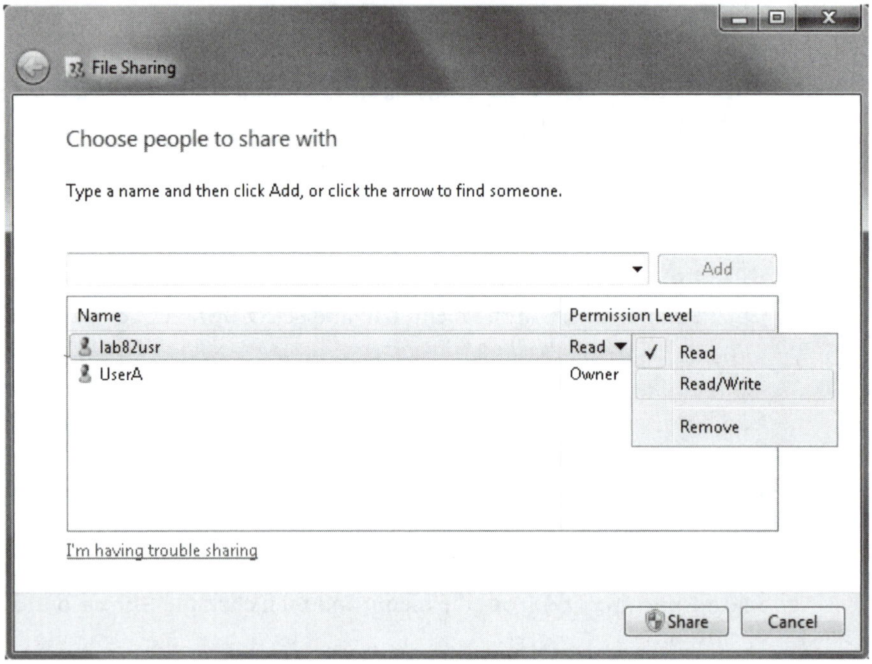

Figure 8-3 Configuring a user's permission to a shared folder
© *Cengage Learning 2012*

4. Confirm that your lab partner has reached Step 4 in the exercise. Write down the UNC path that your lab partner recorded in Step 3.h for the shared folder on his or her computer: _____.

5. Confirm that the LAB8-2 folder is shared on your computer from the command line, as detailed in the following steps:

   a. Click **Start**, **All Programs**, **Accessories**, and then click **Command Prompt**.

   b. At the command prompt, type **hostname** and press **Enter** to display the computer's host name. The computer's network name can be specified using a UNC path, which can be written in its simplest form as *hostname*, where *hostname* is typically the name returned by the hostname command. Record the UNC path to your machine by entering the computer's hostname here: _____.

   c. At the command prompt, type **net view** *hostname*, where *hostname* is the name recorded in Step 5.b, and press **Enter**. This shows the list of shared resources on your computer, as shown in Figure 8-4. Note that LAB8-2 is present in the list of shared resources on your computer.

   d. To see a full list of all shared folders, including hidden ones, type **net view** ***hostname* /ALL**, where *hostname* is the name recorded in Step 5.b, and press **Enter**.

   e. Close the command prompt window.

6. Click **Start**, click **Control Panel**, and then click **View network status and tasks** below the Network and Internet heading.

7. When the Network and Sharing Center window opens, confirm that the network connection listed below *View your active networks* is currently configured as a Work network location, as shown in Figure 8-5. If the network connection is set to *Public*

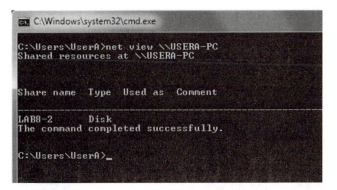

Figure 8-4   Specifying a UNC path target for a net view command
© *Cengage Learning 2012*

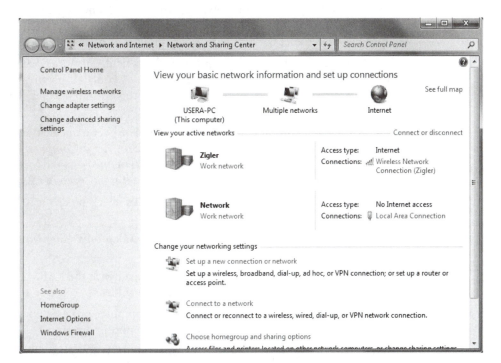

Figure 8-5   Confirming that all active networks are configured as a Work network location
© *Cengage Learning 2012*

8

network or *Home network*, it must be changed to a *Work network* location, as detailed in the following steps:

a. Click the **Public network** or **Home network** link below the network's name in the Network and Sharing Center window.

b. In the Set Network Location window that opens, click the **Work network** option. Note the statement explaining what you can see on the network and what other computers can see.

c. Click the **Close** button to save the change and close the Set Network Location window.

d. If the computer has multiple network interfaces, repeat Steps 7.a–c for each network interface that is not set to a Work network location.

8. Click the link **Change advanced sharing settings** on the left side of the Network and Sharing Center window. In the Advanced Sharing settings window that appears, record the current settings under the **Home or Work (current profile)** heading, as detailed in the following steps:

   a. Network discovery _____

   b. File and printer sharing _____

   c. Public folder sharing _____

   d. Password protected sharing _____

9. Close the Advanced sharing settings window. Confirm with your lab partner that he or she has reached Step 9 in the activity.

10. Your lab partner's computer has a hostname, as detailed in Step 5.b. of his or her lab activity. Record that hostname here:_____

11. Connect to your lab partner's computer over the network and authenticate yourself as user lab82usr on his or her computer. This connection will be validated by creating a new document on a shared folder on your partner's computer, as detailed in the following steps:

    a. Click **Start** and in the *Search programs and files* field, type *TargetComputerName*, where *TargetComputerName* is the hostname of your lab partner's computer from Step 10. Press **Enter** to establish a connection to your lab partner's computer.

    b. A Windows Security dialog box will appear asking you to enter credentials that will grant you access to your lab partner's computer. The User name field must be specified in the format *TargetComputerName\Username*, where *TargetComputerName* is the name of your lab partner's computer in Step 10 and *Username* is a valid local account on that computer. In the dialog box *User name* field, type *TargetComputerName***lab82usr**.

    c. Do not select the **Remember my credentials** check box. If it is selected, clear the check box.

    d. In the *Password* field of the Windows Security dialog box, enter **workpass** and click the **OK** button.

    e. Note that the computer browser window will open with the LAB8-2 share visible as a folder in the window. Double-click the **LAB8-2** folder.

    f. Right-click anywhere on the right side of the computer browser window and point to **New**, and then click **Text Document** from the pop-up menu.

    g. Change the name of the new text document from New Text Document to **Lab82Document** and press **Enter** to save the change.

    h. Double-click **Lab82Document** to open the file in Notepad. Enter the text **"This text will write to my lab partner's computer"**, followed by your student name.

    i. Close Notepad and click the **Save** button when prompted to save changes.

12. Authenticated connections to shared network resources are left open until the connection is closed, such as when a user logs off their current session. Confirm that logging off will force you to reauthenticate to your lab partner's computer, as detailed in the following steps:

    a. Close the computer file browser window.

    b. Repeat Step 11.a, but note that this time you are *not* prompted for a login username and password. Double-click **LAB8-2 share** to confirm that you still have access to the shared folder on your partner's computer.

    c. Close the computer file browser window.

    d. Log out by clicking **Start** and then selecting **Log off** from the start menu.

e. Log on to User*x*-PC.

f. Repeat Step 11.a, but note that this time you are prompted for a login username and password. The previously authenticated connection has been closed. Click **Cancel** to abort the connection attempt.

13. You will establish a connection to the shared folder on your lab partner's computer using the Map Network Drive Wizard, and you will configure your computer to remember the user ID and password required to reestablish the connection, as detailed in the following steps:

a. Click **Start** and then click **Computer** from the Start menu.

b. In the menu bar of the Computer file browser window, click **Map network drive**.

c. Click the **Drive** drop-down arrow, and select **R:**.

d. In the Folder field, type \\ followed by the hostname of your lab partner's computer from Step 10, followed by **\LAB8-2**. Refer to Figure 8-6 for an example of the settings used to connect to a computer called USERA-PC.

e. Click the **Connect using different credentials** check box to select that option.

f. Confirm that the **Reconnect at logon** check box is already selected. If it is not, select it.

g. Click the **Finish** button.

h. A Windows Security dialog box will appear asking you to enter credentials that will grant you access to your lab partner's computer. The User name field must be specified in the format *TargetComputerName\Username*, where *TargetComputerName* is the name of your lab partner's computer in Step 10 and *Username* is a valid local account on that computer. In the dialog box *User name* field, type *TargetComputerName* **lab82usr**. Refer to Figure 8-7 for an example of the settings used to authenticate to a computer called USERA-PC.

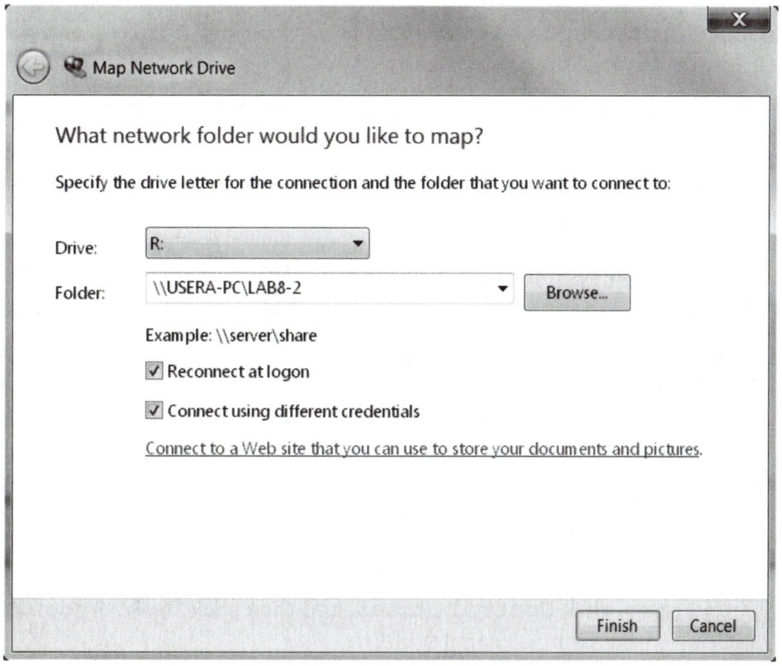

Figure 8-6 Sample settings to map a network location to a drive letter using the Map Network Drive Wizard

© Cengage Learning 2012

Figure 8-7 Sample settings to authenticate to a computer called USERA-PC

© Cengage Learning 2012

    i. Click to select the **Remember my credentials** check box.

    j. In the *Password* field of the Windows Security dialog box, enter **workpass** and click the **OK** button.

    k. The computer file browser window opens to browse files on drive R:. Double-click the **Lab82Document** file and confirm that your student name is present in the text.

    l. Close Notepad and all open computer file browser windows.

14. When a user decides to store credentials to resources such as shared folders, they are stored in the user's profile. There are two ways to access those stored credentials, the Stored User Names and Passwords utility and Credential Manager. Confirm that the stored credentials can be accessed and modified with these utilities, as detailed in the following steps:

    a. Click **Start**, point to **All Programs**, click **Accessories**, and then click **Command Prompt**.

    b. At the command prompt, type **rundll32.exe keymgr.dll,KRShowKeyMgr** and press **Enter** to start the Stored User Names and Passwords utility.

    c. Click the name of your partner's computer in the list of stored credentials to highlight it.

    d. Click the **Edit** button.

    e. In the Password field, type the text **failpass** and click the **OK** button.

    f. Click the **Close** button to close the Stored User Names and Passwords utility.

    g. Confirm the current session to your lab partner's computer is still active by clicking **Start**, entering the text **R:** in the *Search programs and files* field, and then pressing **Enter**. The computer file browser window will open to display the file contents of your lab partner's computer.

    h. Close all open windows and log out.

    i. Log on to User*x*-PC. Note the error message displayed from the system tray that not all network drives could be reconnected.

    j. Click **Start**, click **Control Panel**, and then click **User Accounts and Family Safety** in the Control Panel window.

    k. In the User Accounts and Family Safety window, click **Credential Manager**.

    l. In the Credential Manager window, note the Windows Credentials section and your partner's computer name listed below it. Refer to Figure 8-8 for an example of

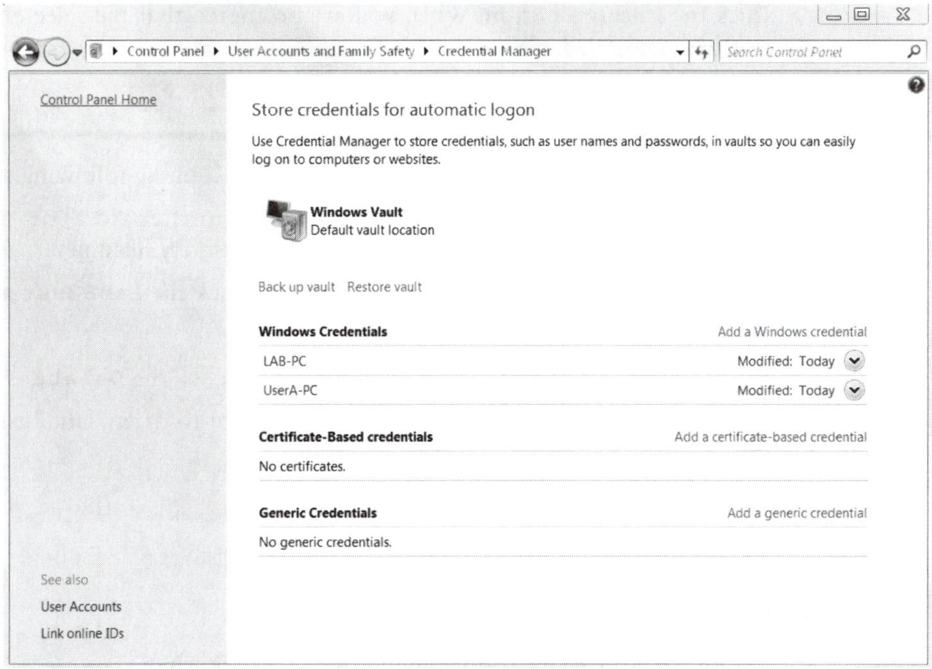

Figure 8-8   Credential Manager window

© Cengage Learning 2012

     the Credential Manager window showing stored Window's credentials for multiple computers. Click your lab partner's computer name.

m. The credentials stored for the computer will be displayed below the computer's name. Click the **Edit** link below the credentials.

n. Confirm that the content in the User name field matches the username format from Step 11.b; if the username format does not match, correct it.

o. In the Password field, type **workpass** and then click the **Save** button.

p. Close all open windows and log out.

q. Log on to User*x*-PC. Note that there is no longer an error message displayed from the system tray stating that not all network drives could be reconnected.

15. When a mapped drive letter is set to reconnect when the user logs on, that setting is stored in the user's profile on the computer. If the mapping is no longer desired, it can be removed. If the stored credential is no longer required, it can be removed as well, as detailed in the following steps:

a. Click **Start** and then click **Computer**.

b. In the right pane, below the section called Network Location, right-click drive letter **(R:)**.

c. Click **Disconnect** in the pop-up menu.

d. Click **Start**, point to **All Programs**, click **Accessories**, and then click **Command Prompt**.

e. At the command prompt, type **rundll32.exe keymgr.dll,KRShowKeyMgr** and press **Enter** to start the Stored User Names and Passwords utility.

f. In the Stored User Names and Passwords window, click the name of your lab partner's computer to highlight it.

g. Click the **Remove** button. When you are prompted that the selected logon information will be deleted, click the **OK** button.

h. Click the **Close** button.

16. Close all open windows.

17. Remove the lab82usr from your computer, as detailed in the following steps:

a. Click **Start**, click **Control Panel**, and then click **Add or remove user accounts** below the User Accounts and Family Safety heading.

b. In the Manage Accounts window that appears, click the **lab82usr** account.

c. Click the **Delete the account** link.

d. When you are prompted to keep lab82usr's files, click the **Delete Files** button.

e. When you are asked if you are sure that you want to delete lab82usr's account, click the **Delete Account** button.

f. Close the Manage Accounts window.

18. Log off the computer.

Certification Objectives

Objectives for MCTS Exam #70-680: Windows 7, Configuring:

- Configuring Network Connectivity: Configure network settings
- Configuring Access to Resources: Configure shared resources
- Configuring Access to Resources: Configure authentication and authorization

Review Questions

1. A UNC path is identified by the characters that start the path's identity. Which of these prefixes identifies a UNC path?

a. file://

b. //

c. http://

d. \\

2. Stored User Names and Passwords is a graphical tool that accesses credentials that are also available through the_____ graphical utility.

a. Explorer

b. Key Manager

c. regedit

d. Credential Manager

3. When users open a shared folder on a remote computer, the credentials used to log on to their own computers (i.e., *username* and password) must match the credentials on the remote computer. True or False?

4. Which of the following commands allow an administrator to edit a cached set of user credentials that is being used to authenticate to a shared folder located on a company server?

a. rundll32.exe keymgr.dll,KRShowKeyMgr

b. rundll32.exe certmgr.dll,KRShowKeyMgr

c. rundll32.exe keymgr.dll,ShowKeyMgr

d. rundll32.exe certmgr.dll,ShowKeyMgr

5. In an environment where you are supporting a small network of 25 Windows 7 computers and one server that has multiple shared folders, what are the disadvantages of using mapped drive letters that reconnect when the users log on?

Lab 8.3: Using Windows Calculator with IPv4 Addresses

Objectives

The objective of this activity is to use the Windows Calculator to perform basic operations related to the conversion and mathematical manipulation of decimal and binary numbers that are typically encountered in IPv4 addressing.

Materials Required

This lab requires the following:

- A physical computer or virtual machine running Windows 7 that is configured as User*x*-PC or as specified by your instructor

Estimated completion time: **30 minutes**

Activity Background

You can use the Programmer mode of Windows Calculator to review common subnet mask values, including the comparison of their binary and decimal representations. You then can use it to apply the subnet mask value to an IPv4 address to determine the corresponding network address. If two computers are on the same local area network, they should be able to talk directly to each other without having to communicate through a router. In that case, those computers should have the same network address as part of their IPv4 address.

Depending on IP addresses and the respective subnet mask value, it is not always obvious that two computers actually share the same network address. Using the Windows Calculator to determine network addresses can be fast and easy once the process is known.

Activity

1. Log on to User*x*-PC.

2. Click **Start**, point to **All Programs**, click **Accessories**, and then click **Calculator**. By default, Windows Calculator opens in Standard mode, as shown in Figure 8-9.

3. In the Calculator window, click the **View** menu and select **Scientific**. Unlike the calculators in previous versions of Windows, note that the Scientific mode for the Windows 7 calculator does not include binary or hexadecimal operations.

4. In the Calculator window, click the **View** menu and select **Programmer**. This will update the Calculator window with binary and hexadecimal features, as shown in Figure 8-10.

5. Note that the default number setting is Dec (which stands for Decimal). Type the value **224** and click the **Bin** option (which stands for Binary). Note that the display changes to the binary number 1110 0000, with a space inserted every four binary digits on the display to improve readability.

6. Click the **Dec** option and note that the binary number on the display converts back to the decimal value 224.

8

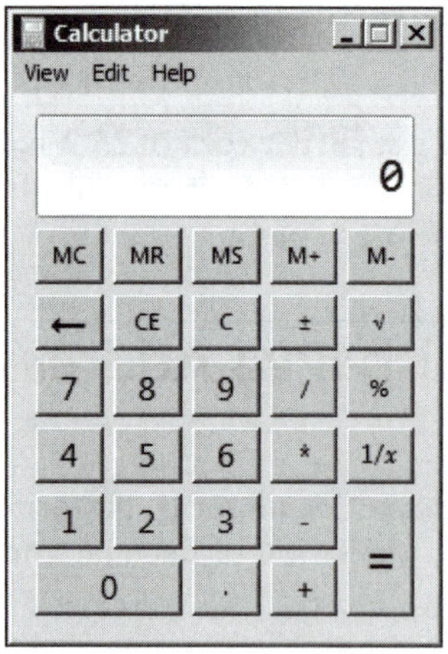

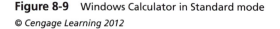

Figure 8-9 Windows Calculator in Standard mode
© Cengage Learning 2012

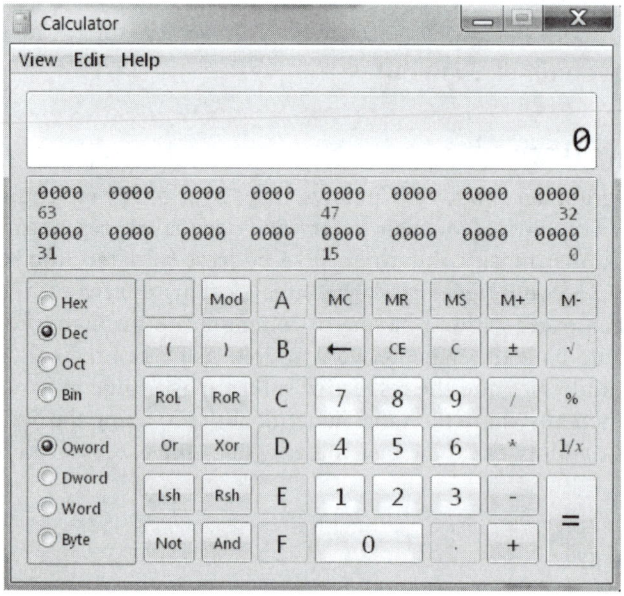

Figure 8-10 Windows Calculator in Programmer mode
© Cengage Learning 2012

7. Several decimal numbers are commonly encountered in IPv4 addressing, specifically with subnet mask values. The Windows Calculator can be used to convert those decimal numbers to binary, as detailed in the following steps:

   a. Click the **C** button, located above the number 9 button, to clear the display.

   b. Enter the decimal number **255**.

   c. Click the **Bin** option and note that the decimal number on the display converts to a binary number.

   d. Click the **Dec** option and note that number on the display returns to 255.

   e. For each of the following decimal numbers, use Steps 7.a to 7.d to convert it to its binary form and record the binary number in the space next to it. (*Note:* Always write the binary equivalent as an eight-digit number, adding leading zeros if necessary to make up eight binary digits. A space after each four-digit set is optional.)

255 _____

254 _____

252 _____

248_____

240 _____

224_____

192 _____

128 _____

0 _____

8. IPv4 subnet masks are a 32-bit binary value. Given a subnet mask value in binary, the value can be converted into dotted decimal notation. For the 32-bit subnet mask value 1111 1111 1111 1111 1111 1111 1000 0000 (spaces have been inserted to aid readability), the procedure to convert the value to dotted decimal notation is detailed in the following steps:

   a. Record the first eight binary bits of the subnet mask value (starting from the leftmost side of the 32-bit binary value): _____. Using the findings in Step 7.e, record the equivalent decimal value: _____. Note that this number represents the first octet (i.e., 8 bits) of the subnet mask value.

   b. Record the next eight binary bits of the subnet mask value: _____. Using the findings in Step 7.e, record the equivalent decimal value: _____. Note that this number represents the second octet of the subnet mask value.

   c. Record the next eight binary bits of the subnet mask value: _____. Using the findings in Step 7.e, record the equivalent decimal value: _____. Note that this number represents the third octet of the subnet mask value.

   d. Record the next eight binary bits of the subnet mask value: _____. Using the findings in Step 7.e, record the equivalent decimal value: _____. Note that this number represents the fourth octet of the subnet mask value.

   e. The dotted decimal notation equivalent of the 32-bit binary value is written in the format "1st octet . 2nd octet . 3rd octet . 4th octet". Using the decimal octet values from Steps 8.a–d, write the equivalent dotted decimal notation for the original subnet mask value (i.e. 1111 1111 1111 1111 1111 1111 1000 0000): _____ . _____ . _____ . _____

9. IPv4 subnet mask values can also be written in Classless Inter-Domain Routing (CIDR) format. CIDR notation for a subnet mask adds a "/" to the end of a network interface's IPv4 address, followed by a decimal number. That decimal number represents the number of binary digit ones (i.e., "1") in the subnet mask's 32-bit binary value. This is a possible representation because the subnet mask's 32-bit binary value has a string of ones that stop at a specific point and become zeros for the remainder of the 32-bit value. Given the subnet mask value 1111 1111 1111 1111 1111 1100 0000 0000, count and record the number of binary digits that are ones: / _____

10. The number of binary digits that are ones in a decimal value can be determined by converting the decimal value into its binary equivalent and then simply counting the ones in that binary value. Next to each of the following decimal values, use the converted binary values in Step 7.e as a reference and record the number of binary digits that are equal to one in that number's corresponding binary representation:

255 _____

254 _____

252 _____

248 _____

240 _____

224 _____

192 _____

128 _____

0 _____

11. A subnet mask that is represented in dotted decimal notation can be converted into CIDR notation by determining the number of binary ones in each decimal value and determining the total number of ones in the subnet mask. Consider the subnet mask value 255.255.240.0. This can be converted to CIDR notation, as detailed in the following steps:

   a. Using the values recorded in Step 10 for reference, write down the number of ones found in the binary representation of the first octet (i.e., 255): _____

   b. Using the values recorded in Step 10 for reference, write down the number of ones found in the binary representation of the second octet (i.e., 255): _____

   c. Using the values recorded in Step 10 for reference, write down the number of ones found in the binary representation of the third octet (i.e., 240): _____

   d. Using the values recorded in Step 10 for reference, write down the number of ones found in the binary representation of the fourth octet (i.e., 0): _____

   e. The CIDR value is the total number of ones from Step 11.a to d: _____ + _____ + _____ + _____ = / _____

12. When a subnet mask is specified using CIDR notation (i.e., /n), it can be rewritten as the corresponding binary value by determining how many ones and zeros make up the 32-bit value. The number of ones to write matches the number specified in the CIDR notation (i.e., n). The number of zeros to write is 32-n. The binary number is written left to right, starting with the required number of ones, followed by the required number of zeros. Once the 32-bit binary representation is determined, the dotted decimal notation can be determined from that. For the subnet mask /13, determine the corresponding binary and dotted decimal equivalents, as detailed in the following steps:

   a. The number of ones to write in the 32-bit binary representation is 13 (i.e., n = 13). Determine the number of zeros to write: _____

   b. Write the subnet mask value in binary form by writing 13 ones, followed by the required number of zeros: _____

   c. Rewrite the binary number from Step 12.b by inserting decimal points after every 8 bits: _____ . _____ . _____ . _____

   d. Using Step 7.e as reference, convert each group of 8 bits from Step 12.c to its decimal equivalent in the corresponding position: _____ . _____ . _____ . _____

13. An IPv4 address contains two pieces of information, the network address and the host address. The subnet mask is applied using a mathematical process called ANDing. The Windows Calculator can be used to calculate the network address given an IP address and a subnet mask in dotted decimal notation. For the IP address 189.1.215.98 and subnet mask 255.255.240.0, determine the network address with the Windows Calculator, as detailed in the following steps:

   a. Click the **C** button, located above the number 9 button, to clear the display.

   b. Using the first octet from the IP address (i.e., 189) and the subnet mask (i.e., 255), start the analysis by entering the decimal number **189**.

c. Click the **And** button

d. Enter the decimal number **255**.

e. Press **Enter** and record the result as the first octet of the network address:
_____

f. Using the second octet from the IP address (i.e., 1) and the subnet mask (i.e., 255), enter the decimal number **1**. Click the **And** button. Enter the decimal number **255**.

g. Press **Enter** and record the result as the second octet of the network address:
_____

h. Using the third octet from the IP address (i.e., 215) and the subnet mask (i.e., 240), enter the decimal number **215**. Click the **And** button. Enter the decimal number **240**.

i. Press **Enter** and record the result as the third octet of the network address:
_____

j. Using the fourth octet from the IP address (i.e., 98) and the subnet mask (i.e., 0), enter the decimal number **98**. Click the **And** button. Enter the decimal number **0**.

k. Press **Enter** and record the result as the fourth octet of the network address:
_____

l. A network address value is written in the format "1st octet . 2nd octet . 3rd octet . 4th octet". Using the octet values from Steps 13.e, 13.g, 13.i and 13.k, write the network address in the following spaces: _____ . _____ . _____ . _____

14. In the Calculator window, click the **View** menu and select **Standard**.

15. Close Windows Calculator and log off the computer.

Certification Objectives

Objectives for MCTS Exam #70-680: Windows 7, Configuring:

- Configuring Network Connectivity: Configure IPv4 network settings

Review Questions

1. Given the binary number 1010 1111 1111 1011 1000 1000 1100 0001, what is the matching dotted decimal representation?

a. 175.255.136.193

b. 175.251.184.193

c. 175.255.184.193

d. 175.251.136.193

2. A subnet mask is identified using the CIDR notation /28. Which one of the following dotted decimal numbers is an equivalent representation?

a. 255.255.255.0

b. 255.255.240.0

c. 255.255.255.240

d. 255.255.255.112

3. Given the IPv4 address 15.251.93.4 and a subnet mask of 255.255.255.0, what is the matching 32-bit binary representation of the IPv4 address?

a. 1111 1111 1011 101 1101 100

b. 0000 1111 1111 1011 0101 1101 0000 0100

    c. 1111 1111 1111 1111 1111 1111 0000 0000

    d. 0000 1111 1111 1011 0101 1101 0000 0000

4. Given the IPv4 address 190.200.150.30 and a subnet mask of 255.255.252.0, what is the network address identified by those values?

    a. 190.200.148.0

    b. 190.200.150.28

    c. 190.200.148.28

    d. 190.200.150.0

5. Three computers are connected to the same local area network and should not require a router to directly communicate with each other. All three computers have the subnet mask specified as the CIDR value /20. Computer A has the IP addresses 172.31.17.2. Computer B has the IP address 172.31.26.2. Which of the following IP addresses can be assigned to Computer C so that these three computers consider themselves on the same network?

    a. 172.31.0.2

    b. 172.31.15.31

    c. 172.31.48.2

    d. 172.31.31.31

Lab 8.4: Configuring Windows Remote Management in a Workgroup

Objectives

The objective of this activity is to examine the process of enabling Windows Remote Management for the purposes of enabling commands to be executed on a remote computer.

Materials Required

This lab requires the following:

- A physical computer or virtual machine running Windows 7 that is configured as User*x*-PC or as specified by your instructor
- A lab partner with a physical computer or virtual machine running Windows 7 that is configured as User*x*-PC or as specified by your instructor

Estimated completion time: **30 minutes**

Activity Background

Commands can be remotely executed on a Windows 7 computer that has the Windows Remote Management (WinRM) system enabled and configured. This activity will examine the procedure used to both enable and configure WinRm on a Windows 7 computer that is part of a workgroup. Specific properties of the WinRM services and the Windows Firewall are examined to highlight important dependencies and settings.

Activity

1. Log on to User*x*-PC as User*x*.

2. Create a new user account on your computer that will be used by your lab partner to authenticate with administrative access to your computer, as detailed in the following steps:

    a. Click **Start**, click **Control Panel**, and then click **Add or remove user accounts** below the User Accounts and Family Safety heading.

    b. In the Manage Accounts window that appears, click the **Create a new account** link.

    c. Enter the name **lab84usr** as the new user account name. Click **Administrator**.

    d. Click the **Create Account** button to create the user.

    e. When the Manage Accounts windows reappears, click the **lab84usr** icon.

    f. When the Change an Account window appears, click the **Create a password** link.

    g. When the Create Password window appears, enter **workpass** in the *New password* field.

    h. Enter **workpass** in the *Confirm new password* field.

    i. Click the **Create password** button.

    j. Close the Change an Account window.

3. Click **Start**, **All Programs**, **Accessories**, and then right-click **Command Prompt**.

4. Select the option **Run as administrator** from the pop-up menu. Click **Yes** when User Account Control asks if you want to allow the program to make changes to the computer.

5. At the command prompt, type **ipconfig** and press **Enter** to display your computer's IP address information. Record the IPv4 address of your primary network connection: _____ . _____ . _____ . _____ .

6. Write down the IPv4 address your lab partner recorded when he or she reached Step 4: _____ . _____ . _____ . _____ .

7. At the command prompt, type **hostname** and press **Enter** to display your computer's host name: _____ .

8. Write down the computer name your lab partner recorded when he or she reached Step 6: _____ .

9. Attempt to ping your lab partner's computer to confirm that your partner's computer name resolves to the correct IP, as detailed in the following steps:

    a. At the command prompt, type **ping -4** followed by a space.

    b. Type your lab partner's computer name from Step 8.

    c. Press **Enter** to run the command. Note the error message stating that a response was not received and the request timed out. This is expected since the remote machine's Windows Firewall will block the ping request by default.

10. Click **Start**, click **Control Panel**, and then click **View network status and tasks** below the Network and Internet heading.

11. When the Network and Sharing Center window opens, confirm that the network connection listed below *View your active networks* is currently configured as a Work network location. If the network connection is not set to *Work network,* it must be changed for WinRM functionality to be fully enabled, as detailed in the following steps:

    a. Click the **Public network** or **Home network** link below the network's name in the Network and Sharing Center window.

8

b. In the Set Network Location window that opens, click the **Work network** option. Note the statement explaining what you can see on the network and what other computers can see.

c. Click the **Close** button to save the change and close the Set Network Location window.

d. If the computer has multiple network interfaces, repeat Steps 10.a-c for each network interface that is not set to a Work network location.

e. Close the Network and Sharing Center window.

12. In the Administrator: Command Prompt window, confirm if your computer has the Windows Remote Management (WinRM) service enabled by typing the command **winrm enumerate winrm/config/listener** and then press **Enter**. Because the WinRM software is uninitialized on your computer, an error message should be displayed.

13. Configure the WinRM server system on your computer, as detailed in the following steps:

a. Type the command **winrm quickconfig** and press **Enter**.

b. Note the changes WinRM quick configuration is suggesting for your computer. When prompted to make these changes, type **Y** and then press **Enter**.

c. After the first changes have completed successfully, the WinRM setup will suggest additional changes. Note the suggested changes, particularly the IP addresses on the machine that will accept remote management requests. When promoted to make these changes, type **Y** and then press **Enter**. Note the final report of what changes have been made to your computer.

d. Confirm that the WinRM service is enabled by typing the command **winrm enumerate winrm/config/listener** and then pressing **Enter**.

e. Because your Windows 7 computer is not domain joined, WinRM must be configured to trust all local workstations on the local area network without validating their identity. Type the case-sensitive command **winrm set winrm/config/client @ {TrustedHosts="<local>"}** and then press **Enter**.

14. Confirm that your lab partner has completed the lab up to Step 13.e. If your lab partner has not completed the WinRM quick configuration fully, any attempt to run commands on his or her remote computer will fail. When your lab partner has completed Step 13, run remote commands on your lab partner's computer through the WinRM system, as detailed in the following steps:

a. Type the command **winrs -r:*TargetComputerName* -u:lab84usr -p:workpass "dir c:\"**, where *TargetComputerName* is the name of your lab partner's computer, which was recorded in Step 7, and then press **Enter**. Note that the *-u* parameter identifies a user account on the remote computer, the *-p* parameter is the password for that account, and the command to run remotely on your lab partner's computer is found between the double quotation marks. After a few seconds' pause, a directory listing of your lab partner's C:\ folder will be displayed in the Command Prompt window.

b. Type the command **winrs -r:*TargetComputerName* -u:lab84usr -p:workpass "netsh interface ipv4 show interface"**, where *TargetComputerName* is the name of your lab partner's computer, which was recorded in Step 8, and then press **Enter**. Note that a list of network interfaces and their general properties are displayed for your lab partner's computer.

c. Close the Command Prompt window.

15. Confirm the WinRM service settings, as detailed in the following steps:

    a. Click **Start** and in the *Search programs and files* box, enter **SERVICES.MSC**, and then press **Enter**.

    b. In the right pane of the Services window that opens, scroll to the **Windows Remote Management (WS-Management)** service.

    c. Double-click the service name to open its properties.

    d. Record the service name displayed on the General tab: _____

    e. Record the Startup type displayed on the General tab: _____

    f. Record the system component on which this service depends. The component is listed on the Dependencies tab: _____ and _____.

    g. Close the service's properties window.

    h. Close the Services window.

16. Confirm the Windows firewall changes that have been made as part of the WinRM quick configuration, as detailed in the following steps:

    a. Click **Start**, click **Control Panel**, and then click **View network status and tasks** below the Network and Internet heading.

    b. When the Network and Sharing Center window opens, click the Windows Firewall link found in the lower-left corner of the window.

    c. In the Windows Firewall window, click the **Advanced settings** link.

    d. In the Windows Firewall with Advanced Security window that opens, scroll the middle pane to the bottom.

    e. Below the heading *View and create firewall rules*, click the **Inbound Rules** link.

    f. Scroll to the bottom of the list of *Inbound Rules* and identify the Windows Remote Management rule that has the Profile type set to Private and the Enabled property set to Yes. Double-click the rule name to open its properties.

    g. Record the rule name displayed on the General tab: _____

    h. Record the Action setting displayed on the General tab: _____

    i. Click the **Protocols and Ports** tab. Record the Local port setting: _____

    j. Record the remote port setting: _____

    k. Click the **Advanced** tab. Record the profiles to which this rule applies (i.e., a selected profile has a check mark next to the name if it is selected): _____

    l. Click the **Customize** button in the Interface types section of the Advanced tab. Record the interface types to which this rule applies:_____

    m. Click the **OK** button to close the Customize Interface Types window.

    n. Click the **OK** button to close the Windows Remote Management (HTTP-In) Properties window.

    o. Close all open windows.

17. Remove the lab84usr from your computer, as detailed in the following steps:

    a. Click **Start**, click **Control Panel**, and then click **Add or remove user accounts** below the User Accounts and Family Safety heading.

    b. In the Manage Accounts window that appears, click the **lab84usr** account.

    c. Click the **Delete the account** link.

8

    d. When you are prompted to keep lab84usr's files, click the **Delete Files** button.

    e. When you are asked if you are sure that you want to delete lab84usr's account, click the **Delete Account** button.

    f. Close the Manage Accounts window.

18. Log off the computer.

Certification Objectives

Objectives for MCTS Exam #70-680: Windows 7, Configuring:

- Configuring Network Connectivity: Configure remote management
- Configuring Network Connectivity: Configure Windows Firewall

Review Questions

1. The Windows Remote Management service listens by default on what IP address?

    a. IPv4 loopback

    b. IPv6 loopback

    c. Assigned IPv4 and IPv6 addresses

    d. All addresses

2. The Windows Remote Management service listens by default on what port in Windows 7?

    a. 80

    b. 443

    c. 5985

    d. 6200

3. What service must be running for the Windows Remote Management service to accept remote operation requests?

    a. HTTPS

    b. RPS

    c. IIS

    d. WinRM

4. An administrator would like to reprogram all Windows 7 workstations on the local network with new static IPv4 addresses. The workstations are configured as part of a workgroup. The administrator has not configured any of the computers to receive remote operation commands. What steps would you advise the administrator to take so that the task can be completed remotely? What command utility would you recommend the administrator use to update IPv4 addresses on the remote computers?

5. The Windows Remote Management service depends on what other services to be running? (select two)

    a. HTTP

    b. NativeWiFi Filter

    c. Remote Procedure Call

    d. NDIS Usermode I/O Protocol

CHAPTER NINE

USER PRODUCTIVITY TOOLS

Labs included in this chapter:

- Lab 9.1 Securing a Shared Printer

- Lab 9.2 Troubleshooting Printers and Print Jobs

- Lab 9.3 Creating a Document Library

- Lab 9.4 Using Internet Explorer Security Features

Microsoft MCTS Exam #70-680 Objectives

Objective	Lab
Configure shared resources	9.1, 9.2
Configure file and folder access	9.3
Configure Internet Explorer	9.4

Lab 9.1: Securing a Shared Printer

Objectives

The object of this activity is to configure a shared printer and then control access to it.

Materials Required

This lab requires the following:

- A physical computer or virtual machine running Windows 7 that is configured as User*x*-PC or as specified by your instructor

Estimated completion time: **10 minutes**

Activity Background

Computers running Windows 7 are capable of using both local and network printers. After a printer has been installed in Windows 7, it can be shared with other users on the network. By default, each printer allows all users to print. You can modify the permissions on a printer to allow only specific users the ability to print.

Activity

1. Log on to User*x*-PC as **User*x***.

2. Install a new printer, as detailed in the following steps:

   a. Click **Start** and click **Devices and Printers**.

   b. In the Devices and Printers window, click **Add a printer**.

   c. In the Add Printer window, click **Add a local printer**.

   d. On the Choose a printer port page, in the Use an existing port box, select **LPT1: (Printer Port)** and click **Next**.

   e. On the Install the printer driver page, in the Manufacturer area, click **Canon**.

   f. In the Printers area, click **Canon Inkjet iP100 series** and then click **Next**.

   g. On the Type a printer name page, in the Printer name box, type **SecurePrinter** and click **Next**.

   h. On the Printer Sharing page, click **Share this printer so that others on your network can find and use it** and then click **Next**.

   i. On the You've successfully added SecurePrinter page, clear the **Set as the default printer** check box and click **Finish**.

   j. In the Devices and Printers window, verify that SecurePrinter is listed.

3. Allow only User*x* to print to SecurePrinter, as detailed in the following steps:

   a. Right-click **SecurePrinter** and click **Printer Properties**.

   b. In the SecurePrinter Properties window, on the Security tab, read the default permissions, as shown Figure 9-1.

   c. In the Group or user names box, click **Everyone** and then click **Remove**.

   d. Click **OK**.

4. Test enforcement of permissions on SecurePrinter, as detailed in the following steps:

   a. Switch to Standard1 with a password of FirstPW.

   b. Click **Start**, point to **All Programs**, click **Accessories**, and click **Notepad**.

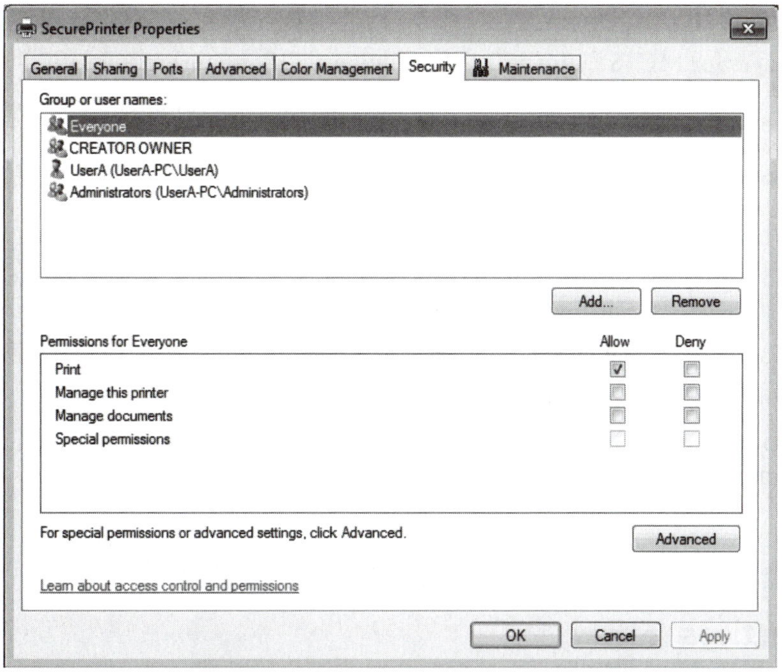

Figure 9-1 Default security settings for a printer
© Cengage Learning 2012

 c. In Notepad, type **This is my message**.

 d. Click the **File** menu and click **Print**.

 e. In the Print window, in the Select Printer area, click **Secure Printer** and then click **Print**.

 f. Click the **printer** icon on the taskbar.

 g. Read the contents in the SecurePrinter - LPT1: window, as shown in Figure 9-2. Notice that the printer is not responding because Standard1 does not have permission to use the printer. The content of the error message that appears is dependent on the printer driver that you are using.

 h. Click **Cancel Printing**.

 i. Close Notepad and do not save the changes.

 j. Log off as Standard1.

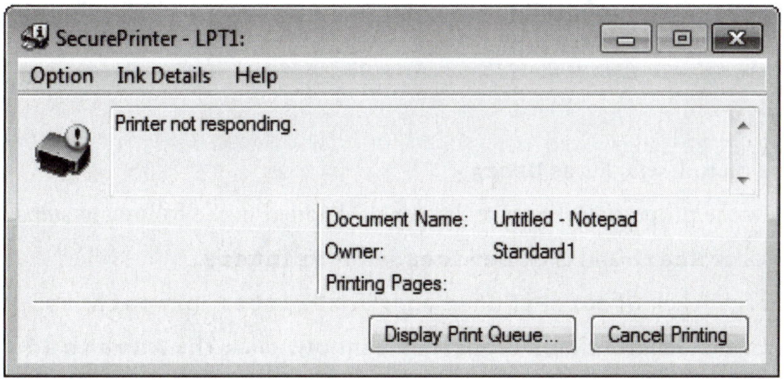

Figure 9-2 Error printing
© Cengage Learning 2012

9

Certification Objectives

Objectives for MCTS Exam #70-680: Windows 7, Configuring:

- Configuring Access to Resources: Configure shared resources

Review Questions

1. What are the different ways you can obtain printer drivers?

2. How does the printer installation process vary for a printer connected to a USB port instead of a parallel port?

3. What is a parallel port?

4. Which icon indicates that a printer is being shared?

5. Do you need to share a printer that is used by two people logging on to the same computer?

Lab 9.2: Troubleshooting Printers and Print Jobs

Objectives

The objective of this activity is to identify how to troubleshoot printers and print jobs.

Materials Required

This lab requires the following:

- A physical computer or virtual machine running Windows 7 that is configured as User*x*-PC or as specified by your instructor

- Completion of Lab 9.1

Estimated completion time: **10 minutes**

Activity Background

A print job is created each time you send a document to a printer. Each print job is stored locally on your computer before being sent to the printer. This printing process is controlled by the spooler service.

When the printing process is not working properly, print jobs can become corrupted. A print spooler might not be able to print a corrupted print job or it may print it incorrectly. In some cases a corrupted print job may prevent other jobs from printing and cause the computer to freeze or run very slowly.

Activity

1. Log on to User*x*-PC as **User*x***.

2. View the properties of Secure Printer, as detailed in the following steps:

   a. Click **Start** and click **Devices and Printers**.

   b. Right-click **SecurePrinter** and click **Printer properties**.

   c. In the SecurePrinter Properties window, click the **Advanced** tab, as shown in Figure 9-3.

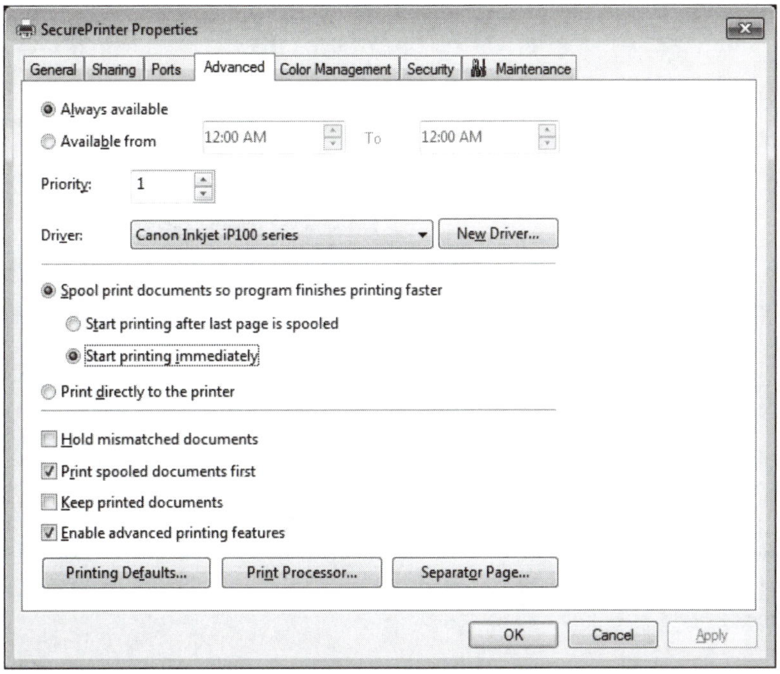

Figure 9-3   Printer Properties, Advanced tab
© Cengage Learning 2012

    d. Click **Start printing after last page is spooled**. This option is used when there have been problems generating the print job and you want to be sure that the entire print job is created before printing is started.

    e. Click **Print directly to the printer**. This option can sometimes avoid problems with print job generation, but it will prevent you from using the application that is printing until the entire print job is printed.

3. Review the print processor options, as detailed in the following steps:

    a. Click the **Print Processor** button.

    b. Read the contents of the Print Processor window, as shown in Figure 9-4. Print processors are programs that control how a print job is generated. The BJ Print Processor4 was installed at part of the printer driver. Generally you should keep the same print processor, but sometimes, changing the default data type can resolve printing issues from a single application.

    c. In the Print Processor window, click **Cancel**.

4. Print a test page, as detailed in the following steps:

    a. In the SecurePrinter Properties window, click the **General** tab.

    b. Click **Print Test Page**.

    c. In the pop-up window informing you that a test page has been sent to your printer, click **Close**.

    d. In the SecurePrinter – LPT1: window, notice that there is an option to display the print queue. This window is generated by the printer driver. Not all printers will generate a pop-up message like this.

    e. Close the SecurePrinter – LPT1: window.

    f. In the SecurePrinter Properties window, click **Cancel**.

9

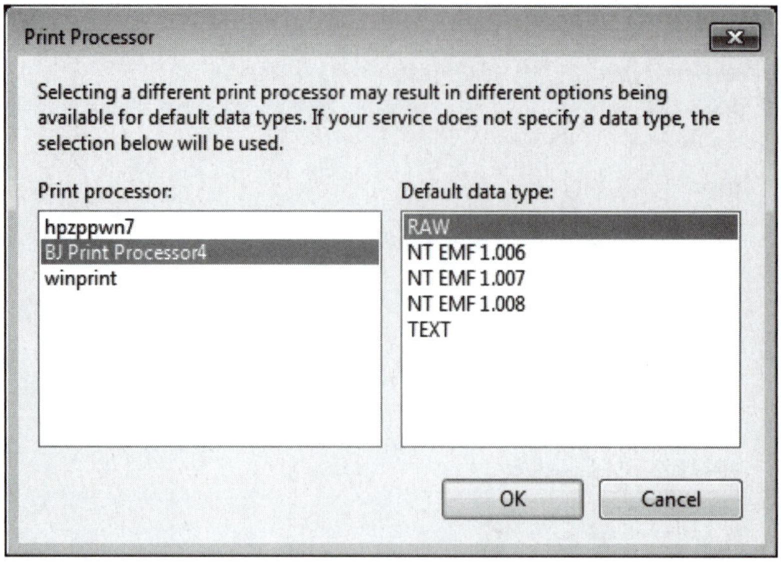

Figure 9-4   Print Processor window
© *Cengage Learning 2012*

5. View the options available for a print job, as detailed in the following steps:

   a. Click **Start** and click **Devices and Printers**.

   b. In the Devices and Printers window, identify any changes to the icon for SecurePrinter. The icon for SecurePrinter now has a warning symbol on it to indicate that there is an error.

   c. Right-click **SecurePrinter** and click **See what's printing**.

   d. Read the contents of the SecurePrinter window, as shown in Figure 9-5.

   e. Right-click **Test Page** to read the options available for managing the print job. Notice that you can Pause, Restart, or Cancel the job.

   f. In the context menu for Test Page, click **Properties**.

   g. In the Test Page Properties window, click each tab and view the options that can be modified for a print job. Options on the General tab are standard options provided by Windows 7. Other tabs are controlled by the printer driver.

   h. Click **Cancel**.

   i. Close the Secure Printer window.

   j. Close the Devices and Printers window.

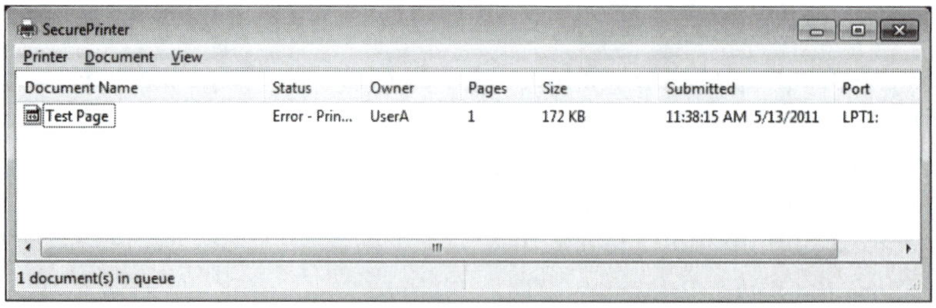

Figure 9-5   Print queue for SecurePrinter
© *Cengage Learning 2012*

6. View the results of a stopped Print Spooler service, as detailed in the following steps:

   a. Click **Start**, right-click **Computer**, and click **Manage**.

   b. In the Computer Management window, expand **Services and Applications**, and click **Services**.

   c. Scroll down in the list of services and click **Print Spooler**.

   d. Read the description of the Print Spooler services and click **Stop**.

   e. Click **Start** and click **Devices and Printers**.

   f. In the Devices and Printers window, read the list of printers. Notice that none of the printers are listed.

   g. Close the Devices and Printers window.

7. Delete print job files from the hard drive, as detailed in the following steps:

   a. Click **Start** and click **Computer**.

   b. Browse to C:\Windows\System32\Spool and read the contents of the folder. Printer drivers for installed printers are located in the drivers folder. Print jobs are stored in the PRINTERS folder.

   c. Double-click the PRINTERS folder.

   d. In the warning window, click **Continue** to give yourself access.

   e. Read the files displayed in Windows Explorer. A print job is composed of two files, as shown in Figure 9-6.

   f. Select and delete the two files in Windows Explorer. These two files have the extension SHD and SPL. Click **Yes** when prompted to move them to the Recycle Bin.

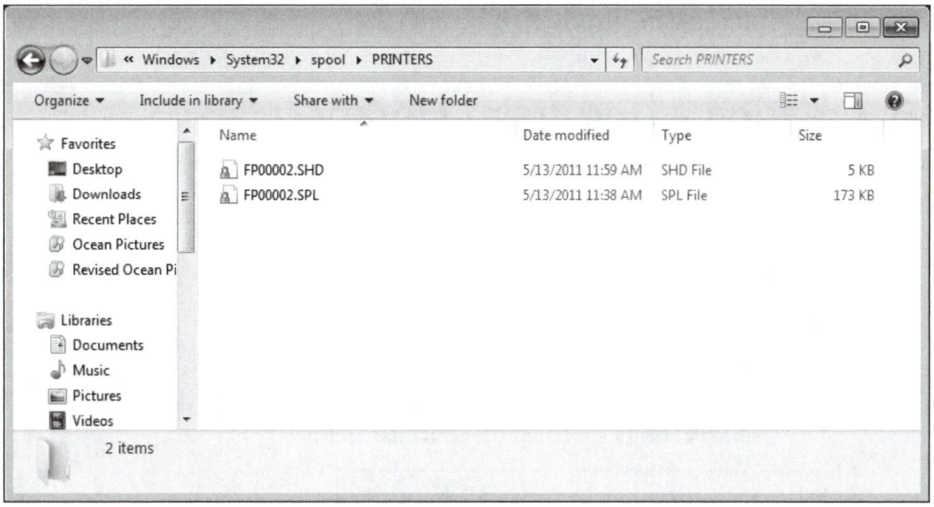

Figure 9-6   Files for a print job
© *Cengage Learning 2012*

9

8. Start the Print Spooler service and view the queue for Secure Printer, as detailed in the following steps:

   a. In the Computer Management window, expand **Services and Applications**, and click **Services**.

   b. Scroll down in the list of services and click **Print Spooler** and click **Start**.

    c. Close Computer Management.

    d. Click **Start** and click **Devices and Printers**.

    e. Right-click **SecurePrinter** and click **See what's printing**.

    f. Read the contents of the queue for SecurePrinter. Notice that no jobs are listed.

    g. Close the SecurePrinter window.

    h. Close Devices and Printers.

Certification Objectives

Objectives for MCTS Exam #70-680: Windows 7, Configuring:

- Configuring Access to Resources: Configure shared resources

Review Questions

1. You have been called to a user's computer where the printers are not visible in Devices and Printers. What is a likely cause of this problem?

2. A printer on a Windows 7 computer is unstable and sometimes fails to completely render a print job. This results in partially completed print jobs being sent to the printer and wasting paper. How can you ensure that partially completed print jobs are not sent to the printer?

3. You are printing a 900-page print job to a printer that you expect to take 30 minutes to complete. You have a much smaller print job that is urgent. How can you print the urgent print job immediately to the same printer?

4. A Windows 7 computer has a corrupted print job that is preventing all other print jobs from printing. You are unable to cancel the corrupted print job. How can you remove the corrupted print job?

5. What is the file structure of a print job?

Lab 9.3: Creating a Document Library

Objectives

The objective of this activity is to create a new document library that holds files from multiple folders.

Materials Required

This lab requires the following:

- A physical computer or virtual machine running Windows 7 that is configured as User*x*-PC or as specified by your instructor

> Estimated completion time: **10 minutes**

Activity Background

Document libraries are a new feature in Windows 7. A document library allows you to pull multiple folders together and present them as a single folder structure. You would do this for folders with related content. For example, an application may generate reports for a project in Folder1, but you have other related documents in Folder2. A document library for the project can display content from both folders in a single location. A document library can even contain shared folders on a network.

Activity

1. Log on to User*x*-PC as **User*x***.

2. Create several folders for a Windows 7 upgrade project, as detailed in the following steps:

   a. Click **Start**, point to **All Programs**, click **Accessories**, and click **Command Prompt**.

   b. Type **md C:\Win7Reports** and press **Enter**.

   c. Type **md %userprofile%\documents\Win7Project** and press **Enter**.

   d. Type **md C:\MigrationTools** and press **Enter**.

   e. Close the command prompt.

3. Create a new document library for the Windows 7 upgrade project, as detailed in the following steps:

   a. Click **Start** and click **Computer**.

   b. In the left pane of Windows Explorer, click **Libraries**.

   c. Review the list of libraries that exist by default.

   d. Click **New library**.

   e. Type **Win7Upgrade** and press **Enter** to rename the library.

4. Add folders to the Win7Upgrade library, as detailed in the following steps:

   a. Right-click **Win7Upgrade** and click **Properties**.

   b. In the Win7Upgrade Properties window, in the Optimize this library for list box, select **Documents**.

   c. Click **Include a folder**.

   d. In the Include Folder in Win7Upgrade window, in the Folder box, type **C:\Win7Reports** and click **Include folder**.

   e. Click **Include a folder**.

   f. In the Include Folder in Win7Upgrade window, in the Folder box, type **C:\MigrationTools** and click **Include folder**.

   g. Click **Include a folder**.

   h. In the Include Folder in Win7Upgrade window, click **Documents**, click **Win7Project** and then click **Include folder**.

   i. Review the contents of the Win7Upgrade Properties window. Notice that a check mark appears beside Win7Reports (C:), as shown in Figure 9-7.

5. Change the default save location for the library, as detailed in the following steps:

   a. In the Win7 Upgrade Properties window, click the **Win7Project** folder.

   b. Click **Set save location**. Notice that the check mark now appears beside the Win7Project folder.

   c. Click **OK**.

6. Change how contents are displayed in the Win7Upgrade library, as detailed in the following steps:

   a. In Windows Explorer, in the left pane, click **Win7Upgrade**.

   b. Read the contents of the right pane. Notice that all three folder locations are listed.

   c. In the upper-right corner, in the Arrange by box, select **Name**.

   d. Read the contents of the right pane. Notice that the three folder locations are no longer listed.

9

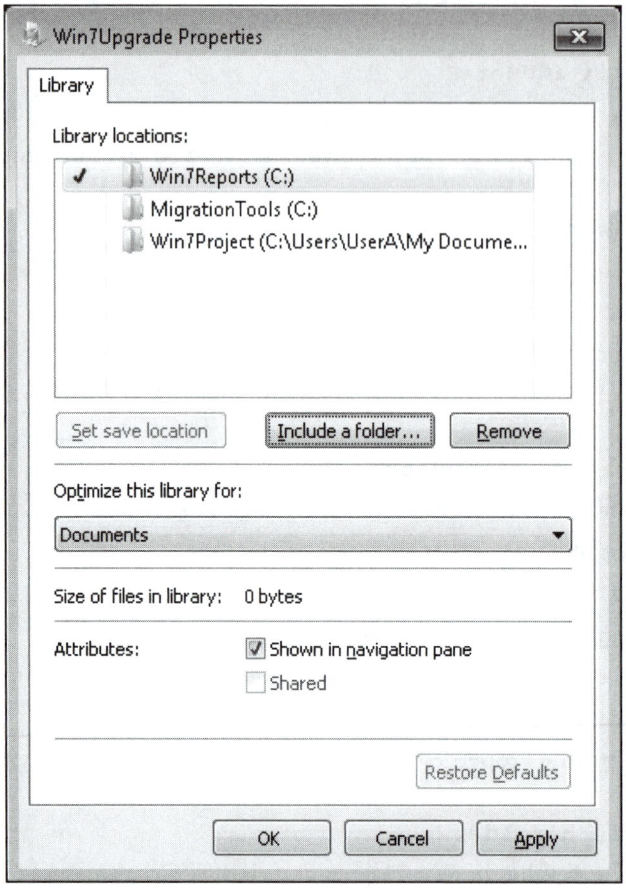

Figure 9-7   Properties of a library
© Cengage Learning 2012

7. Create a new document in the Win7Upgrade library, as detailed in the following steps:

   a. In the right pane, right-click an open area, point to **New,** and click **Text Document**.

   b. Type **ProjectPlan** and press **Enter** to rename the document.

   c. Right-click **ProjectPlan.txt** and click **Properties**.

   d. In the ProjectPlan.txt Properties window, on the General tab, read the Location of the file. Notice that it is located in the default save location.

   e. Click **Cancel**.

8. Close all open windows.

Certification Objectives

Objectives for MCTS Exam #70-680: Windows 7, Configuring:

* Configuring Hardware and Applications: Configure file and folder access

Review Questions

1. What is the purpose of creating a library?

2. Can a library include network folders?

3. How can you identify the default save location for a library?

4. Why would you vary the type of files for which a library is optimized?

5. What benefit is there to arranging files by methods other than Folder?

Lab 9.4: Using Internet Explorer Security Features

Objectives

The objective of this activity is to identify and use security features in Internet Explorer 8.

Materials Required

This lab requires the following:

- A physical computer or virtual machine running Windows 7 that is configured as User*x*-PC or as specified by your instructor

Estimated completion time: **15 minutes**

Activity Background

Internet Explorer 8 includes several features to make Web browsing safe and prevent the installation of malicious software (malware). These features include security zones in Internet Options, Pop-up Blocker, the ability to manage add-ons, SmartScreen Filter, and privacy settings.

Internet Explorer 8 is the version of Internet Explorer included with Windows 7.

Activity

1. Log on to User*x*-PC as **User*x***.

2. On the taskbar, click the **Internet Explorer** icon.

3. Test the Pop-up Blocker, as detailed in the following steps:

    a. In Internet Explorer, click the **Tools** menu, point to **Pop-up Blocker**, and click **Pop-up Blocker Settings**.

    b. Read the information in the Pop-up Blocker Settings window. Notice that pop-ups are not allowed from any Web site.

    c. Click **Cancel**.

    d. In the address bar, type **http://www.popuptest.com** and press **Enter**.

    e. Under the Common pop-up techniques heading, click the **Multi-Popup Test #2** link.

    f. Notice that no pop-ups are displayed, but an information bar is displayed at the top of the Web page.

    g. Click the yellow information bar and read the available options. Notice that you have the option to temporarily or permanently allow pop-ups from this site.

    h. Click the **Back** button.

4. Review security settings for zones in Internet Explorer, as detailed in the following steps:

    a. Click the **Tools** menu and click **Internet Options**.

    b. In the Internet Options window, click the **Security** tab.

    c. Click each zone and read the information about each.

9

5. Review the privacy settings in Internet Explorer, as detailed in the following steps:

   a. Click the **Privacy** tab.

   b. Read the current configuration. Notice that the default setting for the Internet zone is Medium.

   c. Move the slider to each possible setting and read the description of each.

6. Review advanced security in Internet Explorer, as detailed in the following steps:

   a. Click the **Advanced** tab.

   b. Scroll down to the Security heading and read the available options. In most cases, these options do not need to be modified.

   c. Click **Restore advanced settings**. This option is useful if you are experiencing problems after modifying advanced settings and cannot remember the original settings.

   d. Click **OK**.

7. Use SmartScreen filter to check the current Web site, as detailed in the following steps:

   a. Click the **Safety** menu, point to **SmartScreen Filter**, and click **Check This Website**.

   b. In the SmartScreen Filter window, read the warning and click **OK**.

   c. Read the response indicating that the site has not been reported, and click **OK**.

8. Install the Flash plug-in, as detailed in the following steps:

   a. In the address bar, type **http://www.adobe.com** and press **Enter**.

   b. Scroll down to the Download section, and click **Adobe Flash Player**.

   c. On the Adobe Flash Player page, click **Download now**.

   d. Read the instructions on the Web page.

   e. Click the information bar and click **Install This Add-on for All Users on This Computer**.

   f. In the User Account Control window, click **Yes**.

   g. Wait a few minutes while Adobe Flash Player and Google Toolbar are downloaded.

   h. In the Adobe Flash Player 10.3 Installer window, select the **I have read and agree to the terms of the Flash Player License Agreement** check box and click **Install**.

   i. When the installation is complete, click **Done**.

   j. Close the Adobe Download Manager window.

9. Verify successful installation of Adobe Flash Player, as detailed in the following steps:

   a. In the address bar, type **http://www.adobe.com/software/flash/about** and press **Enter**.

   b. In the Version Information box, read the installed version of Adobe Flash Player.

   c. Right-click the graphic at the top of the screen. This is a flash animation and displays a context menu for flash animations that includes options such as Quality and Play.

10. Disable the Adobe Flash Played add-on, as detailed in the following steps:

    a. Click the **Tools** menu and click **Manage Add-ons**.

    b. In the Manage Add-ons window, read the list of installed add-ons, as shown in Figure 9-8. Notice that add-ons from Adobe and Google are installed.

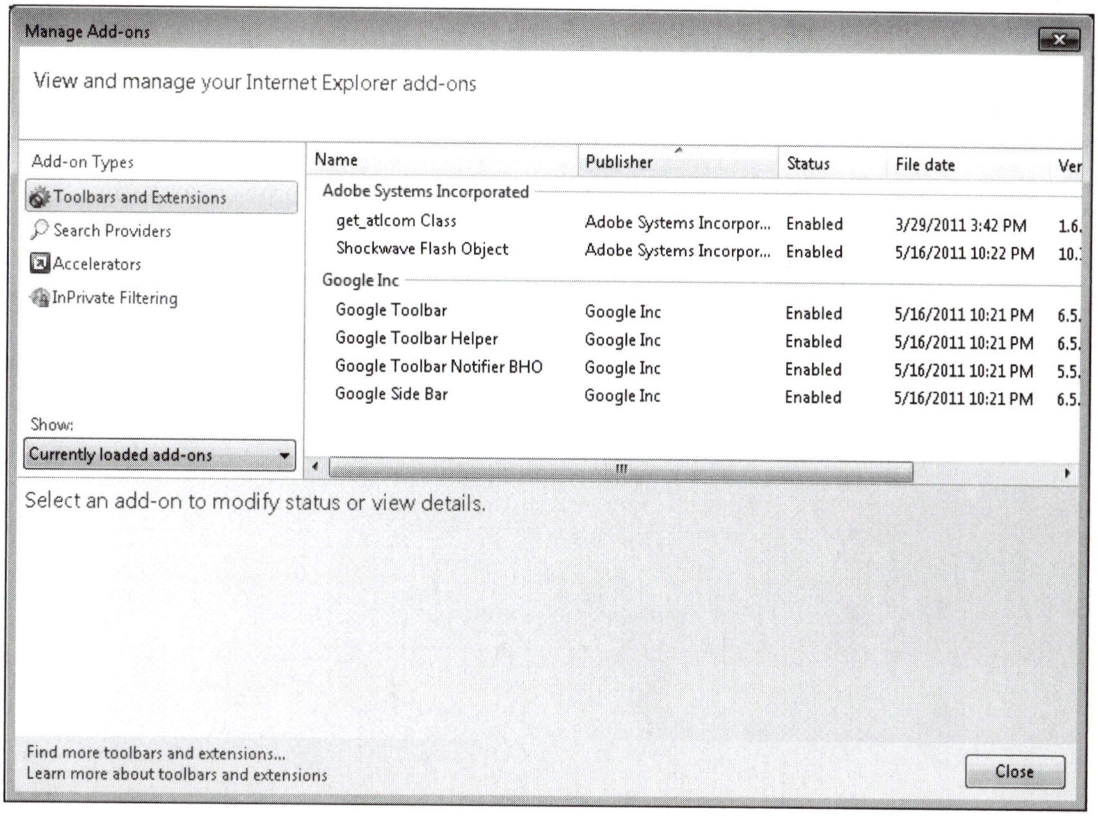

Figure 9-8   Manage Add-ons window
© Cengage Learning 2012

    c. Right-click the **Shockwave Flash Object** add-on, and click **Disable**.

    d. Click **Close**.

    e. In Internet Explorer, press **F5** to refresh the page. Notice that the graphic and version are no longer displayed.

11. Reset Internet Explorer settings, as detailed in the following steps.

    a. Click the **Tools** menu and click **Internet Options**.

    b. In the Internet Options window, click the **Advanced** tab.

    c. Under Reset Internet Explorer settings, click **Reset**.

    d. In the Reset Internet Explorer Settings window, read the warning and then click **Reset**.

    e. In the Reset Internet Explorer Settings window, click **Close**.

    f. In the Internet Explorer window, read the message and click **OK**.

    g. Close Internet Explorer.

Certification Objectives

Objectives for MCTS Exam #70-680: Windows 7, Configuring:

- Configuring Hardware and Applications: Configure Internet Explorer

9

Review Questions

1. What is a reason that you would allow pop-ups from a Web site?

2. A user is complaining that a Web site is not retaining options between viewing sessions. Can this be a result of privacy settings?

3. Is a Web site safe if SmartScreen does not detect a problem with it?

4. Why would you want to disable an add-on?

5. Internet Explorer is displaying random pop-up advertisements related to any Web site that you are visiting. You think that this is due to malware installed as an add-on, but you cannot locate it in Manage Add-ons. How can you remove the malware?

CHAPTER TEN

PERFORMANCE TUNING

Labs included in this chapter:

- Lab 10.1 Managing Power Plans
- Lab 10.2 Working with POWERCFG
- Lab 10.3 Using Windows Troubleshooting Wizards to Influence Performance

Microsoft MCTS Exam #70-680 Objectives

Objective	Lab
Configure performance settings	10.1, 10.2
Monitor systems	10.3

Lab 10.1: Managing Power Plans

Objectives

The object of this activity is to configure basic and advanced settings as part of a custom power plan.

Materials Required

This lab requires the following:

- A physical computer or virtual machine running Windows 7 that is configured as User*x*-PC or as specified by your instructor

Estimated completion time: 30 minutes

Activity Background

Power plans control how power and performance are balanced for a computer system. Power plan settings are presented using a basic format by default, which provides only a few settings to manage. Laptop systems include separate settings for *on battery* and *on AC power*. You can use advanced power plan settings to implement specific control over how individual hardware components are managed.

   (*Note*: Some settings may be unavailable if you are using a virtual machine instead of a physical computer to run Windows 7.)

Activity

1. Log on to User*x*-PC.

2. Click **Start** and then click **Control Panel**.

3. Click **Hardware and Sound**, and then click **Power Options**.

4. In the Power Options window, note the three power plans that are available. Record which plan is currently selected: _____. If necessary, click **Show Additional Plans** to display the High performance plan.

5. Create a new custom power plan and make it active, as detailed in the following steps:

   a. Click the **Create a power plan** link.

   b. Confirm that the **Balanced** plan is already selected. If it is not, click to select it. This will be the base plan used to define the starting settings for your new custom power plan.

   c. In the Plan name field, replace the text *My Custom Plan 1* with **LAB10-1 Power Plan**.

   d. Click the **Next** button.

   e. In the Edit Plan Settings window, click the **Turn off the display** drop-down arrow and select **1 minute** from the list.

   f. Click the **Put the computer to sleep** drop-down arrow and select **2 minutes** from the list, as shown in Figure 10-1.

   g. Click the **Create** button. The window will update to display the Power Options window. Note that the new power plan is currently selected and active.

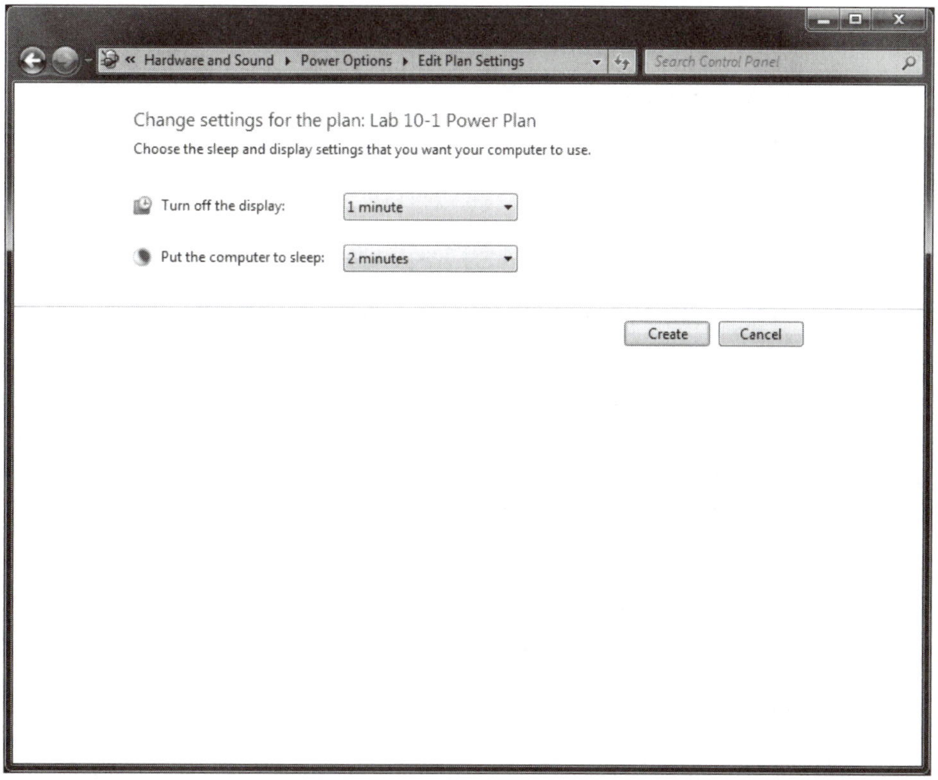

Figure 10-1 Basic power plan settings
© Cengage Learning 2012

6. Confirm that the plan settings work as expected, as detailed in the following steps:

   a. Wait one minute without touching the keyboard or mouse. Confirm that the monitor goes to sleep.

   b. Wait a second minute, without touching the keyboard or mouse, and confirm that the computer enters a sleep state. Note that the computer may take 15 to 30 seconds past the second minute to fully enter the sleep state.

   c. Move the mouse to wake the computer.

   d. Enter your password to log back in to the computer.

7. Additional advanced power settings are available for each plan. For example, the Lab 10-1 power plan that was created in Step 5.c can be changed to not require a password when the computer wakes up from a sleep state, and multimedia settings can be maximized for power savings, as detailed in the following steps:

   a. In the Power Options window, click the **Change plan settings** link next to *LAB 10-1 Power Plan*.

   b. Click the **Change advanced power settings** link.

   c. A new Power Options window with Advanced settings will open, with the active plan displayed by default, as shown in Figure 10-2. If the settings are dimmed in the window, click the **Change settings that are currently unavailable** link; otherwise, proceed to the next step.

10

Figure 10-2 Power Options window with Advanced settings
© *Cengage Learning 2012*

d. In the Power options window, change the setting for the *Require a password on wakeup* to **No**. If your computer is a laptop, there will be two subsettings for this advanced setting, *On battery* and *Plugged in*. In that case, change both settings to **No**.

e. Scroll down the list of advanced settings until you reach **Multimedia Settings**.

f. Click the plus sign next to Multimedia Settings to expand the sub settings. Click the plus sign next to **When sharing media** and **When playing video** to expand those settings, as seen in Figure 10-3.

g. Click the **When sharing media** drop-down arrow, and select **Allow the computer to sleep**.

h. Click the **When playing video** drop-down arrow and select **Optimize power savings**.

i. Click the **OK** button to save the changes and close the Power Options window.

8. Confirm that the updated advanced plan settings work as expected, as detailed in the following steps:

a. Wait one minute without touching the keyboard or mouse. Confirm that the monitor goes to sleep.

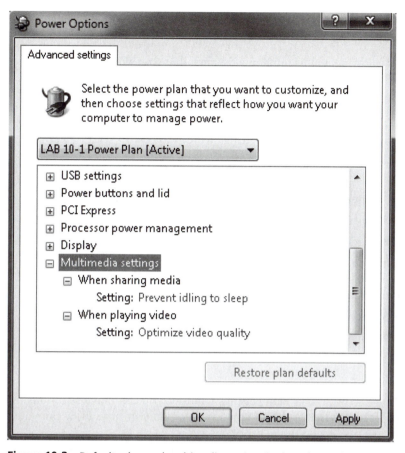

Figure 10-3   Default advanced multimedia settings in the Advanced Power Options window

© Cengage Learning 2012

    b. Wait a second minute, without touching the keyboard or mouse, and confirm that the computer enters a sleep state. Note that the computer may take 15 to 30 seconds past the second minute to fully enter the sleep state.

    c. Move the mouse to wake the computer. Note that you do not need to enter your password to log back in to the computer.

  9. To avoid having the computer go to sleep, update the Lab 10-1 Power Plan settings, as detailed in the following steps:

    a. In the Edit Plan Settings window, if the settings are dimmed, click the **Change settings that are currently unavailable** link; otherwise, proceed to the next step.

    b. Click the **Put the computer to sleep** drop-down arrow, and select **Never** from the list.

    c. Click the **Save changes** button. The window will be updated to display the Power Options window. Note that the updated power plan is still selected and active.

  10. Close all windows and log out.

10

Certification Objectives

Objectives for MCTS Exam #70-680: Windows 7, Configuring:

- Monitoring and Maintaining Systems that Run Windows 7: Configure performance settings

Review Questions

1. Using the basic Edit Plan Settings window, you can set a power plan so that it can turn off the display after as little as _____.

   a. 30 seconds

   b. 1 minute

   c. 5 hours

   d. 8 hours

2. Using the basic Edit Plan Settings window, you can set a power plan so that it can turn off the display after as much as _____. (Choose the longest setting that is possible.)

   a. 30 seconds

   b. 1 minute

   c. 5 hours

   d. 8 hours

3. Using the basic Edit Plan Settings window, you can make selections for a power plan so that it turns off a display after a certain amount of time. How can you choose an amount of time that is not on the list of choices?

4. In the advanced power plan settings, the hard disk can be configured to turn off after a period of inactivity. True or false?

5. In the advanced power plan settings, which of these settings can be assigned to the Power button action setting? (Select all that apply.)

   a. Restart

   b. Do nothing

   c. Hibernate

   d. Sleep

Lab 10.2: Working with POWERCFG

Objectives

The objective of this activity is to use the POWERCFG command-line utility to configure power settings and to analyze the power configuration of a computer.

Materials Required

This lab requires the following:

- A physical computer or virtual machine running Windows 7 that is configured as User*x*-PC or as specified by your instructor
- Completion of Lab 10.1

Estimated completion time: **40 minutes**

Activity Background

Power limits and consumption are important to the performance of a computer system. For example, a wireless network card can be configured to use less power, but this also reduces the range of the wireless network. Many devices, such as batteries, modems, network cards, and processors, can report power issues and identify their power consumption. The POWERCFG utility has the ability to analyze power- and performance-related issues, and it can report its findings in an HTML-formatted report. Because it is a command-line tool, it is well suited to scripting.

The activity of the computer system and its hardware influences the power analysis report generated by POWERCFG. The energy analysis report is intended to be run when the computer system is idle, not when it is actively being used by the user. Some activities run in the background; note that the computer can be active with processes that might not be obvious to the user.

Activity

1. Log on to User*x*-PC.

2. Click **Start**, and in the *Search programs and files* field, type the text **CMD** and then press **Enter**.

3. Type the command **POWERCFG –ENERGY** and then press **Enter**. Note the error message that is displayed.

4. Record the current directory of C:, as specified in the command prompt: _____

5. Close the command window.

6. Click **Start**, and in the *Search programs and files* field, type the text **CMD** and then right-click the **CMD** program listed at the top of the Start menu. Select **Run as administrator** from the pop-up menu that appears.

7. In the User Account Control window that appears, click the **Yes** button to allow the program to run.

8. Record the current directory of C:, as specified in the command prompt: _____

9. Note the difference between the current directory recorded in Step 4 and the one recorded in Step 8.

10. In the command window, type the command **POWERCFG –ENERGY** and then press **Enter**. Note that the command will take 60 seconds to complete. A full report will be written to a HTML file, with its name and location identified at the end of the screen summary, as shown in Figure 10-4.

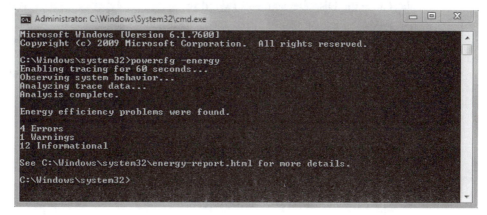

Figure 10-4   POWERCFG –ENERGY command output to screen
© Cengage Learning 2012

10

11. The default location for the HTML report is a system folder. You can specify a different location, as detailed in the following steps:

    a. In the command window, type the command **POWERCFG -ENERGY -OUTPUT c:\users\userx\LAB10-2-EREPORT-A.HTML** and press **Enter**, and then press the **Spacebar**. Note that this path is based on the profile of the currently logged-on user, as identified in Step 4.

12. Click **Start**, and in the *Search programs and files* field, type **c:\users\userx\LAB10-2-EREPORT-A.HTML**, and then press **Enter**.

13. Internet Explorer will open the file specified in Step 12. Review the report and note that the main sections of the report include a machine summary, errors, warnings, and information. Close the Internet Explorer window.

14. The length of time the energy analysis is allowed to run can be changed from the default of 60 seconds to obtain a broader view of the power consumption on the computer, as detailed in the following steps:

    a. Click **Start** and then **Computer**.

    b. Right-click the **Local Disk (C:)** icon, and select **Properties** from the pop-up menu.

    c. Click to select the **Tools** menu.

    d. Click the **Defragment now** button. The Disk Defragmenter window will open. Defragmenting the drive is being used to generate different results in the report.

    e. In the command window, type the command **POWERCFG -ENERGY -OUTPUT c:\users\userx\LAB10-2-EREPORT-B.HTML -DURATION 180**, but do not run the command until specified later in this activity.

    f. In the Disk Defragmenter window, click the **Defragment disk** button.

    g. In the command window, press **Enter** to run the POWERCFG command. Note that the power analysis will run for 120 seconds (i.e., 2 minutes).

    h. Click **Start**, and in the *Search programs and files* field, type **c:\users\userx\LAB10-2-EREPORT-B.HTML** and then press **Enter**.

    i. The energy analysis report will open in Internet Explorer. Scroll down to the **Errors** section. Review the list of power-related errors in the report. In most cases, the report will identify that processor utilization is high and that svchost.exe (using defrag.svc.dll) is responsible for a high percentage of that utilization.

    j. Close the Internet Explorer window.

    k. Close the Disk Defragmenter window.

    l. Close the Local Disk (C:) Properties window.

    m. Close the Computer file browser window.

15. The POWERCFG utility can be used to configure power setting from the command line. For example, you can set the amount of inactivity before the monitor is put into sleep to 3 minutes, as detailed in the following steps:

    a. In the command window, type **POWERCFG -CHANGE -MONITOR-TIMEOUT-AC 3** and then press **Enter**. Note that this will update the active power plan's monitor timeout when the computer is plugged in.

    b. Wait for three minutes to confirm the setting works as expected.

    c. Move the mouse to restore the screen.

16. The POWERCFG can also be used to report on devices and their power configuration settings. For example, to list the devices that have the ability to wake the computer from any sleep state, type the command **POWERCFG -DEVICEQUERY WAKE_FROM_ANY** and then press **Enter**.

17. If a device has the ability to wake the computer, that ability still might not be enabled for that device. You can use a POWERCFG command to identify those devices with that ability enabled. Type the command **POWERCFG -DEVICEQUERY WAKE_ARMED** and then press **Enter**. Note that the list of devices with that feature enabled is different from the list reported in Step 16.

18. To review other POWERCFG options, type **POWERCFG /?** and press **Enter**.

19. Close all windows.

20. Log off the computer.

Certification Objectives

Objectives for MCTS Exam #70-680: Windows 7, Configuring:

- Monitoring and Maintaining Systems that Run Windows 7: Configure performance settings

Review Questions

1. What user privilege level is required to run the POWERCFG –ENERGY command?

2. What file format is used for the POWERCFG energy analysis report by default?
   a. TXT
   b. HTML
   c. XML
   d. RTF

3. The POWERCFG utility can analyze a computer for energy efficiency and energy-related properties using the _____ command-line option.
   a. DEVICEQUERY
   b. OUTPUT
   c. DURATION
   d. ENERGY

4. The POWERCFG utility can report energy efficiency and energy-related properties, including CPU usage during the monitoring interval. True or False?

5. Which of the following POWERCFG command-line options will alter the number of seconds the utility will examine system activities that impact power efficiency?
   a. TIMER
   b. TRACE
   c. DURATION
   d. OUTPUT

10

Lab 10.3: Using Windows Troubleshooting Wizards to Influence Performance

Objectives

The objective of this activity is to use the built-in Windows Troubleshooting wizards to confirm that a system is healthy so that it can operate at peak performance.

Materials Required

This lab requires the following:

- A physical computer or virtual machine running Windows 7 that is configured as User*x*-PC or as specified by your instructor
- Completion of Lab 10.2

Estimated completion time: **30 minutes**

Activity Background

Even simple problems can have an impact on Windows performance. When a problem is detected by the system or a user, the issue can be analyzed by wizards called troubleshooters. Troubleshooters contain predetermined tests, questions, and logic to help analyze the computer. Updated troubleshooters are available online and can be downloaded automatically to analyze the computer with increased accuracy. This activity will exercise several troubleshooters, as well as identify some essential controls that influence the behavior of these troubleshooting wizards.

Activity

1. Log on to User*x*-PC.
2. Click **Start**, click **Control Panel**, and then under System and Security, click **Find and fix problems**. This will open the Troubleshooting window, as shown in Figure 10-5.
3. Select the **Get the most up-to-date troubleshooters from the Windows Online Troubleshooting service** check box, if necessary.
4. Below System and Security, click the **Check for performance issues** link.
5. When the Performance window opens, click the **Advanced** link. Deselect the option **Apply repairs automatically**.
6. Click the **Next** button. The system will run performance checks based on the script built into the performance troubleshooter.
7. Click the **View detailed information** link.
8. Review the list of performance issues that were checked. Hover the mouse cursor over **Check disk was run during system startup** and note the pop-up description of the test.
9. Scroll down and under Potential issues that were checked, click **Power Plan is set to Power saver**. The screen automatically scrolls down to the detection details for that test. Read the description of that test to understand why it is important when checking for maximum performance.
10. Click the **Next** button to return to the troubleshooter summary screen.

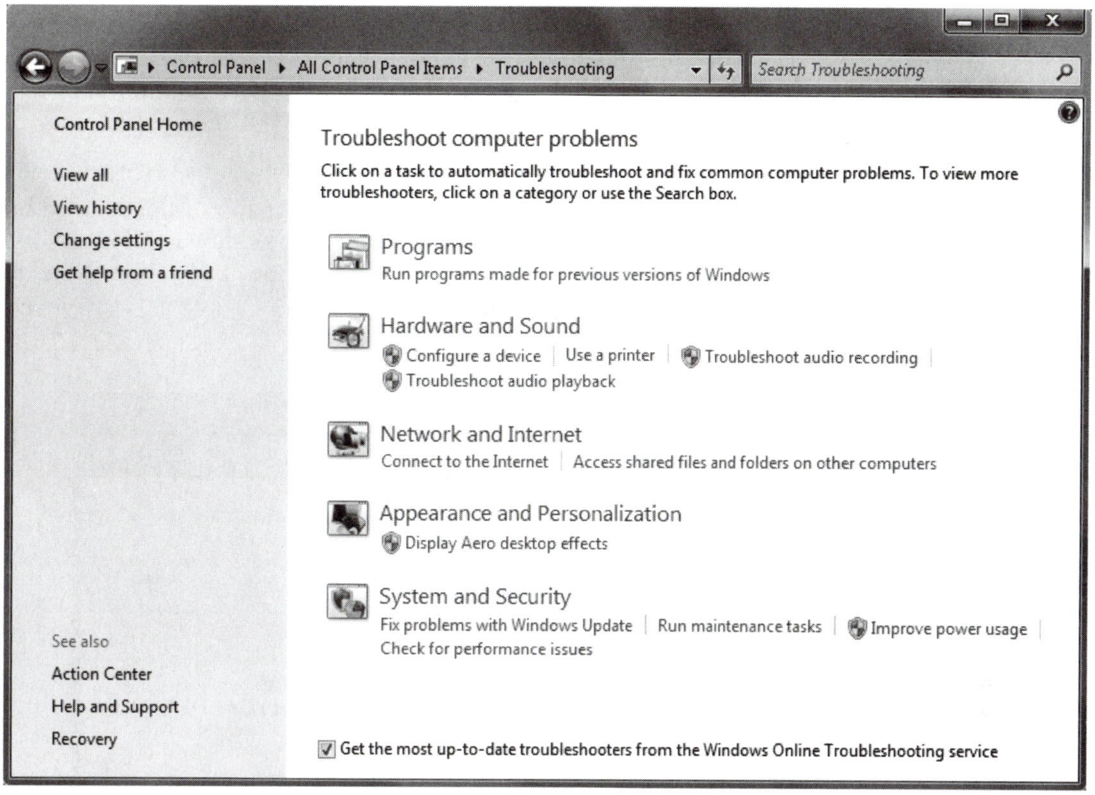

Figure 10-5 Troubleshooting window in Control Panel
© *Cengage Learning 2012*

11. Click the **Close** button to close the performance troubleshooter. If the Close button is not available, click **Cancel**.

12. Below System and Security in the Troubleshooting window, click the **Run maintenance tasks** link and click **Advanced**.

13. Click the **Run as administrator** link.

14. When the System Maintenance window reopens, click the **Advanced** link. Deselect the **Apply repairs automatically** option.

15. Click the **Next** button to start the system maintenance troubleshooter.

16. Click the **View detailed information** link.

17. Review the list of system maintenance issues that were checked. Under Potential issues that were checked, click **System time is incorrectly set**. The screen automatically scrolls down to the detection details for that test. Note the description that time measurement is important for a properly operating system.

18. Click the **Next** button to return to the troubleshooter summary screen.

19. Click the **Close** button to close the system maintenance troubleshooter. If the Close button is unavailable, click **Cancel**.

20. Below System and Security in the Troubleshooting window, click the **Improve power usage** link.

21. When the Power window opens, click the **Advanced** link. Deselect the **Apply repairs automatically** option.

10

22. Click the **Next** button to start the power troubleshooter.

23. The power troubleshooter will detect that the system sleep setting is disabled. This issue will be presented under the heading *Time before computer goes to sleep is too long.* Deselect the **Restore the default sleep setting for the computer** option.

24. Click the **View detailed information** link.

25. Note that the found issues are presented at the top of the detailed information, and a warning icon is placed to draw your attention, as shown in Figure 10-6. Click the **Time before computer goes to sleep is too long** issue. Note the description that power usage may be affected.

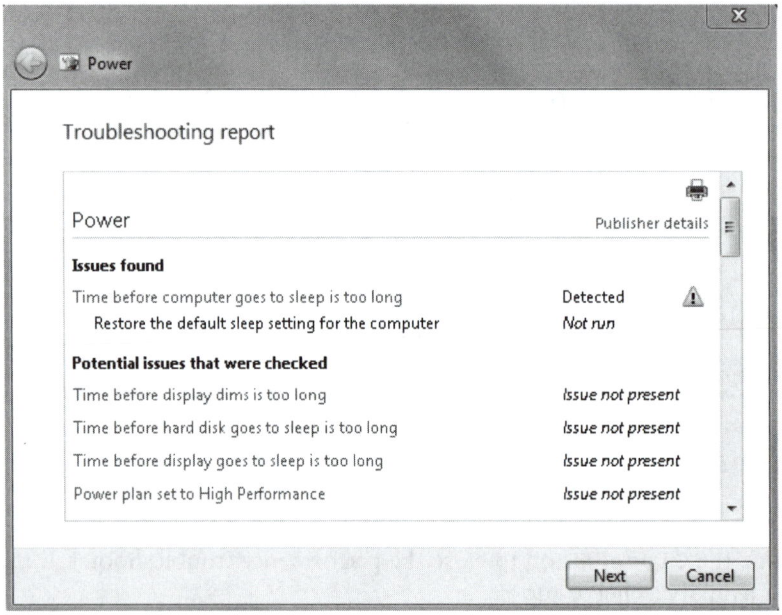

Figure 10-6 Issues found by the power troubleshooter
© Cengage Learning 2012

26. Click the **Next** button to return to the troubleshooter summary screen.

27. Click the **Cancel** button to close the power troubleshooter.

28. In the Troubleshooting window, click the **Change settings** link.

29. Confirm that the setting for windows to check for routine maintenance issues is set to **On**. Clear the **Allow troubleshooting to begin immediately when started** option. Click **OK** to save the change.

30. In the Troubleshooting window, click the **View all** link. A window will appear that lists all computer troubleshooters, as shown in Figure 10-7.

31. Click the **Search and Indexing** troubleshooter.

32. When the Search and Indexing window opens, click the **Advanced** link. Click the link to **Run as administrator**.

33. When the Search and Indexing window reopens, click the **Advanced** link. Deselect the option **Apply repairs automatically**.

34. Click the **Next** button to start the troubleshooter.

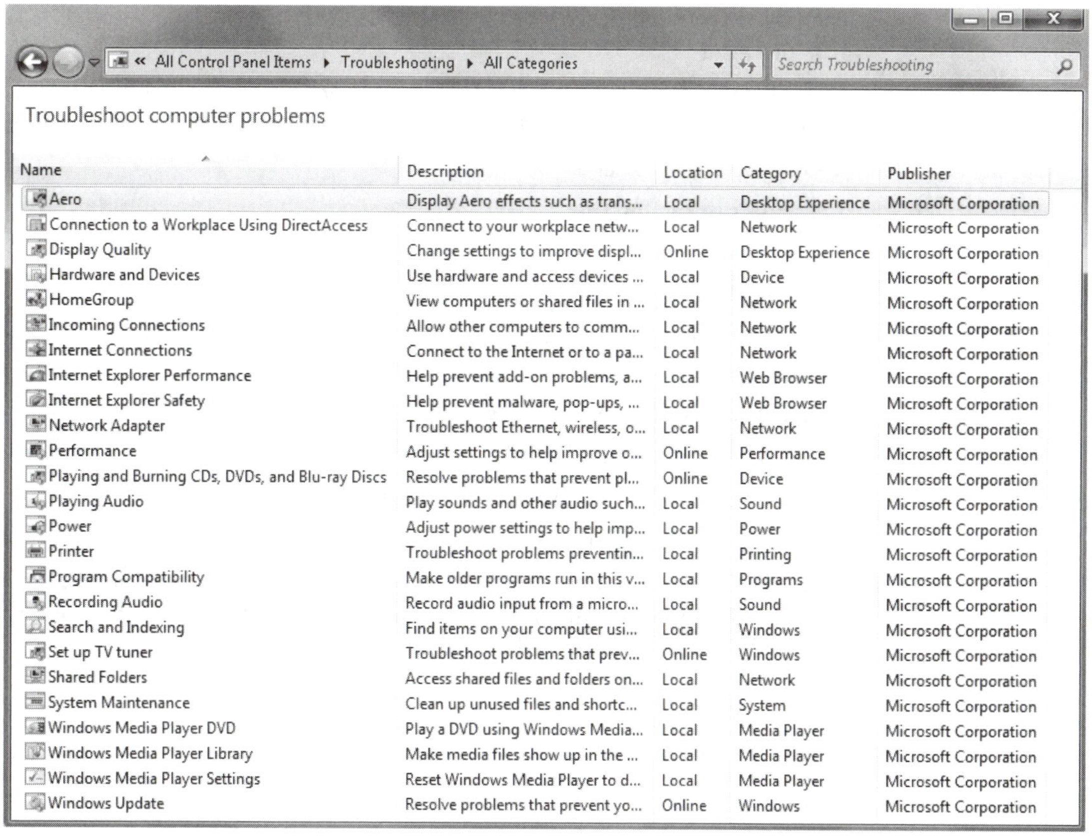

Name	Description	Location	Category	Publisher
Aero	Display Aero effects such as trans...	Local	Desktop Experience	Microsoft Corporation
Connection to a Workplace Using DirectAccess	Connect to your workplace netw...	Local	Network	Microsoft Corporation
Display Quality	Change settings to improve displ...	Online	Desktop Experience	Microsoft Corporation
Hardware and Devices	Use hardware and access devices ...	Local	Device	Microsoft Corporation
HomeGroup	View computers or shared files in ...	Local	Network	Microsoft Corporation
Incoming Connections	Allow other computers to comm...	Local	Network	Microsoft Corporation
Internet Connections	Connect to the Internet or to a pa...	Local	Network	Microsoft Corporation
Internet Explorer Performance	Help prevent add-on problems, a...	Local	Web Browser	Microsoft Corporation
Internet Explorer Safety	Help prevent malware, pop-ups, ...	Local	Web Browser	Microsoft Corporation
Network Adapter	Troubleshoot Ethernet, wireless, o...	Local	Network	Microsoft Corporation
Performance	Adjust settings to help improve o...	Online	Performance	Microsoft Corporation
Playing and Burning CDs, DVDs, and Blu-ray Discs	Resolve problems that prevent pl...	Online	Device	Microsoft Corporation
Playing Audio	Play sounds and other audio such...	Local	Sound	Microsoft Corporation
Power	Adjust power settings to help imp...	Local	Power	Microsoft Corporation
Printer	Troubleshoot problems preventin...	Local	Printing	Microsoft Corporation
Program Compatibility	Make older programs run in this v...	Local	Programs	Microsoft Corporation
Recording Audio	Record audio input from a micro...	Local	Sound	Microsoft Corporation
Search and Indexing	Find items on your computer usi...	Local	Windows	Microsoft Corporation
Set up TV tuner	Troubleshoot problems that prev...	Online	Windows	Microsoft Corporation
Shared Folders	Access shared files and folders on...	Local	Network	Microsoft Corporation
System Maintenance	Clean up unused files and shortc...	Local	System	Microsoft Corporation
Windows Media Player DVD	Play a DVD using Windows Media...	Local	Media Player	Microsoft Corporation
Windows Media Player Library	Make media files show up in the ...	Local	Media Player	Microsoft Corporation
Windows Media Player Settings	Reset Windows Media Player to d...	Local	Media Player	Microsoft Corporation
Windows Update	Resolve problems that prevent yo...	Online	Windows	Microsoft Corporation

Figure 10-7 List of all categories for troubleshooting computer problems
© Cengage Learning 2012

35. When you are prompted to identify the problems you noticed, click to select **`Search or indexing is slowing down the computer`**.
36. Click the **`Next`** button to start the troubleshooter scanning for problems.
37. Click the **`Close`** button to close the troubleshooter.
38. Close the troubleshooting window and log off the computer.

Certification Objectives

Objectives for MCTS Exam #70-680: Windows 7, Configuring:

- Monitoring and Maintaining Systems that Run Windows 7: Monitor systems

Review Questions

1. The Performance troubleshooter tests for which of the following conditions? (Select all that apply.)
   a. SuperFetch is not running.
   b. System time is incorrectly set.
   c. Disk volume errors.
   d. Power plan is set to Power saver.

10

2. The power troubleshooter saves a detailed HTML report to C:\WINDOWS\SYSTEM32. True or False?

3. To enable the users to browse for troubleshooters available from the Windows Online Troubleshooting service, which link should you select in the Troubleshooting window?

   a. Get help from a friend

   b. Connect to the Internet

   c. Fix problems with Windows Update

   d. Change settings

4. You would like to confirm all changes recommended by a troubleshooting wizard before they are applied. Which setting must be disabled for you to make this confirmation?

   a. Run as administrator

   b. Apply repairs automatically

   c. Try troubleshooting as an administrator

   d. Explore additional options

5. When the power troubleshooter detects that the time before the computer goes to sleep is too long, the setting could be reconfigured in the troubleshooter by specifying the number of minutes as a custom value. True or False?

APPLICATION SUPPORT

Labs included in this chapter:

- Lab 11.1 Configuring a Local Mandatory Profile

- Lab 11.2 Working with File Extensions and the Programs Used to Open Them

- Lab 11.3 Running Applications in a Different Security Context or a Different Processor Priority

Microsoft MCTS Exam #70-680 Objectives

Objective	Lab
Configure application restrictions	11.1
Configure file and folder access	11.2
Configure authentication and authorization	11.3
Configure performance settings	11.3

Lab 11.1: Configuring a Local Mandatory Profile

Objectives

The object of this activity is to configure a local mandatory user profile, to ensure a predictable application environment for a specific user.

Materials Required

This lab requires the following:

- A physical computer or virtual machine running Windows 7 that is configured as User*x*-PC or as specified by your instructor

Estimated completion time: **30 minutes**

Activity Background

A user's personal application settings are typically stored in his or her user profile. This includes many custom settings that define how applications and the user interface behave. The user profile is locally stored as a subfolder of C:\USERS, and typically given the same name as the user's account. When a user customizes his or her application settings, the majority of those changes are saved in the local user profile. In the user's profile, the file NTUSER.DAT stores registry settings specifically for that user account. Any registry changes for that user are applied to that file in his or her local profile. The other folders in the local user profile include application settings as well as the user's own data folders, such as My Documents, Desktop, and Favorites.

To ensure that applications run with predictable settings, administrators can configure a standardized profile, called a mandatory profile, that is used each time a user logs in. The profile is customized before it is used to build a mandatory profile. When the user logs in, the mandatory profile is copied to the user's local profile, providing a preconfigured application experience. The user can customize his or her profile, but all changes are lost when the user logs out. The next time the user logs in, all settings return to what is configured in the mandatory profile. This lab looks at how a local mandatory profile is provisioned and how a user account is configured to use that mandatory profile.

Activity

1. Log on to User*x*-PC.

2. Create a new user account on your computer that will be used to test profile updates, as detailed in the following steps:

   a. Click **Start**, click **Control Panel**, and then and then click **Add or remove user accounts** below the User Accounts and Family Safety heading.

   b. In the Manage Accounts window that appears, click the link **Create a new account**.

   c. Enter the name **lab11usr** as the new user account name. Confirm that the **Standard user** selection is already selected.

   d. Click the **Create Account** button to create the user.

   e. When the Manage Accounts windows reappears, click the **lab11usr** icon.

   f. When the Change an Account window appears, click the **Create a password** link.

   g. When the Create Password window appears, enter **workpass** in the *New password* field.

   h. Enter **workpass** in the *Confirm new password* field.

   i. Click the **Create password** button.

   j. Close the Change an Account window.

3. Log out as the current user.

4. Log in as the user **lab11usr** specifying **workpass** as the password.

5. Change the background and color scheme, as detailed in the following steps:

   a. Right-click anywhere on the desktop.

   b. Select **Personalize** from the pop-up menu.

   c. In the Personalization window that opens, click **Desktop Background** to open the Desktop Background window.

   d. Click a desktop background image that is different from the one that is currently active.

   e. Click the **Save changes** button.

   f. Click **Window Color** to open the Window Color and Appearance window.

   g. Note the current color scheme. Click a different color square to select a different color scheme.

   h. Click the **Save changes** button.

   i. Close the Personalization window.

6. Log out as lab11usr.

7. Log in with the original user account used at the start of this lab. Note that the desktop background image and windows color scheme is different from the customized settings for lab11usr.

8. Protected files and folders must be revealed to allow advanced customizations of user profiles, as detailed in the following steps:

   a. Click **Start, Computer,** and then double-click the **Local Disk (C:)** icon.

   b. Double-click the folder **Users** and then double-click the folder **lab11usr.**

   c. When the system prompts you that you do not have permissions to access the folder, click the **Continue** button to permanently allow access to the folder.

   d. Press the **Alt** key on the keyboard. A toolbar will appear in the computer browser window, as shown in Figure 11-1.

   e. Click **Tools** in the menu bar and then click to select **Folder options.**

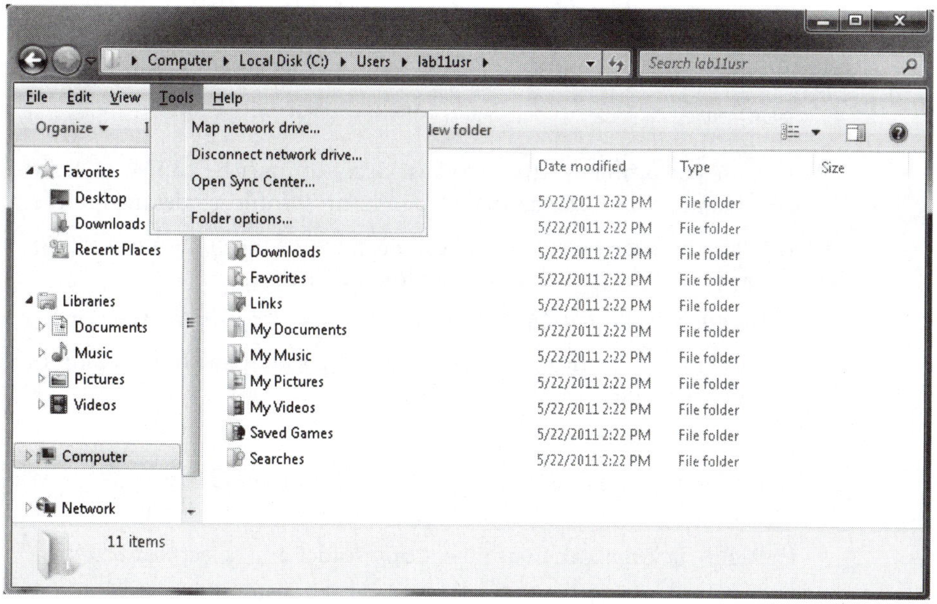

Figure 11-1 Computer file browser window with the menu bar displayed
© *Cengage Learning 2012*

f. Click to select the **View** tab.

g. Click to select the option **Show hidden files, folders, and drives**.

h. Click to uncheck the option **Hide protected operating system files**, and when prompted to confirm that you really want to see these files, click **Yes**.

i. Click to uncheck the option **Hide extensions for known file types**, as shown in Figure 11-2.

j. Click **OK** to save your changes and close the Folder Options window. Note that the number of files and folders shown in the computer file browser window has increased.

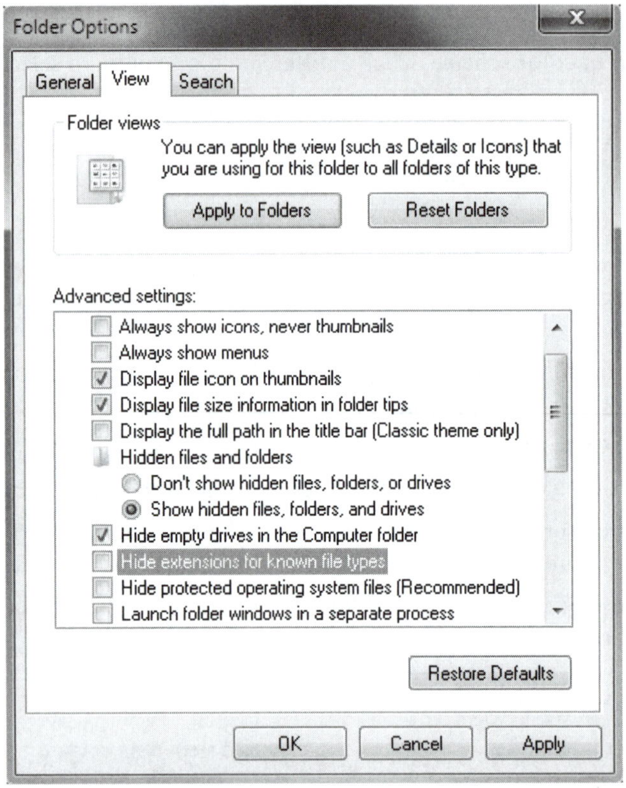

Figure 11-2 Folder options selected to show files and display known file extensions
© *Cengage Learning 2012*

9. The current profile for the lab11usr account must be copied to a different location and configured so it can be used as a mandatory profile, as detailed in the following steps:

a. Click the left-arrow button at the top left of the computer file browser window to go back one folder level in the window to C:\Users.

b. Right-click the **lab11usr** folder and select **Copy** from the pop-up menu.

c. Place the mouse over unused space in the right pane of the computer file browser window and right-click the mouse.

d. Select **Paste** from the pop-up menu.

e. By default, you are not able to create folders in C:\Users. When you are prompted to confirm this action, click the **Continue** button to allow it to proceed.

f. Right-click the **lab11usr – Copy** folder and select **Rename** from the pop-up menu.

g. Type **lab11usr-Mandatory.v2** as the new folder name, and then press **Enter** to save the change. Note that the .v2 extension is required for a folder to be used as a source for mandatory profiles.

11

h. When you are prompted to confirm this action, click the **Continue** button to allow the process to proceed.

i. Double-click the **lab11usr-Mandatroy.v2** folder to open it.

j. In the list of files and folders, locate the file NTUSER.DAT. Right-click **NTUSER .DAT** and select **Rename** from the pop-up menu.

k. Change the filename from NTUSER.DAT to **NTUSER.MAN** and press **Enter**.

l. When you are prompted with a warning that changing file extensions may make the file unusable, click the **Yes** button to continue. Note that NTUSER.DAT must be renamed NTUSER.MAN for a mandatory profile.

m. When you are prompted to confirm the name change, click the **Yes** button.

n. When you are prompted to confirm the name change of a system file, click the **Yes** button.

10. Configure the user lab11usr account to use the mandatory profile created in Step 9, as detailed in the following steps:

a. Click **Start**, right-click **Computer**, and then click **Manage** in the pop-up menu.

b. In the Computer Management window that appears, in the left pane, click **Local Users and Groups** below System Tools.

c. In the middle pane, double-click the **Users** folder.

d. Double-click the **lab11usr** account in the middle pane.

e. In the lab11usr Properties window, click to select the **Profile** tab.

f. In the Profile path field, type **C:\USERS\LAB11USR-MANDATORY**, as shown in Figure 11-3. Note that the folder's extension, .v2, is not included when specifying a mandatory profile in a user account's attributes.

g. Click **OK** to save the change.

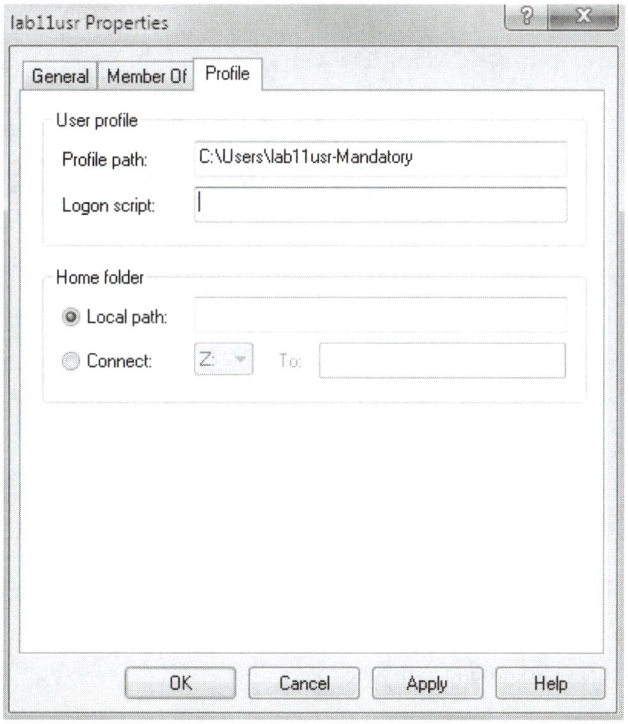

Figure 11-3   Configuring a user's profile directory
© Cengage Learning 2012

11. Log out as the current user.

12. Log in as the user **lab11usr** specifying **workpass** as the password.

13. Change the background and color scheme, as detailed in the following steps:

    a. Right-click anywhere on the desktop.

    b. Select **Personalize** from the pop-up menu.

    c. In the Personalization window that opens, click **Desktop Background** to open the Desktop Background window.

    d. Click the drop-down control next to Picture location and select **Solid Colors** from the list, as shown in Figure 11-4.

    e. Click a color square of your choice to select it.

    f. Click the **Save changes** button.

    g. Click **Window Color** to open the Window Color and Appearance window.

    h. Note the current color scheme. Click a different color square to select a different color scheme.

    i. Click the **Save changes** button.

    j. Close the Personalization window.

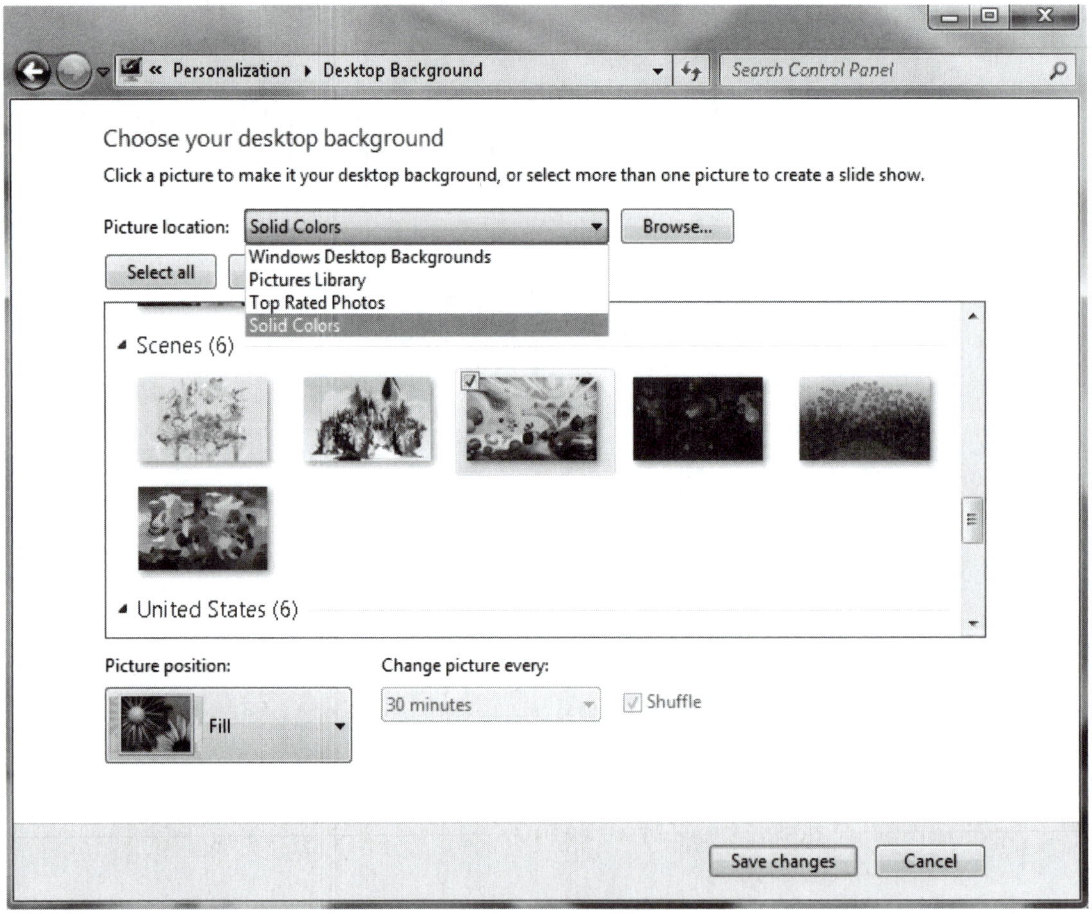

Figure 11-4 Configuring a user's background with solid colors
© Cengage Learning 2012

14. Log out as the current user.

15. Log in as the user **lab11usr** specifying **workpass** as the password.

16. Note that the background and color changes made in Step 13 are not preserved. The settings have changed back to those configured in Step 5 when they were copied to this user's mandatory profile in Step 9.

17. Log out as lab11usr.

18. Log in with the original user account used at the start of this lab.

19. Change the background for a user account that is not configured with a mandatory profile, as detailed in the following steps:

    a. Right-click anywhere on the desktop.

    b. Select **Personalize** from the pop-up menu.

    c. In the Personalization window that opens, click **Desktop Background** to open the Desktop Background window.

    d. Click the **Picture location** drop-down arrow and select **Solid Colors** from the list.

    e. Click a color square of your choice to select it.

    f. Click the **Save changes** button. Note that the background image has been replaced with the selected color.

    g. Close the Personalization window.

20. Log out as the current user.

21. Log in with the original user account used at the start of this lab. Note that the background customization made in Step 19 has been preserved. The mandatory profile behavior is only observed for lab11usr.

22. Log out as the current user.

Certification Objectives

Objectives for MCTS Exam #70-680: Windows 7, Configuring:

- Configuring Hardware and Applications: Configure application restrictions

Review Questions

1. When a mandatory profile is created, the registry file NTUSER.DAT in that mandatory profile is renamed to which of the following filenames?

    a. NTUSER.DAT.v2

    b. NTUSER.MAN

    c. Mandatory-NTUSER.DAT

    d. Mandatory.v2-NTUSER.MAN

2. When a mandatory profile is created, the mandatory profile path in the file system must end with what extension?

    a. No extension required

    b. DAT

    c. .v2

    d. .MAN

3. When a mandatory profile is specified for a user account's properties, the mandatory profile path attribute must end with what extension?

   a. No extension required

   b. DAT

   c. .v2

   d. .MAN

4. To reveal the Tools menu in the Computer browser window, which key on the keyboard do you need to press first?

   a. SHIFT

   b. ALT

   c. Windows key

   d. None at all

5. You cannot see NTUSER.DAT in a user's profile directory. Which of the following is part of the process of allowing you to see the file?

   a. Launch folder windows in a separate process.

   b. Hide extensions for known file types.

   c. Show hidden files, folders, and drives.

   d. Hide protected operating system files.

Lab 11.2: Working with File Extensions and the Programs Used to Open Them

Objectives

The objective of this activity is to reveal how file extensions are associated with programs so that the programs can open them. This activity also covers how those programs can be modified.

Materials Required

This lab requires the following:

- A physical computer or virtual machine running Windows 7 that is configured as User*x*-PC or as specified by your instructor
- Completion of Lab 11.1

   | Estimated completion time: | **15 minutes** |

Activity Background

File extensions are assigned to the end of a filename, and they include any text following the last period on the right side of the filename. Some files are executable programs and others are simply data files. The file extensions are used by the operating system to tell one type of file apart from another. Instructions on what program to use to open a data file, or how a program should run, are stored in the registry. There are several ways to reveal or change how a file extension is treated for a user or a computer. This activity looks at common tools and methods used to manage file extensions and their associations.

11

Activity

1. Log on to User*x*-PC.

2. Modify the program that is used to open a specific file type—in this case, files with the extension .txt—as detailed in the following steps:

   a. Click **Start**, click **Control Panel**, and then click **Programs**.

   b. Below the heading Default Programs, click the **Make a file type always open in a specific program** link.

   c. In the Set Associations window, looking in the Name column, scroll to the **.txt** extension, as shown in Figure 11-5.

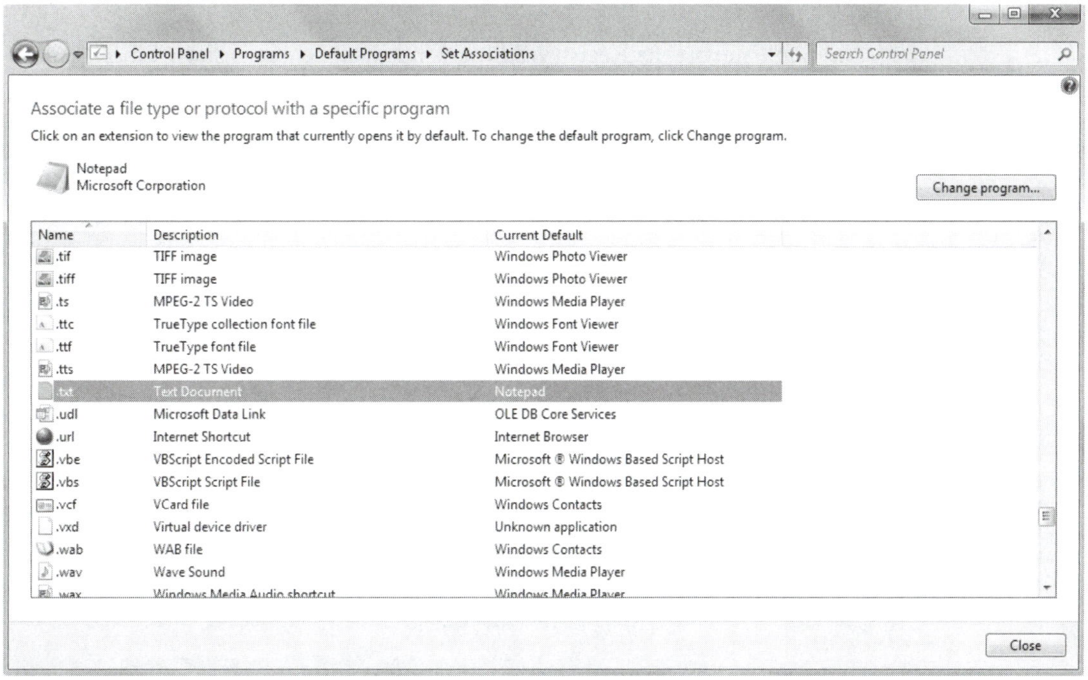

Figure 11-5 Displaying programs associated with a file extension from Control Panel
© Cengage Learning 2012

   d. Click the **Change program** button.

   e. In the Open with window that opens, below the heading Recommended Programs, click the **Wordpad** icon to select it.

   f. Click **OK** to save the selection. When the Set Associations window updates itself, confirm that the .txt file extension is now associated with the Wordpad application as its current default application.

   g. Click the **Close** button to close the Set Associations window.

   h. Close the **Programs** window.

   i. Right-click the desktop and highlight **New** from the pop-up menu.

   j. Click to select **Text Document** from the side menu.

   k. Replace the name New Text Document with **Lab11-2TextDocument** and press **Enter** to save the change.

l. Double-click the file **Lab11-2TextDocument.txt** and confirm that the file opens in Wordpad instead of Notepad.

m. Close Wordpad.

3. The registry contains default settings for what programs open a specific file type. Those settings can be customized for a user, as they were using the procedure in Step 2. Identify the default program that is used to open .txt files through the registry editor and confirm the default and customized settings for two different user accounts, as detailed in the following steps:

a. Click **Start**, click **All Programs**, click **Accessories**, and then click **Run**.

b. In the Open field, type **regedit** and then press **Enter**.

c. When you are prompted by User Account Control for permission to continue, click **Yes**.

d. Confirm that the Registry Editor window appears, as shown in Figure 11-6.

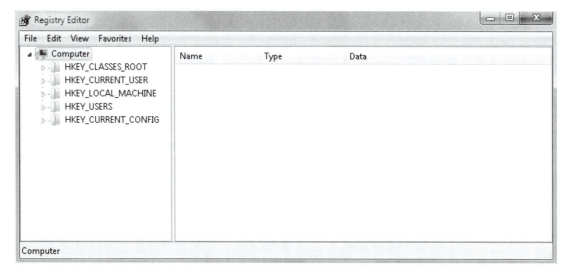

Figure 11-6 Registry Editor window
© Cengage Learning 2012

e. In the left pane of the Registry Editor window, double-click the folder **HKEY_CLASSES_ROOT**. This will expand that level of the registry and show a list of registry keys below it, named after file extensions, as shown in Figure 11-7.

f. Scroll down the list of file extensions below HKEY_CLASSES_ROOT until the **.txt** folder is visible.

g. Double-click the **.txt** folder. Confirm that two folders are now displayed below the .txt folder in the left pane.

h. Click the **ShellNew** folder to select it.

i. In the right-pane, click the **ItemName** registry value. Record the value data assigned to the ItemName: _____.

j. Click **OK** to close the Edit String window without making any changes.

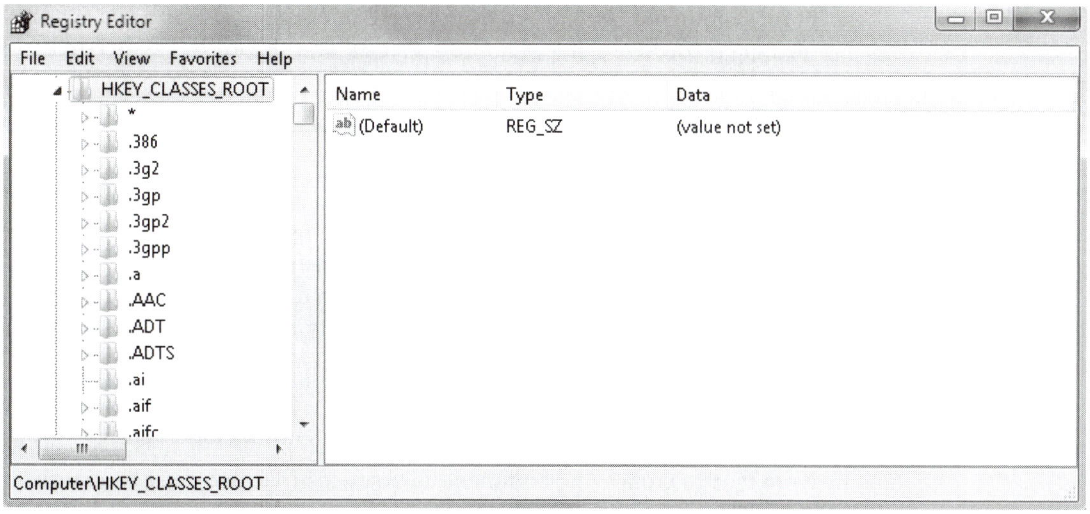

Figure 11-7 Registry Editor window with HKEY_CLASSES_ROOT expanded
© *Cengage Learning 2012*

    k. Close the Registry Editor window.

    l. Log off as the current user.

    m. Log in as the user **lab11usr** specifying **workpass** as the password.

    n. Right-click the desktop and highlight **New** from the pop-up menu.

    o. Click to select **Text Document** from the side menu.

    p. Replace the name New Text Document with **Lab11usrTextDocument** and press **Enter** to save the change.

    q. Double-click the file **Lab11usrTextDocument.txt** and confirm that the file opens in Notepad.

    r. Close the Notepad window.

    s. Log off as the current user.

    t. Log in with the original user account used at the start of this lab.

    u. Double-click the file **Lab11-2TextDocument.txt** and confirm that the file opens in Wordpad instead of Notepad.

    v. Close the Wordpad window.

4. Confirm the default command used to open a specific file type using command-line utilities, as detailed in the following steps:

    a. Click **Start**, click **All Programs**, click **Accessories**, and then click **Command Prompt**.

    b. In the Command Prompt window, type **ASSOC** and then press **Enter**. This will list all known extensions and the type of file associated with each extension.

    c. In the Command Prompt window, type **ASSOC .txt** and then press **Enter**. This will only list the type of file associated with the given extension. Record the associated file type: _____.

    d. In the Command Prompt window, type **FTYPE** and then press **Enter**. This will list the default command used to open each specific file type.

  e. In the Command Prompt window, type **FTYPE** followed by a space and then type the file type recorded in Step 4.c. Press **Enter** and record the associated command used to open that file type: _____. Compare this value to the one recorded in Step 3.i.

  f. Close the Command Prompt window.

5. When a command is issued in the Command Prompt window without a file extension specified, the system must locate an executable using a list of extensions stored in the PATHEXT environment variable. The extensions are tried one at a time, in order, until an executable program with that name is located. Confirm which extensions are used to locate an executable program and then modify the list for a single user to include the extension .PS1, as detailed in the following steps:

  a. In the Command Prompt window, type **SET PATHEXT** and press **Enter**. Confirm that the current PATHEXT variable data does not include .PS1.

  b. Note that the following command is case sensitive and must be entered as uppercase text. Type the command **SET PATHEXT=%PATHEXT%;.PS1** and press **Enter**.

  c. Type the command **SET PATHEXT** and press **Enter**. Confirm that the current PATHEXT variable data now includes .PS1 at the end of the string of extensions. The SET command will only modify environment values in the current session of the Command Prompt window.

  d. Close the Command Prompt window.

  e. Repeat Step 4.a, and then type the command **SET PATHEXT** and press **Enter**. Note that the PATHEXT variable no longer includes the .PS1 extension.

  f. To make permanent changes to an environment variable from the command prompt, use the SETX command instead of SET. Note that the following command is case sensitive and must be entered as uppercase text. Type the command **SETX PATHEXT %PATHEXT%;.PS1** and press **Enter**. (As you type, make sure that you place a space before the first percent sign.) Confirm that the utility reports a success message. By default, the SETX command will store changes to the HKEY_CURRENT_USER portion of the registry. The SETX change will not take effect until the Command Prompt window session is restarted.

  g. Close the Command Prompt window.

  h. Repeat Step 4.a, type the command **SET PATHEXT**, and press **Enter**. Note that the PATHEXT variable now includes the .PS1 extension.

  i. Close the Command Prompt window.

  j. Log off as the current user.

  k. Log in as the user **lab11usr** specifying **workpass** as the password.

  l. Repeat Step 4.a, type the command **SET PATHEXT**, and press **Enter**. Note that the PATHEXT variable does not include the .PS1 extension.

  m. Log off as the current user.

  n. Log in with the original user account used at the start of this lab.

  o. Repeat Step 4.a, type the command **SET PATHEXT**, and press **Enter**. Note that the PATHEXT variable includes the .PS1 extension. The change made in Step 5.f is persistent for this user.

  p. Type the command **SETX /?** and press **Enter** to see the full help listing for this utility.

  q. Close the Command Prompt window.

6. Log off the computer.

Certification Objectives

Objectives for MCTS Exam #70-680: Windows 7, Configuring:

* Configuring Access to Resources: Configure file and folder access

Review Questions

1. Which one of the following commands will update the PATHEXT environment variable to include its original contents plus the file extension .RUN?

   a. SET PATHEXT=%PATHEXT%;.RUN

   b. SET PATH+=.RUN

   c. SETX PATHEXT=%PATHEXT%.RUN

   d. SETX PATH %PATHEXT%;.RUN

2. What command-line utility is used to display the default command used to open a specific file type?

   a. SETX

   b. ASSOC

   c. PATHEXT

   d. FTYPE

3. What command-line utility is used to display the file type linked to a specific file extension?

   a. SETX

   b. ASSOC

   c. PATHEXT

   d. FTYPE

4. The registry hive that includes details about filename associations is called _____.

   a. HKEY_LOCAL_MACHINE

   b. HKEY_CLASSES_ROOT

   c. HKEY_USERS

   d. HKEY_CURRENT_CONFIG

5. Which of the following SETX command-line options will update environment variables systemwide instead of just for the current user?

   a. /HKEY_LOCAL_MACHINE

   b. /P

   c. /M

   d. /U

Lab 11.3: Running Applications in a Different Security Context or a Different Processor Priority

Objectives

The objective of this activity is to change the security context an application uses or alter the processor priority when the application runs.

Materials Required

This lab requires the following:

- A physical computer or virtual machine running Windows 7 that is configured as User*x*-PC or as specified by your instructor
- Completion of Lab 11.2

Estimated completion time: **25 minutes**

Activity Background

Applications run, by default, with normal processor priority and the same security context as the user or process that started them. There are several methods that can be used to change how a program runs with different privileges, including administrator level or that of another user. Windows features, including Windows games and the telnet client, will be activated temporarily for the purposes of this lab.

Activity

1. Log on to User*x*-PC.

2. Install some Windows components that are currently not installed, which will be used to test application-launching methods, as detailed in the following steps:

   a. Click **Start**, click **Control Panel**, and then click **Programs**.

   b. Below the heading Programs and Features, click the **Turn Windows features on or off** link. The Windows Features window will open, but it may take 30 seconds or more to populate with an application list, as shown in Figure 11-8.

Figure 11-8 Windows Features window, listing active and inactive features
© Cengage Learning 2012

   c. Click the + symbol next to **Games**. This will expand the Games list to show all of the games that can be installed.

   d. Click the **Chess Titans** selection box.

   e. Scroll down the list of Windows Features and click the **Telnet Client** selection box.

    f. Click the **OK** button to save the changes and activate those Windows features. Note that the installation of those features may take some time to complete.

    g. Close the Programs window.

3. Run the telnet client as an administrator, as detailed in the following steps:

    a. Click **Start** and then click **Computer**.

    b. Double-click the **Local Disk (C:)** icon.

    c. Double-click the **Windows** folder.

    d. Double-click the **System32** folder.

    e. Scroll down the list of files and folders to locate and highlight the file **telnet.exe**.

    f. Right-click the file and select **Run as administrator** from the pop-up menu.

    g. When you are prompted by User Account Control for permission to continue, click the **Yes** button.

    h. When the telnet application starts, type the command **?** and press **Enter**.

    i. Type the command **quit** and press **Enter** to close the Telnet client window.

4. Run the telnet client as a different user, as detailed in the following steps:

    a. In the computer file browser window, confirm that the file **telnet.exe** is highlighted.

    b. Hold down the **SHIFT** key, then while you are holding the key, right-click **telnet.exe** and select **Run as different user** from the pop-up menu. Release the SHIFT key.

    c. In the Windows Security dialog box that opens, type **lab11usr** for the User name.

    d. Type **workpass** for the Password.

    e. Click **OK** to authenticate as that user and launch the program in that user's security context.

    f. When the telnet application starts, type the command **status** and press **Enter**.

    g. Type the command **quit** and press **Enter** to close the Telnet client window.

5. Start the Notepad utility using the START command to modify the starting window size and processor priority, as detailed in the following steps:

    a. Click **Start**, click **All Programs**, click **Accessories**, and then click **Command Prompt**.

    b. Type the command **START /?** and then press **Enter**. Review the help screen contents.

    c. Type the command **START /MAX NOTEPAD.EXE** and then press **Enter**. Note that Notepad starts with the window maximized.

    d. Close the Notepad window.

    e. Click **Start**, and in the *Search programs and files* field, type **taskmgr.exe** and press **Enter** to start Task Manager.

    f. Click the **Processes** tab to select it.

    g. Click **View** in the Windows Task Manager menu bar, and click **Select Columns** from the menu.

    h. In the Select Process Page Columns window, scroll to **Base Priority** and click the box next to it to select it.

    i. Click **OK** to save the change.

    j. Click the column name **Base Pri** to sort the column with high-priority processes at the top of the window and normal-priority processes at the bottom, as shown in Figure 11-9.

    k. Minimize the Windows Task Manager window.

    l. In the Command Prompt window, type the command **START /ABOVENORMAL NOTEPAD.EXE** and then press **Enter**. Minimize the Notepad window.

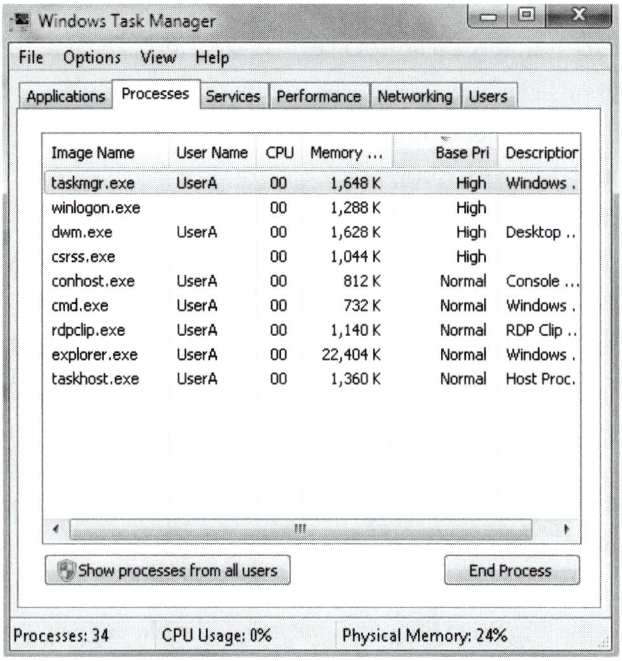

Figure 11-9 Processes in Windows Task Manager sorted by priority
© *Cengage Learning 2012*

> m. Maximize the Windows Task Manager window. Confirm that notepad.exe is now listed as a running process with a base priority of Above Normal.
>
> n. Right-click the **notepad.exe** process, click **Set Priority** from the pop-up menu, and then click **Below Normal** from the side menu.
>
> o. When you are prompted to change the priority of notepad.exe, click the **Change priority** button. Confirm that the position of notepad.exe in the Windows Task Manager window has changed to indicate that it is running with a Below Normal processor priority.
>
> p. close the Notepad window.
>
> q. In the Command Prompt window, type **NOTEPAD.EXE** and press **Enter**.
>
> r. In the Windows Task Manager window, record the Base Priority for the new notepad. exe process: _____.
>
> s. Close the Notepad window.
>
> t. Close the Windows Task Manager window.

6. Start a utility using the runas command, as detailed in the following steps:

   a. Log off as the current user.

   b. Log in as the user **lab11usr**, specifying **workpass** as the password.

   c. Click **Start**, click **All Programs**, click **Accessories**, and then click **Command Prompt**.

   d. Type the command **RUNAS /?** and press **Enter**. Review the help screen contents.

   e. Type the command **DEFRAG C: /A** and press **Enter**. Note the error message that is displayed, as shown in Figure 11-10.

   f. Type the command **RUNAS /user:** followed by the name of your administrator-level local user account, press the **spacebar**, type **"DEFRAG C: /A"** and press **Enter**.

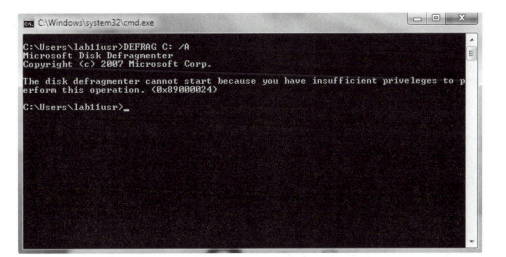

Figure 11-10   Running DEFRAG with insufficient privileges
© *Cengage Learning 2012*

g. Type the password for the user account you specified in Step 6.f and press **Enter**. The RUNAS command will open a new window to run the program with the credentials provided. Once the program completes, the new window will close automatically.

h. Type the command **RUNAS /user:** followed by the name of your administrator-level local user account, press the **spacebar**, type **/savecred "DEFRAG C: /A"** and press **Enter**.

i. Type the password for the user account you specified in Step 6.h and press **Enter**. Once the program completes, the Defrag window will close automatically.

j. Repeat Step 6.h, but note that you are no longer prompted for a password. The /save-cred parameter recorded the user credentials the first time they were used and is now using those cached values.

k. Click **Start**, in the *Search programs and files* field, type **Credential Manager**, and press **Enter** to start Credential Manager, as shown in Figure 11-11.

l. In the Credential Manger window, under the Windows Credentials heading, the user account details recorded by RUNAS in Step 6.h will be listed. Double-click the user account name to expand its details.

m. Select the **Remove from vault** link for that user account. Note that the Edit option is also available to correct the password if it changes at a later date.

n. When you are prompted to confirm the permanent deletion of the credential from the vault, click the **Yes** button.

o. Close the Credential Manager window.

p. Close the Command Prompt window.

q. Log off as the current user.

r. Log in with the original user account used at the start of this lab.

7. Remove the games and telnet client utility installed in Step 2, as detailed in the following steps:

a. Click **Start**, click **Control Panel**, and then click **Programs**.

b. Below the heading Programs and Features, click the **Turn Windows features on or off** link.

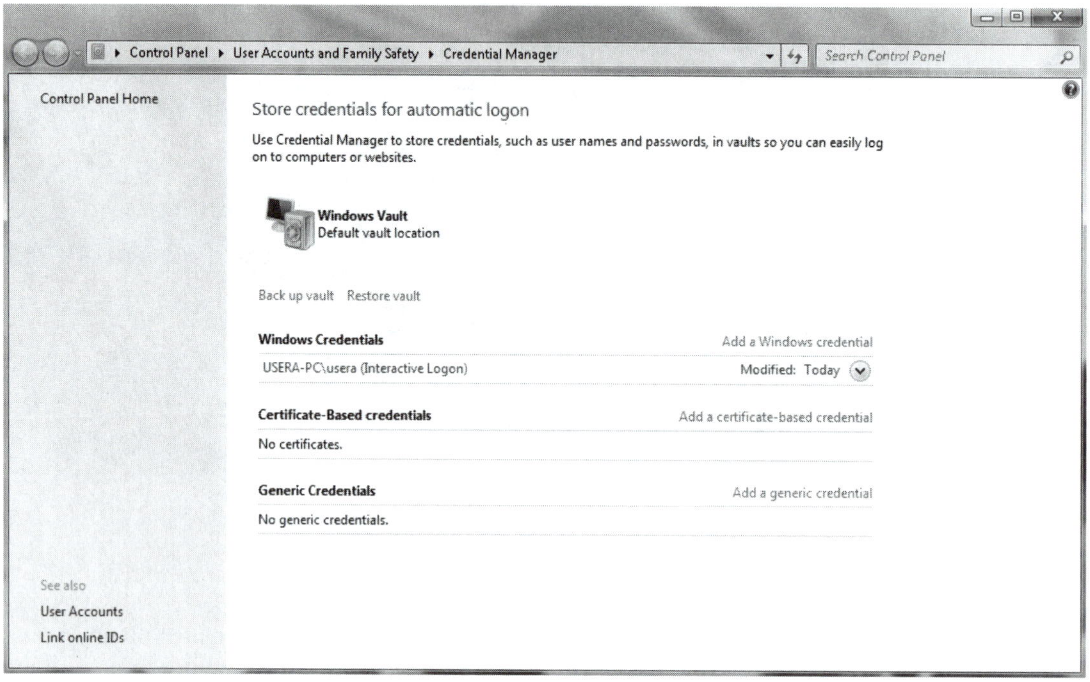

Figure 11-11 Credential Manager window
© Cengage Learning 2012

    c. Click the **+** symbol next to **Games**.

    d. Click the selection box next to **Chess Titans** to deselect it.

    e. Scroll down the list of Windows Features and deselect the selection box next to **Telnet Client**.

    f. Click the **OK** button to save the changes and deactivate those Windows features.

    g. Close the Programs window.

8. Delete the user lab11usr, originally created in Lab 11.1 Step 2, as detailed in the following steps:

    a. Click **Start**, click **Control Panel**, and then click **Add or remove user accounts** below the User Accounts and Family Safety heading.

    b. In the Manage Accounts window that appears, click the **lab11usr** account.

    c. Click the link **Delete the account**.

    d. When you are prompted to keep lab11usr's files, click the **Delete Files** button.

    e. When you are asked if you are sure that you want to delete lab84usr's account, click the **Delete Account** button.

    f. Close the Manage Accounts window.

9. Restore the default file and folder view that was originally modified in Lab 11.1 Step 8, as detailed in the following steps:

    a. Click **Start**, in the *Search programs and files* field, type **Folder Options**, and press **Enter** to open the Folder Options window.

    b. Click the **View** tab to select it.

    c. In the Advanced settings section, click **Don't show hidden files, folders, or drives**.

d. Click **Hide extensions for known file types**.

e. Click **Hide protected operating system files**.

f. Click **OK** to save those changes.

10. Delete the **Lab11-2TextDocument** file from the desktop.

11. Log off the computer.

Certification Objectives

Objectives for MCTS Exam #70-680: Windows 7, Configuring:

- Configure Access to Resources: Configure authentication and authorization
- Monitoring and Maintaining Systems that Run Windows 7: Configure performance settings

Review Questions

1. To run a program from the Start menu with the context of a user that is not currently logged in, what key on the keyboard must be pressed first?

   a. SHIFT

   b. ALT

   c. Windows key

   d. None at all

2. To run a program from the Start menu with the context of an administrator, what key on the keyboard must be pressed first?

   a. SHIFT

   b. ALT

   c. Windows key

   d. None at all

3. A program can be started with a high-level processor priority using which one of the following?

   a. Credential Manager

   b. RUNAS

   c. Windows Task Manager

   d. START

4. A program can be started with its windows maximized using which one of the following?

   a. Credential Manager

   b. RUNAS

   c. Windows Task Manager

   d. START

5. A program can be run with different privileges from those of the currently logged-on user using which of these methods? (Select all that apply.)

   a. START /savecred

   b. RUNAS

   c. Run as Administrator

   d. Run as another user

CHAPTER TWELVE

DISASTER RECOVERY AND TROUBLESHOOTING

Labs included in this chapter:

- Lab 12.1 Identifying and Resolving Problems with Event Viewer
- Lab 12.2 Resolving Startup Problems
- Lab 12.3 Controlling Service Startup
- Lab 12.4 Backing Up and Restoring

Microsoft MCTS Exam #70-680 Objectives

Objective	Lab
Monitor systems	12.1
Configure system recovery options	12.2, 12.3
Configure backup	12.4
Configure file recovery options	12.4

Lab 12.1: Identifying and Resolving Problems with Event Viewer

Objectives

The object of this activity is to use Event Viewer to identify and resolve a problem.

Materials Required

This lab requires the following:

- A physical computer or virtual machine running Windows 7 that is configured as User*x*-PC or as specified by your instructor

Estimated completion time: **15 minutes**

Activity Background

Windows 7 records system activity in event logs. Each event log contains a specific type of system activity. The Application log contains information about application operation, warnings, and errors. The System log contains information about operating system operation, warnings, and errors.

Event Viewer is the administrative tool included in Windows 7 to view the contents of event logs. You can use Event Viewer when you are trying to resolve problems with applications or Windows 7. The events in the event logs may give you enough information to quickly identify the problem. Alternatively, you may need to search on the Internet to identify whether anyone else has experienced a similar problem and what he or she did to resolve it.

Activity

1. Log on to User*x*-PC as **User*x***.

2. Review the logs in Event Viewer, as detailed in the following steps:

   a. Click **Start**, in the Search programs and files box, type **Event Viewer**, and press **Enter**.

   b. In Event Viewer, expand **Windows Logs** and read the list of logs.

   c. Click the **Security** log and review the events that are listed.

   d. Expand **Applications and Services Logs** and read the list of logs.

   e. Expand **Microsoft**, expand **Windows**, and read the list of logs, as shown in Figure 12-1

3. Stop the Print Spooler service, as detailed in the following steps:

   a. Click **Start**, in the Search programs and files box, type **services.msc**, and press **Enter**.

   b. In Services, scroll down and click the **Print Spooler** service. Notice that this service is started.

   c. Click **Stop**.

4. Locate the event indicating that the Print Spooler service has stopped, as detailed in the following steps:

   a. In Event Viewer, click the **Action** menu and click **Create Custom View**.

   b. In the Create Custom View window, click **By source**.

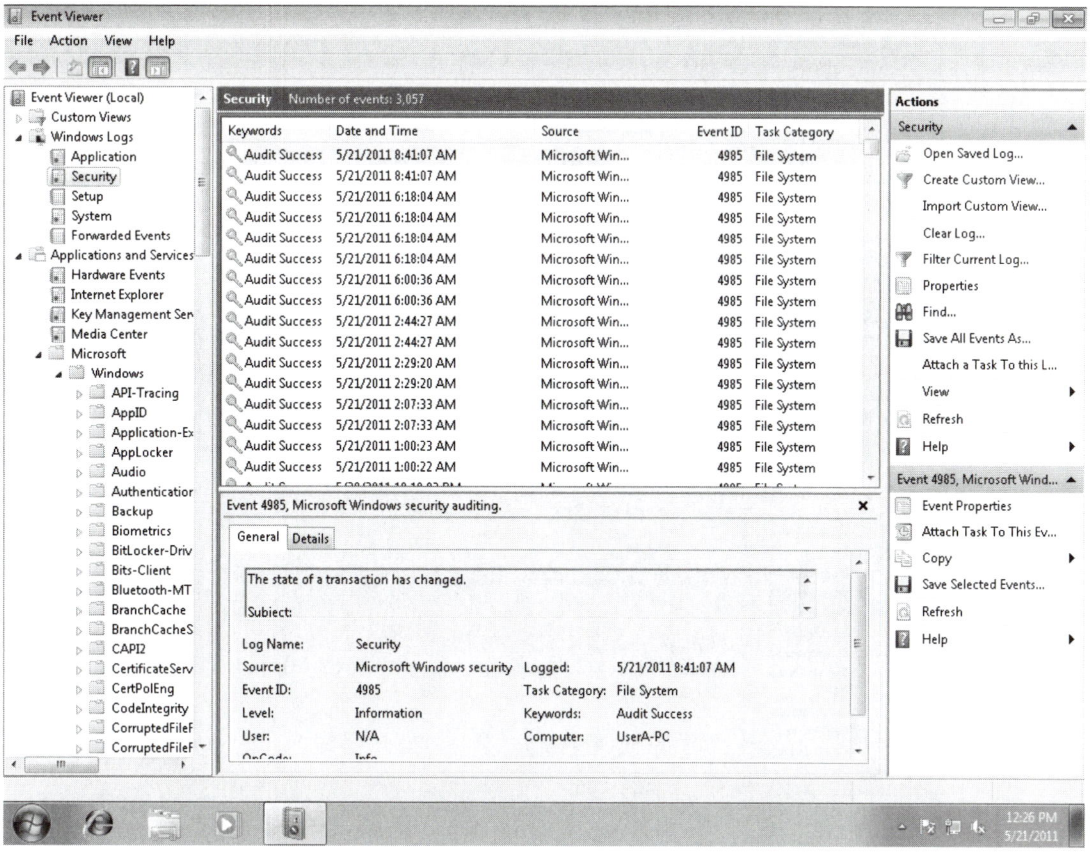

Figure 12-1   Event Viewer logs
© *Cengage Learning 2012*

c. In the Event sources box, select the **Service Control Manager** check box.

d. In the Includes/Excludes Event IDs box, type **7036**.

e. Click **OK**.

f. In the Save Filter to Custom View window, in the Name box, type **Service Start and Stop Events** and click **OK**.

g. Review the contents of the screen. Notice that you are viewing the contents of a custom view that contains only events generated when services start or stop.

h. Scroll through the list of events until you locate the event for stopping the Print Spooler service, as shown in Figure 12-2.

5. Start the Print Spooler service, as detailed in the following steps:

a. In the Services window, click the **Print Spooler** service.

b. Click **Start**.

6. Locate the event indicating that the Print Spooler service has started, as detailed in the following steps:

a. In Event Viewer, press **F5** to refresh the view.

b. Locate the event indicating that the Print Spooler service has started. This event should be first in the list.

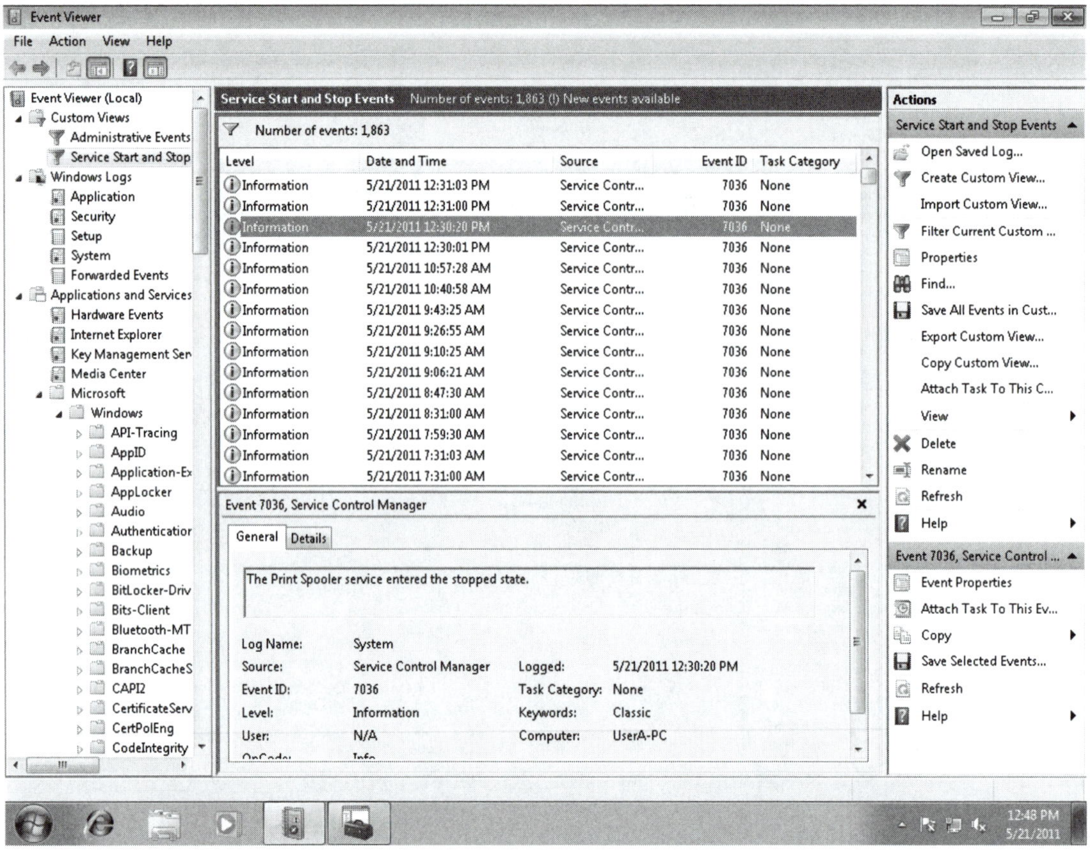

Figure 12-2   Stopped Print Spooler service event
© Cengage Learning 2012

7. Display a message when services are started or stopped, as detailed in the following steps:

   a. In Event Viewer, in the Actions pane, below the Event 7036, Service Control Manager heading, click **Attach Task to This Event**.

   b. In the Create Basic Task Wizard window, in the Name box, type **Display Service Message** and click **Next**.

   c. On the When a Specific Event Is Logged Page, review the information and then click **Next**.

   d. On the Action page, click **Display a message** and click **Next**.

   e. On the Display a Message page, in the Title box, type **Service Event**.

   f. In the Message box, type **A service has been started or stopped** and click **Next**.

   g. On the Summary page, review the settings, and click **Finish**.

   h. Click **OK** to clear the message about how to modify the scheduled task.

8. Test the link between the scheduled task and the event for the stopped Print Spooler service, as detailed in the following steps:

   a. In the Services window, click the **Print Spooler** service.

   b. Click **Stop**.

c. On the taskbar, click the new Service Event icon that has appeared. This displays the message you configured in Step 7.

d. In the Service Event window, click **OK** to close the window.

9. Remove the warning about services starting and stopping, as detailed in the following steps:

a. Click **Start**, in the Search programs and files box, type **task scheduler**, and press **Enter**.

b. In the Task Scheduler window, expand **Task Scheduler Library** and click **Event Viewer Tasks**.

c. Right-click **System_Service Control Manager_7036** and click **Delete**.

d. Click **Yes** to confirm.

e. In the Services window, click the **Print Spooler** service.

f. Click **Start**.

g. Close all open windows.

Certification Objectives

Objectives for MCTS Exam #70-680: Windows 7, Configuring:

- Monitoring and Maintaining Systems that Run Windows 7: Monitor systems

Review Questions

1. What type of events are found in the Security event log?

2. How are the event logs in Applications and Services Logs different from the event logs found in Windows Logs?

3. How do custom views make it easier to find relevant events?

4. You would like to monitor the Print Spooler service and automatically restart it if it fails. Can you do this with a scheduled task linked to event 7036 as used in the lab?

5. Which administrative tool do you use to create and manage scheduled tasks?

Lab 12.2: Resolving Startup Problems

Objectives

The objective of this activity is to identify how to resolve Windows 7 startup problems.

Materials Required

This lab requires the following:

- A physical computer or virtual machine running Windows 7 that is configured as User*x*-PC or as specified by your instructor
- The Windows 7 installation DVD

Estimated completion time: **20 minutes**

Activity Background

One common reason that Windows 7 experiences startup failures is hard drive corruption. When a hard drive begins to fail, files on the hard drive might become corrupted. If the corrupted files are part of Windows 7, you may experience a startup failure. Another common cause of startup failure is damage due to malware.

There are several tools that you can use to resolve startup failures, including the Windows 7 installation DVD and Last Known Good Configuration. In some cases, Windows 7 resolves startup problems automatically.

Activity

1. Log on to User*x*-PC as **User*x***.

2. Make the System Reserved partition accessible through a drive letter, as detailed in the following steps:

   a. Click **Start**, right-click **Computer**, and click **Manage**.

   b. In Computer Management, click **Disk Management**.

   c. On Disk 0, right-click the **System Reserved** partition and click **Change Drive Letter and Paths**.

   d. In the Change Drive Letter and Paths for System Reserved window, click **Add**.

   e. In the Add Drive Letter or Path window, select the drive letter **W** and click **OK**.

   f. Right-click the **System Reserved (W:)** partition, and click **Open**.

   g. Press the **Alt** key to display the toolbar.

   h. Click the **Tools** menu and click **Folder options**.

   i. On the **View** tab, clear the **Hide protected operating system files (Recommended)** check box.

   j. Click **Yes** to clear the warning, and then click **OK**.

   k. Read the list of files on the System Reserved partition. Notice that bootmgr is listed here. This file controls the Windows 7 boot process. The Boot folder contains the boot configuration database that stores information used by bootmgr.

3. Delete bootmgr to break the Windows 7 boot process, as detailed in the following steps:

   a. Right-click **bootmgr** and click **Properties**.

   b. In the bootmgr Properties window, on the **Security** tab, click **Advanced**.

   c. In the Advanced Security Settings for bootmgr window, on the **Owner** tab, click **Edit**.

   d. In the Change owner to box, click **Administrators** and then click **OK**.

   e. Click **OK** to close the warning window.

   f. In the Advanced Security Settings for bootmgr window, click **OK**.

   g. In the bootmgr Properties window, on the Security tab, click **Edit**.

   h. In the Permissions for bootmgr window, click **Administrators**, select **Allow Full control**, and click **OK**.

   i. In the bootmgr Properties window, click **OK**.

   j. In Windows Explorer, right-click **bootmgr** and click **Delete**.

4. Restart your computer. Notice that your computer is unbootable, as shown in Figure 12-3.

5. Boot your computer from the Windows 7 installation DVD, as detailed in the following steps:

   a. If necessary, place the Windows 7 installation DVD in your computer.

   b. Press **Ctrl+Alt+Del** to restart your computer.

   c. When prompted to Press any key to boot from CD or DVD, press a key.

Figure 12-3   Boot error after deleting bootmgr
© Cengage Learning 2012

6. Start the System Recovery Options from the Windows 7 installation DVD, as detailed in the following steps:

a. In the Install Windows window, click **Next** to accept the default language settings.

b. Click **Repair your computer**.

c. In the System Recovery Options window, shown in Figure 12-4, click **Use recovery tools that can help fix problems starting Windows** and then click **Next**.

d. In the System Recovery Options window, shown in Figure 12-5, read the list of available recovery tools.

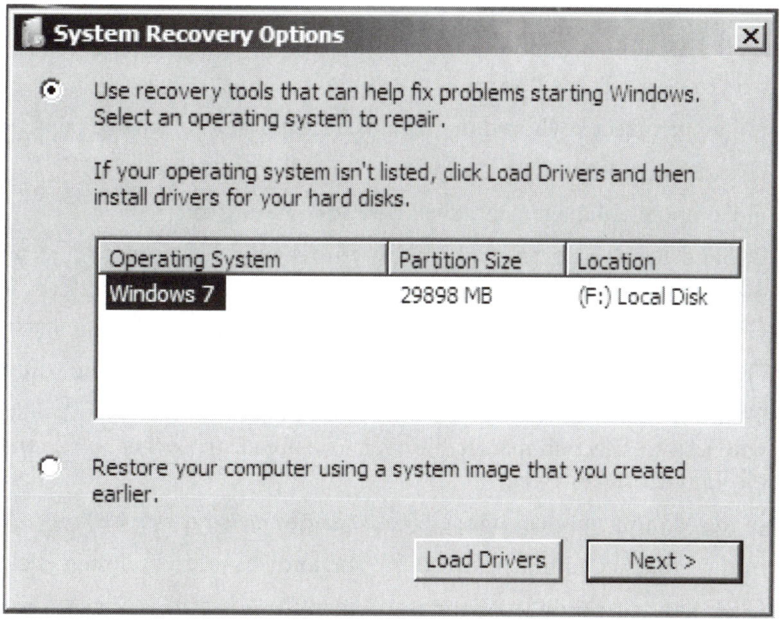

Figure 12-4   Selecting an operating system to repair
© Cengage Learning 2012

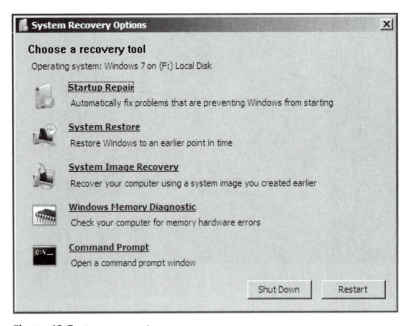

Figure 12-5 Recovery tools
© Cengage Learning 2012

7. Repair the boot process automatically with Startup Repair, as detailed in the following steps:

a. Click **Startup Repair**.

b. In the Startup Repair window, click **Click here for diagnostic and repair details**.

c. Scroll through the report and read the root cause. The root cause is listed as Boot manager is missing or corrupt.

d. Click **Close**.

e. Click **Finish**.

8. Log on to User*x*-PC as **User*x***.

9. Install an incorrect keyboard driver, as detailed in the following steps:

a. Click **Start**, right-click **Computer**, and click **Manage**.

b. In Computer Management, click **Device Manager**.

c. Expand **Keyboards**, right-click your keyboard, and click **Update Driver Software**.

d. Click **Browse my computer for driver software**.

e. Click **Let me pick from a list of device drivers on my computer**.

f. Clear the **Show compatible hardware** check box. To simulate failure for this lab, you need to select an incorrect driver. You are clearing this box so that you are able to pick an incorrect driver.

g. In the Manufacture column, click **(Standard keyboards)**.

h. In the Model column, click **HID Keyboard Device** and then click **Next**.

i. Click **Yes** to acknowledge the warning.

j. Click **Close**.

k. Click **Yes** to restart your computer.

10. Press `Ctrl+Alt+Del` to start logging on. Notice that this does not work because the keyboard driver is incorrect.

11. Use Last Known Good Configuration to recover registry settings to the last successful logon, as detailed in the following steps:

    a. Turn off and then turn on your computer.

    b. During the boot process, press `F8` to display the Advanced Boot Options menu shown in Figure 12-6.

    c. Select `Last Known Good Configuration (advanced)` and press `Enter`.

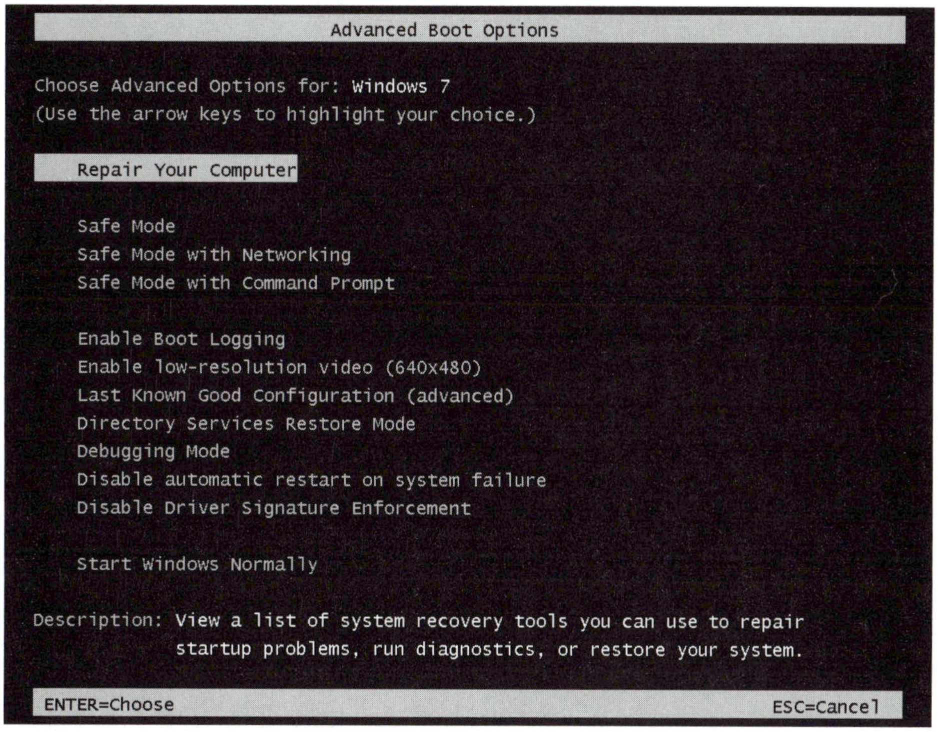

```
                        Advanced Boot Options

Choose Advanced Options for: Windows 7
(Use the arrow keys to highlight your choice.)

    Repair Your Computer

    Safe Mode
    Safe Mode with Networking
    Safe Mode with Command Prompt

    Enable Boot Logging
    Enable low-resolution video (640x480)
    Last Known Good Configuration (advanced)
    Directory Services Restore Mode
    Debugging Mode
    Disable automatic restart on system failure
    Disable Driver Signature Enforcement


    Start Windows Normally

Description: View a list of system recovery tools you can use to repair
            startup problems, run diagnostics, or restore your system.

ENTER=Choose                                            ESC=Cancel
```

Figure 12-6 Advanced Boot Options
© Cengage Learning 2012

12. Log on to User*x*-PC as `User`*x*. You are able to log on this time because the original keyboard driver has been restored.

13. Remove the drive letter for the System Reserved partition, as detailed in the following steps:

    a. Click `Start`, right-click `Computer`, and click `Manage`.

    b. In Computer Management, click `Disk Management`.

    c. Right-click `System Reserved (W:)` and click `Change Drive Letter and Paths`.

    d. In the Change Drive Letter and Paths for W: (System Reserved) window, click `Remove`.

    e. Click `Yes` to confirm.

    f. Click `Yes` to continue.

    g. Close Computer Management.

Certification Objectives

Objectives for MCTS Exam #70-680: Windows 7, Configuring:

- Configuring Backup and Recovery Options: Configure system recovery options

Review Questions

1. Why did you need to assign a drive letter to the System Reserved partition to delete bootmgr?

2. Why did you need to take ownership of bootmgr before you could delete it?

3. Can you think of at least one more way that you could have resolved the missing boot-mgr error other than using Startup Repair?

4. Can you think of at least one more way that you could have resolved the incorrect keyboard driver?

5. When is the Last Known Good Configuration updated?

Lab 12.3: Controlling Service Startup

Objectives

The objective of this activity is to control service startup by using multiple methods.

Materials Required

This lab requires the following:

- A physical computer or virtual machine running Windows 7 that is configured as User*x*-PC or as specified by your instructor

Estimated completion time:	**15 minutes**

Activity Background

A service is software that runs in the background of Windows 7. Many specific tasks required by Windows 7 and applications are performed by services. For example, Windows 7 uses services to resolve DNS names, browse the network, access shared files, and share printers.

A service can be configured to start automatically when Windows 7 starts. This ensures that the service is available after a reboot. Conversely, unnecessary services can be disabled to ensure they do not start and use system resources.

You can control services startup by using the Services administrative tool, System Configuration, or Safe Mode. You can also control services startup by editing the registry. Each tool is applicable in different situations.

Some malware creates services as part of its infection and replication process. Knowing how to stop and remove these services is a useful malware recovery skill.

Activity

1. Log on to User*x*-PC as **User*x***.

2. Review the options for service startup and security, as detailed in the following steps:

   a. Click **Start**, in the Search programs and files box, type **services.msc**, and press **Enter**.

   b. Click the **BranchCache** service.

    c. Read the Startup Type for this service and the Description.

    d. Right-click the **BranchCache** service, and click **Start**.

    e. Right-click the **BranchCache** service, and click **Properties**.

    f. In the BranchCache Properties (Local Computer) window, on the **General** tab, in the **Startup type** box, select **Disabled**, and click **Apply**.

    g. Read the Service status. Notice that the service did not stop automatically when you set the Startup type to disabled.

    h. Click **Stop**. Notice that the Startup type is disabled, as shown in Figure 12-7.

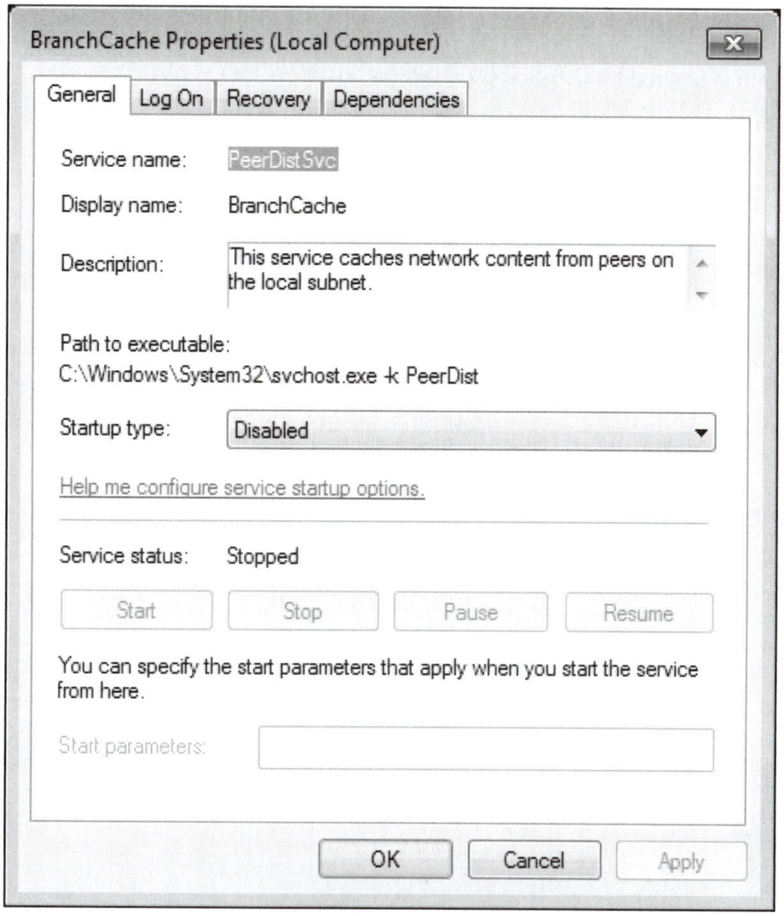

12

Figure 12-7 Service Properties, General tab
© Cengage Learning 2012

    i. Click the **Log On** tab and read the available options. Notice that you can define which account the service logged on as. The privileges and permission granted to the service are based on this account.

    j. Click the **Recovery** tab and read the available options. Notice that you can define what happens when a service fails.

    k. Click the **First failure** box to display the list of available options.

    l. Click the **Dependencies** tab and read the dependencies that exist for this service.

    m. Click **Cancel**.

3. Change the Startup Type for a service in the registry, as detailed in the following steps.

   a. Click **Start**, in the Search programs and files box, type **regedit**, and press **Enter**.

   b. In the User Account Control window, click **Yes**.

   c. In the Registry Editor, browse to **HKEY_LOCAL_MACHINE/SYSTEM/Current ControSet/services/PeerDistSvc**.

   d. Read the registry keys and values for the BranchCache service.

   e. Right-click the **Start** key and click **Modify**.

   f. In the Value data box, type **3** and click **OK**. Valid values are 0 (boot, for drivers only), 1 (system, for drivers only), 2 (automatic), 3 (manual), and 4 (disabled). If the value is 2 and the key DelayedAutostart has a value of 1, then the service starts automatically but is started after other services.

   g. In Services, press **F5** to refresh the view. Notice that the Startup Type for the BranchCache service has changed back to Manual.

   h. Close all open windows.

4. Use System Configuration to control service startup, as detailed in the following steps:

   a. Click **Start**, in the Search programs and files box, type **system configuration**, and press **Enter**.

   b. In System Configuration, read the information on the General tab, as shown in Figure 12-8. Diagnostic startup is similar to Safe Mode. Selective startup uses settings from the other tabs to control which services and applications are started automatically.

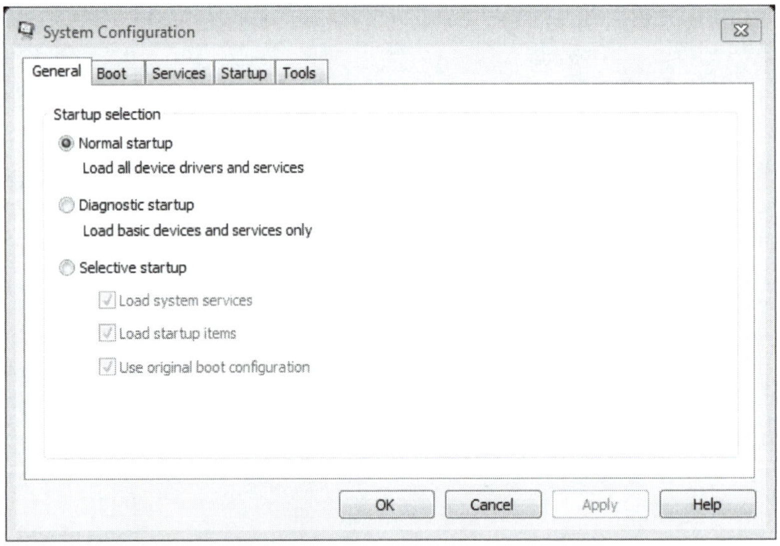

Figure 12-8   System Configuration
© Cengage Learning 2012

   c. Click the **Boot** tab and read the options. Notice that the Boot options area is equivalent to options that you can select from the Advanced Boot Options menu available when pressing F8 during startup.

   d. Click the **Services** tab and read the information. Notice that you can disable services from this location. Disabling services here is equivalent to changing the Startup Type of the service to Disabled in the Services administrative tool.

e. Click the **Startup** tab and read the information. This tab allows you to disable programs that are starting automatically. This includes programs in the Startup folder of the start menu or the Run key in the registry. If your computer has any applications listed on this tab, expand each column so that you can read the details.

f. Click the **Tools** tab and read the list of tools. You can launch these tools directly from within System Configuration.

5. Start your computer in Safe Mode, as detailed in the following steps:

a. On the **Boot** tab, select the **Safe boot** check box and click **OK**.

b. Click **Restart**. Notice that your computer automatically restarts in Safe Mode without pressing F8 during the startup.

c. Log on as **Userx**.

d. Notice that Windows Help and Support opens automatically. Also notice that the screen resolution is reduced and that there is no network connectivity.

e. Read the information about Safe Mode, and close Windows Help and Support.

6. View the running services in Safe Mode, as detailed in the following steps:

a. Click **Start**, in the Search programs and files box, type **services.msc**, and press **Enter**.

b. In Services, click the **Startup Type** column heading. This action sorts the services based on Startup Type.

c. Scroll through the list of services, and read the Status and Startup Type for each service. Notice that many services with a Startup Type of Automatic do not have a Status of Started.

d. Scroll down and click the **Windows Installer** service. Notice that this service is not started automatically in Safe Mode.

e. Right-click the **Windows Installer** service, and click **Start**.

f. Read the error message and then click **OK**. This service cannot be started in Safe Mode.

7. Restart your computer.

8. Log on as **Userx**. Notice that your computer is still in Safe Mode.

9. Enable normal startup for your computer, as detailed in the following steps:

a. Click **Start**, in the Search programs and files box, type **system configuration**, and press **Enter**.

b. In System Configuration, on the General tab, notice that Selective startup is being used.

c. Click **Normal startup** and click **OK**.

d. Click **Restart**.

Certification Objectives

Objectives for MCTS Exam #70-680: Windows 7, Configuring:

- Configuring Backup and Recovery Options: Configure system recovery options

Review Questions

1. What is one reason that you would disable a service?

2. Can you run a program when a service fails?

3. How is System Configuration different from the Services administrative tool?

4. How could Safe Mode be used when trying to remove malware?

5. Can you install or remove software when running in Safe Mode?

Lab 12.4: Backing Up and Restoring

Objectives

The objective of this activity is to back up Windows 7 and restore the system state and data files.

Materials Required

This lab requires the following:

- A physical computer or virtual machine running Windows 7 that is configured as User*x*-PC or as specified by your instructor
- An external USB drive that can be used to store a backup. In a virtualized environment, you can use a second virtual hard drive. Configure the second hard drive as a single NTFS partition using the drive letter W.

Estimated completion time: **60 minutes**

Activity Background

The system state in Windows 7 consists of operating and application files, including the registry and drivers. You can back up the system state by using Windows Backup to create a full backup, by creating a system image, or by creating recovery points.

The best way to recover data files, such as documents, is by using shadow copies. You can also recover data files from a full backup or system image.

Activity

1. Log on to User*x*-PC as **User*x***.

2. Create a document, as detailed in the following steps:

    a. Right-click the **desktop**, point to **New**, and click **Text Document**.

    b. Type **Important** and press **Enter** to rename the file.

    c. Double-click **Important.txt** to open it.

    d. In Notepad, type **This is my important information to back up**.

    e. Close Notepad and click **Save**.

3. Perform a system image of your computer, as detailed in the following steps:

    a. Click **Start**, in the Search programs and files box, type **backup and restore**, and press **Enter**.

    b. In Backup and Restore, click **Create a system image**.

    c. In the Create a system image window, click **On a hard disk**, select the **W:** drive as shown in Figure 12-9, and then click **Next**.

    d. On the Which drives do you want to include in the backup page, read the drives that are available for backup. Notice that the System Reserved partition and C: drive are automatically selected.

    e. Click **Next**.

    f. On the Confirm your backup settings page, click **Start backup**.

    g. Wait for the backup to complete. This may take 5–10 minutes.

    h. When prompted to create a system repair disc, click **No**. You will use the Windows 7 installation DVD later in this activity rather than a system repair disc.

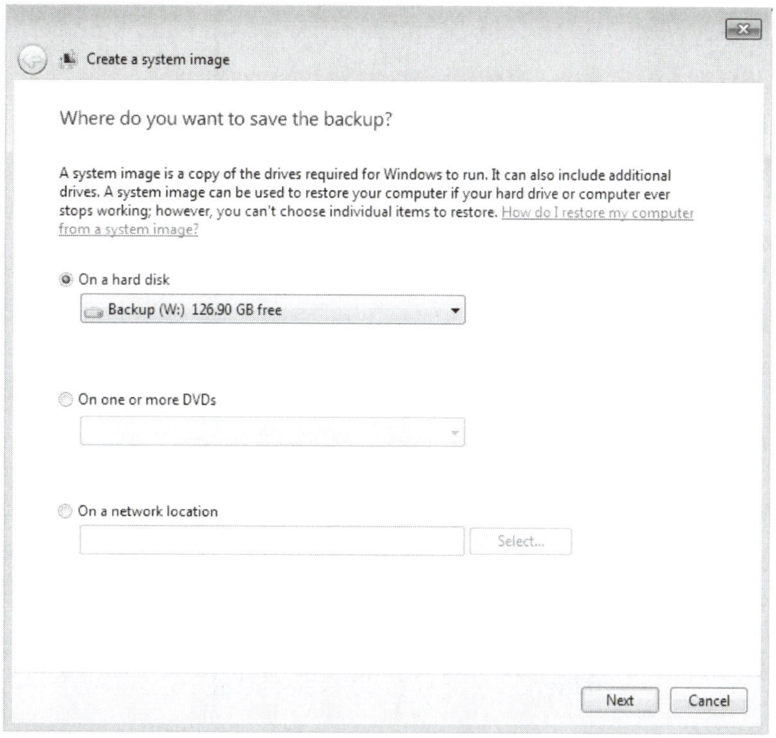

Figure 12-9   Creating a system image
© *Cengage Learning 2012*

    i. In the Create a system image window, click **Close**.

    j. Close Backup and Restore.

4. Modify Important.txt, as detailed in the following steps:

    a. Double-click **Important.txt** to open it.

    b. In Notepad, select the existing text and delete it.

    c. Type **I accidentally deleted the content in my file**.

    d. Close Notepad and click **Save**.

5. Recover the previous version of Important.txt, as detailed in the following steps:

    a. Right-click **Important.txt** and click **Restore previous versions**. This displays previous versions of the file captured by shadow copies, as shown in Figure 12-10. A shadow copy was taken as part of creating the system image.

    b. Select the most recent version of the file and click **Restore**.

    c. In the Previous Versions window, read the warning and click **Restore**.

    d. Click **OK** to close the message about successful restoration.

    e. In the Important.txt Properties window, click **OK**.

6. Verify that the previous version of the file is recovered, as detailed in the following steps:

    a. Double-click **Important.txt** to open it.

    b. In Notepad, read the contents of the file. Note that the important information is restored.

    c. Close Notepad.

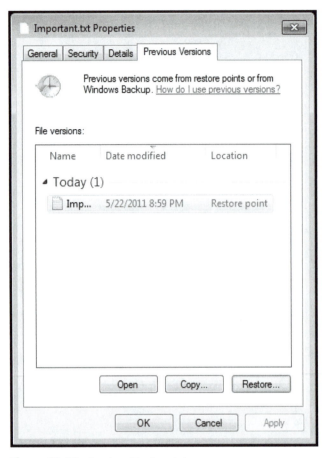

Figure 12-10 Previous Versions tab
© *Cengage Learning 2012*

7. Disable the BranchCache service, as detailed in the following steps:

   a. Click **Start**, in the Search programs and files box, type **services.msc**, and press **Enter**.

   b. Click the **BranchCache** service.

   c. Right-click the **BranchCache** service and click **Properties**.

   d. In the BranchCache Properties (Local Computer) window, on the **General** tab, in the **Startup type** box, select **Disabled**, and click **OK**.

   e. Close Services.

8. Restore a recovery point, as detailed in the following steps:

   a. Click **Start**, in the Search programs and files box, type **system restore**, and press **Enter**.

   b. In the System Restore window, read the information and click **Next**.

   c. Select the most recent restore point, and click **Scan for affected programs**.

   d. Read the results. Notice that no programs or drivers will be affected.

   e. Click **Close**.

   f. Click **Next**.

g. On the Confirm your restore point page, read the information and click Finish.

h. Read the warning and click **Yes** to confirm.

i. After your computer restarts, log on as **User*x***.

j. Read the contents of the System Restore window, and click **Close**.

9. Verify that the BranchCache service is configured for Manual start, as detailed in the following steps:

a. Click **Start**, in the Search programs and files box, type **services.msc**, and press **Enter**.

b. Click the **BranchCache** service.

c. Read the Startup Type for the BranchCache service.

d. Close Services.

10. Make system changes before performing a system image restore, as detailed in the following steps:

a. Right-click **Important.txt** and click **Delete**.

b. In the Delete File window, click **Yes** to confirm.

c. Disable the BranchCache service, as shown in Step 7 of this lab.

11. Perform a system image restore, as detailed in the following steps:

a. If necessary, place the Windows 7 installation DVD in your computer.

b. Restart your computer.

c. When prompted to Press any key to boot from CD or DVD, press a key.

d. In the Install Windows window, click **Next** to accept the default language settings.

e. Click **Repair your computer.**

f. In the System Recovery Options window, click **Restore your computer using a system image that you created earlier** and then click **Next**.

g. In the Re-image your computer window, click **Use the latest available system image(recommended)** and click **Next**. Notice that the drive letter on which the system image is stored may not be W:.

h. On the Choose additional restore options page, shown in Figure 12-11, read the available options and then click **Next**. Notice that you have the option to completely wipe out the existing disk and repartition it.

i. Click **Finish**.

j. Read the warning and click **Yes**.

k. Wait for the system image restore to complete. This may take 10–20 minutes.

12. After the computer restarts, log on as **User*x***.

13. Verify that the system and data are restored, as detailed in the following steps.

a. Notice that Important.txt is on the desktop.

b. Click **Start**, in the Search programs and files box, type **services.msc**, and press **Enter**.

c. Click the **BranchCache** service.

d. Read the Startup Type for the BranchCache service.

e. Close Services.

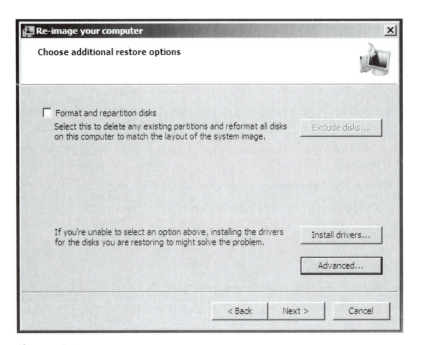

Figure 12-11 Additional restore options
© *Cengage Learning 2012*

Certification Objectives

Objectives for MCTS Exam #70-680: Windows 7, Configuring:

- Configuring Backup and Recovery Options: Configure backup
- Configuring Backup and Recovery Options: Configure file recovery options

Review Questions

1. Can you use a system image to restore individual files?

2. What is the easiest way to recover an individual file that has been deleted?

3. Can you use previous versions to recover a file after a hard drive has failed?

4. How is a system restore different from a system image restore?

5. You are performing a system image restore to a computer with a new hard drive. Should you select the option to format and repartition disks?

ENTERPRISE COMPUTING

Labs included in this chapter:

- Lab 13.1 Using Group Policy to Configure Windows 7

- Lab 13.2 Using USMT to Migrate Profiles

- Lab 13.3 Implementing VHD Boot

Microsoft MCTS Exam #70-680 Objectives

Objective	Lab
Configure Internet Explorer	13.1
Migrate user profiles	13.2
Perform a clean installation	13.3
Configure a VHD	13.3

Lab 13.1: Using Group Policy to Configure Windows 7

Objectives

The object of this activity is to configure Windows 7 by using Group Policy.

Materials Required

This lab requires the following:

- A physical computer or virtual machine running Windows 7 that is configured as Userx-PC or as specified by your instructor

- An Active Directory domain controller for the domain GiganticLifey.local, where y is a number assigned by your instructor, as configured in Activity 13-1 of the *MCTS Guide to Microsoft Windows 7*. The computer name is DCy and Remote Desktop Services (Terminal Services) is enabled.

- Your computer joined to the GiganticLifey.local domain, as configured in Activity 13-2 of the course book

Estimated completion time: **45 minutes**

Activity Background

Windows 7 includes a local Group Policy object (GPO) with many settings that can be used to control the configuration of Windows 7. In a corporate environment with Active Directory, GPOs can be stored in Active Directory. Configuring GPOs in Active Directory is much more efficient because a single GPO can affect all computers and users in the entire organization.

Settings in a GPO are organized into user and computer settings. User settings apply to user accounts in the organizational unit (OU) to which the GPO is linked. Computer settings apply to computer accounts in the OU to which the GPO is linked. For special-use computers, you can use loopback processing to apply the user settings in a GPO that is linked to an OU where the computer account is located.

Activity

1. Log on to Userx-PC as **GiganticLifey\Administrator** with a password of **Passw0rd**.

2. Connect to the server with Remote Desktop Connection, as detailed in the following steps:

   a. Click **Start**, in the Search programs and files box, type **remote desktop connection**, and press **Enter**.

   b. In the Computer box, type **DCy** and press **Enter**.

   c. In the Windows Security window, log on as **GiganticLifey\Administrator** with a password of **Passw0rd**.

3. Create a new OU structure for testing Group Policy application, as detailed in the following steps:

   a. On DCy, click **Start**, point to **Administrative Tools**, and click **Active Directory Users and Computers**.

   b. In Active Directory Users and Computers, if necessary, expand **GiganticLifey.local**.

   c. Right-click **GiganticLifey.local**, point to **New**, and click **Organizational Unit**.

   d. In the New Object – Organizational Unit window, in the Name box, type **Labz**, where z is a number assigned by your instructor, and click **OK**.

e. Right-click **Lab***z*, point to **New**, and click **Organizational Unit**.

f. In the New Object – Organizational Unit window, in the Name box, type **Marketing***z*, where *z* is a number assigned by your instructor, and click **OK**.

g. Right-click **Lab***z*, point to **New**, and click **Organizational Unit**.

h. In the New Object – Organizational Unit window, in the Name box, type **Training***z*, where *z* is a number assigned by your instructor, and click **OK**. When it is complete, your OU structure should be similar to Figure 13-1.

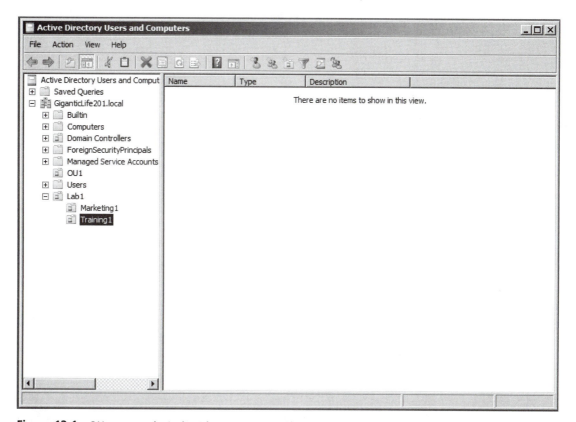

Figure 13-1   OU structure in Active Directory Users and Computers
© *Cengage Learning 2012*

4. Create a user in the Marketing OU, as detailed in the following steps:

a. In Active Directory Users and Computers, right-click **Marketing**, point to **New**, and click **User**.

b. Enter the following information and click **Next**:

- First name: **Shaun**

- Last name: **Smith**

- User logon name **Shaun***z*

c. In the Password and Confirm password boxes, type **Passw0rd**.

d. Clear the **User must change password at next logon** check box, and click **Next**.

e. Click **Finish**.

5. Move your computer account into the Training OU, as detailed in the following steps:

   a. In Active Directory Users and Computers, click the **Computers** container.

   b. Right-click **Userx-PC** and click **Move**.

   c. In the Move window, expand **Labz**, click **Trainingz**, and click **OK**.

   d. Click **Trainingz**. The computer account Userx-PC is here, but it can take up to 90 minutes before Windows 7 picks up this configuration change. A reboot forces the change to happen immediately.

   e. Close Active Directory Users and Computers.

6. Restart your computer, as detailed in the following steps:

   a. Close Remote Desktop and click **OK** when notified that the connection will be disconnected.

   b. Restart your computer.

   c. Log on Userx-PC as **Userx**.

   d. Click **Start**, in the Search programs and files box, type **remote desktop connection**, and press **Enter**.

   e. In the Computer box, type **DCy** and press **Enter**.

   f. In the Windows Security window, log on as **GiganticLifey\Administrator** with a password of **Passw0rd**.

7. The computers in the training room require a shortcut for Microsoft Paint on the desktop. Create a GPO that places a Microsoft Paint shortcut on the desktop for computer accounts in the Training OU, as detailed in the following steps:

   a. On DCy, click **Start**, point to **Administrative Tools**, and click **Group Policy Management**.

   b. In Group Policy Management, expand **Forest: GiganticLifey.local**, expand **Labz**, and click **Trainingz**. Notice that no GPOs are linked to this OU.

   c. Right-click **Trainingz** and click **Create a GPO in this domain, and Link it here**.

   d. In the New GPO window, in the Name box, type **TrainingRoomz** and click **OK**.

   e. Right-click **TrainingRoomz** and click **Edit**.

   f. In Group Policy Management Editor, under Computer Configuration, expand **Preferences**, expand **Windows Settings**, and click **Shortcuts**.

   g. Right-click **Shortcuts**, point to **New**, and click **Shortcut**.

   h. In the New Shortcut Properties window, in the Location box, select **Desktop**.

   i. In the Name box, type **Paint Training**.

   j. In the Target path box, type **C:\Windows\System32\mspaint.exe** and click **OK**. The result is shown in Figure 13-2.

   k. Close Group Policy Management Editor.

8. Users in the Marketing department should have Google as their home page in Internet Explorer. Create a GPO that configures Google as the home page for users in the Marketing OU, as detailed in the following steps:

   a. In Group Policy Management, click the **Marketingz** OU.

   b. Right-click **Marketingz** and click **Create a GPO in this domain, and Link it here**.

Figure 13-2   Group Policy Management Editor
© *Cengage Learning 2012*

13

c. In the New GPO window, in the Name box, type **MarketingUsers***z* and click **OK**. The result will be similar to Figure 13-3.

d. Right-click **MarketingUsers***z* and click **Edit**.

e. In Group Policy Management Editor, under User Configuration, expand **Policies**, expand **Windows Settings**, expand **Internet Explorer Maintenance**, and click **URLs**.

f. Double-click **Important URLs**.

g. In the Important URLs window, select the **Customize Home page URL** check box.

h. In the Home page URL box, type **http://www.google.com** and click **OK**.

i. Close Group Policy Management Editor.

9. By default, a Windows 7 computer downloads new GPOs every 90 minutes. Force your computer to download the new GPOs now, as detailed in the following steps:

a. On Userx-PC, click **Start**, in the Search programs and files box, type **cmd**, and press **Enter**.

b. In the command prompt window, type **gpupdate /force** and press **Enter**.

c. Close the command prompt.

g. Close all open windows.

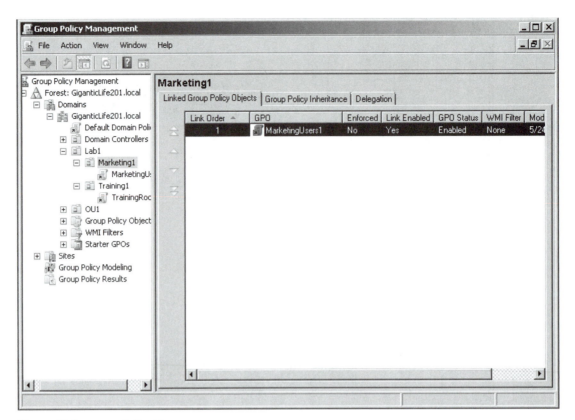

Figure 13-3 Group Policy Management
© *Cengage Learning 2012*

10. Test the application of GPOs to your computer, as detailed in the following steps:

   a. On User*x*-PC, log off and log on as **GiganticLifey\Shaun***z* with a password of **Passw0rd**.

   b. Notice that the Paint Training icon appears on the Desktop, as defined in the TrainingRoom GPO.

   c. On the taskbar, click the **Internet Explorer** icon.

   d. Notice that http://www.google.com is used for the home page, as defined in the MarketingUsers GPO. Depending on your location, you may be redirected to a country-specific version of Google. For example, Canadian users may be redirected to www.google.ca.

   e. Close Internet Explorer.

11. The training room is being used for a technical training course on Microsoft products this week. The home page for all computers in the training room should be directed to http://technet.microsoft.com regardless of which user logs on. Use loopback processing to enable a computer-specific home page for computers in the training room, as detailed in the following steps:

   a. Click **Start**, in the Search programs and files box, type **remote desktop connection**, and press **Enter**.

   b. In the Computer box, type **DC***y* and press **Enter**.

   c. In the Windows Security window, log on as **GiganticLifey\Administrator** with a password of **Passw0rd**.

d. In Group Policy Management, right-click **TrainingRoom***z* and click **Edit**.

e. In Group Policy Management Editor, under User Configuration, expand **Policies**, expand **Windows Settings**, expand **Internet Explorer Maintenance**, and click **URLs**.

f. Double-click **Important URLs**.

g. In the Important URLs window, select the **Customize Home page URL** check box.

h. In the Home page URL box, type **http://technet.microsoft.com** and click **OK**.

i. Under Computer Configuration, expand **Policies**, expand **Administrative Templates**, expand **System**, and click **Group Policy**.

j. In the list of Group Policies, double-click **User Group Policy loopback processing mode**.

k. In the User Group Policy loopback processing mode window, read the information in the Help area and then click **Enabled**.

l. In the Mode box, select **Replace** and click **OK**.

m. Close Group Policy Management Editor.

n. Close Group Policy Management.

12. Test the application of GPOs and loopback processing to your computer, as detailed in the following steps:

a. Restart User*x*-PC and log on as **GiganticLifey\Shaun***z* with a password of **Passw0rd**.

b. Notice that the Paint Training icon appears on the Desktop, as defined in the TrainingRoom GPO.

c. On the taskbar, click the **Internet Explorer** icon.

d. Notice that http://technet.microsoft.com is used for the home page, as defined in the TrainingRoom GPO.

e. Close Internet Explorer.

13. Move your computer account back into the Computers container, as detailed in the following steps:

a. Click **Start**, in the Search programs and files box, type **remote desktop connection**, and press **Enter**.

b. In the Computer box, type **DC***y* and press **Enter**.

c. In the Windows Security window, log on as **GiganticLifey\Administrator** with a password of **Passw0rd**.

d. On DC*y*, click **Start**, point to **Administrative Tools**, and click **Active Directory Users and Computers**.

e. In Active Directory Users and Computers, browse to the **Training***z* OU, right-click **User***x***-PC**, and click **Move**.

f. In the Move window, click the **Computers** container and click **OK**.

g. Close Active Directory Users and Computers.

h. Restart User*x*-PC.

Certification Objectives

Objectives for MCTS Exam #70-680: Windows 7, Configuring:

- Configuring Hardware and Applications: Configure Internet Explorer

Review Questions

1. When are the changes to a GPO saved?

2. Which computers in the GiganticLife.local domain will get a shortcut for Training Paint on the desktop, as defined in the TrainingRoom GPO?

3. Which users in the GiganticLife.local domain will get the http://www.google.com home page in Internet Explorer, as defined in the MarketingUsers GPO?

4. Why did the Internet Explorer home page change after enabling loopback processing?

5. Where should you link a GPO to have the settings apply to all users and computers in the domain?

Lab 13.2: Using USMT to Migrate Profiles

Objectives

The objective of this activity is to identify how to migrate user profiles by using the User State Migration Tool.

Materials Required

This lab requires the following:

- A physical computer or virtual machine running Windows 7 that is configured as User*x*-PC or as specified by your instructor

- The Windows Automated Installation Kit installed, as detailed in Activity 2-1 of *MCTS Guide to Microsoft Windows 7*

- Completion of Lab 13.1

Estimated completion time: **20 minutes**

Activity Background

User profiles contain the user-specific portion of the registry and user-specific files, such as Favorites, My Documents, and some application configuration files. A user profile is typically stored on the local computer on which a user works. When a user gets a new computer, it is common to migrate the profile from the old computer to the new computer.

Windows 7 includes the graphical tool Windows Easy Transfer to migrate user profiles from one computer to another. This tool is effective but not suitable for large corporate environments because it is time consuming to use. Most large migration projects migrate user profiles by using the User State Migration Tool (USMT). USMT can be scripted to speed up the migration process.

Activity

1. Log on to User*x*-PC as `GiganticLifey\Administrator`.

2. Create a folder to store the profile during migration, as detailed in the following steps:

   a. Click **Start** and click **Computer**.

   b. In Windows Explorer, browse to `C:\` and click **New folder**.

   c. Type **ProTemp** and press **Enter** to rename the folder.

   d. Right-click **ProTemp** and click **Properties**.

e. In the ProTemp Properties window, on the **Security** tab, select **Authenticated Users**. Notice that Authenticated Users has Modify permissions to this folder. This is sufficient to store the user profile information.

f. Click **Cancel** and close Windows Explorer.

3. Configure the user profile for Shaun, as detailed in the following steps:

a. Log off and log on as **GiganticLifey\Shaunz** with a password of **Passw0rd**.

b. Right-click the **desktop** and click **Personalize**.

c. Scroll down in the list of themes, and click **Nature**.

d. Close the Personalization window.

4. View the documentation for USMT, as detailed in the following steps:

a. On the taskbar, click the **Internet Explorer** icon.

b. In Internet Explorer, in the address bar, type **http://go.microsoft.com/fwlink/?LinkID=56578** and press **Enter**.

c. In the Quick links section, click the **USMT.xml Files** link.

d. Read the description of the XML files that can be used to control USMT.

e. Close Internet Explorer.

5. View the contents of MigUser.xml, as detailed in the following steps:

a. Click **Start** and click **Computer**.

b. In Windows Explorer, browse to **C:\Program Files\Windows AIK\Tools\USMT\amd64** and double-click **MigUser.xml**. The file opens in Internet Explorer.

c. Scroll down through the MigUser.xml and read the contents. Notice that the file includes comments that describe what each section of the file is doing.

d. Close Internet Explorer and Windows Explorer.

6. Use ScanState to capture the local user profile, as detailed in the following steps:

a. Click **Start**, in the Search programs and files box, type **cmd**, and press **Enter**.

b. In the command prompt window, type **"C:\Program Files\Windows AIK\Tools\USMT\amd64\scanstate.exe" C:\ProTemp** and press **Enter**. If your computer is running the 32-bit version of Windows 7, then substitute x86 for amd64 in the path. Do not change to the folder containing ScanState before running this command or it will fail because Shaun does not have permission to create the log file in that location.

c. When storage of the profile is complete, the screen appears as shown in Figure 13-4.

d. Close the command prompt.

7. Review the captured profile data, as detailed in the following steps:

a. Click **Start** and click **Computer**.

b. In Windows Explorer, browse to **C:\ProTemp\USMT**. The USMT.MIG file in this folder contains the data being migrated.

c. Close Windows Explorer.

8. Configure the user profile for Shaun, as detailed in the following steps:

a. Right-click the **desktop** and click **Personalize**.

b. Scroll down in the list of themes and click **High Contrast #1**.

c. Close the Personalization window.

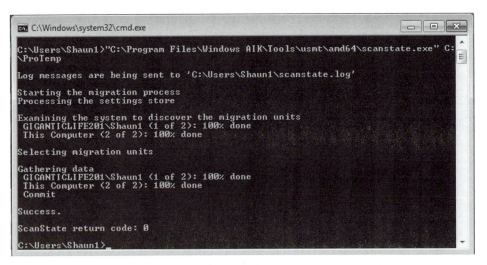

Figure 13-4 Using ScanState to capture a profile
© *Cengage Learning 2012*

9. After a profile is captured with ScanState, you use LoadState to apply the profile to a new computer. Use LoadState to apply the saved profile, as detailed in the following steps:

   a. Click **Start**, in the Search programs and files box, type **cmd**, and press **Enter**.

   b. In the command prompt window, type **"C:\Program Files\Windows AIK\ Tools\USMT\amd64\loadstate.exe" C:\ProTemp** and press **Enter**. If your computer is running the 32-bit version of Windows 7, then substitute x86 for amd64 in the path. Notice that this fails because Shaun does not have sufficient permissions, as shown in Figure 13-5.

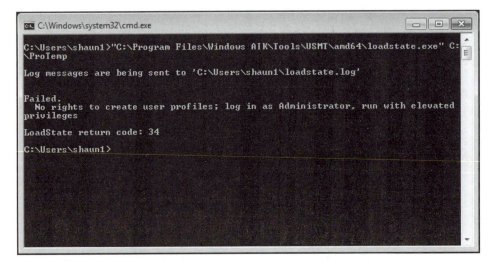

Figure 13-5 Error when running LoadState
© *Cengage Learning 2012*

   c. Log off as Shaun and log on as **GiganticLifey\Administrator** with a password of **Passw0rd**.

   d. Click **Start**, in the Search programs and files box, type **cmd**, and press **Enter**.

e. In the command prompt window, type **"C:\Program Files\Windows AIK\ Tools\USMT\amd64\loadstate.exe" C:\ProTemp** and press **Enter**. If your computer is running the 32-bit version of Windows 7, then substitute x86 for amd64 in the path. Notice that you did not have to specify the name of the user because it is in the migration data.

f. When the profile is applied, log off.

10. Verify that the profile was applied correctly, as detailed in the following steps:

a. Log on as **GiganticLifey\Shaunz** with a password of **Passw0rd**.

b. Review the Desktop theme. The theme is set back to Nature. The Nature theme was contained in the profile that was migrated.

c. Log off.

13

Certification Objectives

Objectives for MCTS Exam #70-680: Windows 7, Configuring:

- Installing, Upgrading, and Migrating to Windows 7: Migrate user profiles

Review Questions

1. Is it typical to store migrating user profile data on the local computer?

2. When running ScanState, a user requires permissions to access the profile storage location. Which permissions are required by the user running ScanState?

3. How do you determine how large of a storage location you require for migrating profiles?

4. What can MigUser.xml be used for?

5. Describe how you could run ScanState during a migration.

Lab 13.3: Implementing VHD Boot

Objectives

The objective of this activity is to configure a dual boot Windows 7 system by booting from VHD.

Materials Required

This lab requires the following:

- A physical computer or virtual machine running Windows 7 that is configured as User*x*-PC or as specified by your instructor
- A partition with at least 15 GB of free space
- Windows 7 installation DVD

Estimated completion time: **60 minutes**

Activity Background

Windows 7 has the ability to mount and access virtual hard disk files (VHDs). When mounted, a VHD is treated as a physical disk. You can partition the VHD and store data on it.

Windows 7 also has the ability to boot from an operating system stored on a VHD file. The boot process is started by the System partition on the physical drive, but an entry in the boot configuration database (BCD) allows bootmgr to mount the VHD file and start the operating system from the VHD file. The VHD file becomes the boot partition.

Booting from a VHD is helpful when dual booting with Windows 7. To dual boot multiple Windows 7 operating system instances, each instance of Windows 7 needs to be stored on a separate partition. Rather than dividing a physical disk into multiple partitions, you can use one large partition with multiple VHD files. Dual booting is useful to have a separate instance of Windows 7 for testing hardware drivers.

Be aware that when a dynamic VHD is used for a VHD boot, it is expanded to full size when you boot from it. The size is reduced when you are not using it as the boot partition.

Activity

1. Log on to User*x*-PC as **User*x***.

2. Verify that there is sufficient free disk space on your C: drive partition to complete the activity.

   a. Click **Start**, in the Search programs and files box, type **disk cleanup**, and press **Enter**.

   b. In the Disk Cleanup: Drive Select window, in the Drives box, select **(C:)** and click **OK**.

   c. In the Disk Cleanup for (C:) window, select all available check boxes and then click **OK**.

   d. Click **Delete Files** to confirm.

   e. Click **Start** and click **Computer**.

   f. In Windows Explorer, review the free disk space on Local Disk (C:).

   g. If the free disk space on Local Disk (C:) is 10 GB or more, then skip to Step 3. If the free disk space on Local Disk (C:) is less than 10 GB, then you can delete the following files created for previous activities and labs:

      • C:\bootcd

      • C:\images

      • C:\wininstall

   h. If there is still not enough free space on your C: drive, then use Steps 2.i through 2.r and delete all unneeded partitions and extend your C: drive.

   i. Click **Start**, right-click **Computer**, and click **Manage**.

   j. In Computer Management, click **Disk Management** and review the existing list of drive letters. All partitions except C: and System Reserved can be deleted.

   k. Right-click an unneeded partition and click **Delete Volume**.

   l. In the warning window, click **Yes**.

   m. Repeat Steps 2.k and 2.l for all remaining unnecessary partitions. Only system Reserved and C: should be left.

   n. Right-click **(C:)** and click **Extend Volume**.

   o. In the Extend Volume Wizard, click **Next**.

   p. By default, all remaining space on Disk 0 is selected for extension. Click **Next**.

   q. On the Completing the Extend Volume Wizard page, click **Finish**. Notice that C: is now one large partition.

   r. Close Computer Management.

3. Create a VHD for operating system installation, as detailed in the following steps:

   a. Click **Start**, right-click **Computer**, and click **Manage**.

   b. In Computer Management, click **Disk Management** and review the existing list of drive letters.

   c. Right-click **Disk Management** and click **Create VHD**.

d. In the Create and Attach Virtual Hard Disk window, type the following, as shown in Figure 13-6:

- Location: **C:\Win7Test.vhd**
- Virtual hard disk size: **15 GB**
- Virtual hard disk format: **Dynamically expanding**

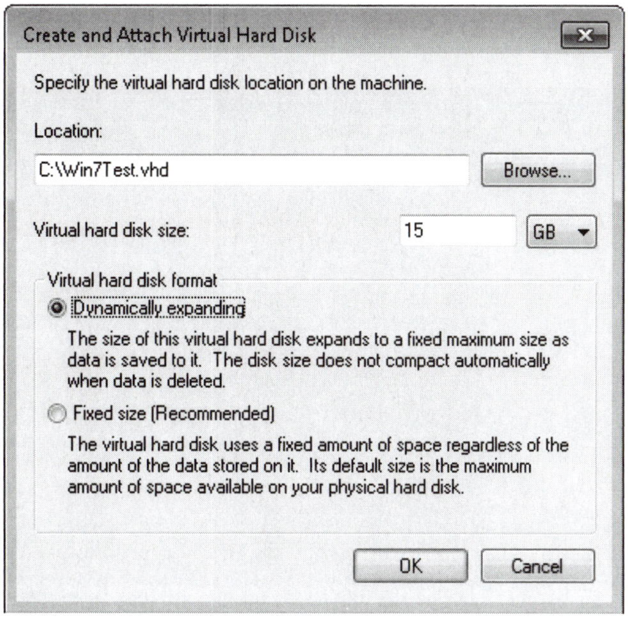

Figure 13-6   Creating a virtual hard disk
© *Cengage Learning 2012*

e. Click **OK** and wait a few seconds for the VHD driver to load.

f. If you have completed Activity 13-7 from the course book on this computer, the VHD is not automatically mounted and an error message appears after a few minutes. This occurs because Activity 13-7 implemented a Group Policy setting that prevents new disk drivers from being loaded. You will boot from the installation DVD and perform any necessary disk operations. If necessary, click **OK** to clear the error message.

4. Mount the VHD to prepare for Windows 7 installation, as detailed in the following steps.

a. If necessary, place the Windows 7 installation DVD in your computer.

b. Restart your computer.

c. When prompted to **Press any key to boot from CD or DVD**, press a key.

d. In the Install Windows window, click **Next** to accept the default language settings.

e. Press **Shift+F10** to open a command prompt.

f. At the command prompt, type **diskpart** and press **Enter**.

g. Type **list volume** and press **Enter**. This displays the volumes on your system. Identify the volume containing your existing windows installation. You can identify this volume by the size (which will be equivalent to your C: drive) and by the Label (which is typically blank). For the remainder of this step, it is assumed that it is drive letter D:

h. Type **select vdisk file=d:\win7test.vhd** and press **Enter**.

i. Type **attach vdisk** and press **Enter**.

j. Close the command prompt.

5. Install Windows 7 to the VHD file, as detailed in the following steps:

   a. In the Install Windows window, click `Install now`.

   b. Select the `I accept the license terms` check box, and click `Next`.

   c. Click `Custom (advanced)`.

   d. Scroll through the list of partitions and select the partition corresponding to the VHD file, as shown in Figure 13-7. You can identify this partition by the Total Size value of 15.0 GB.

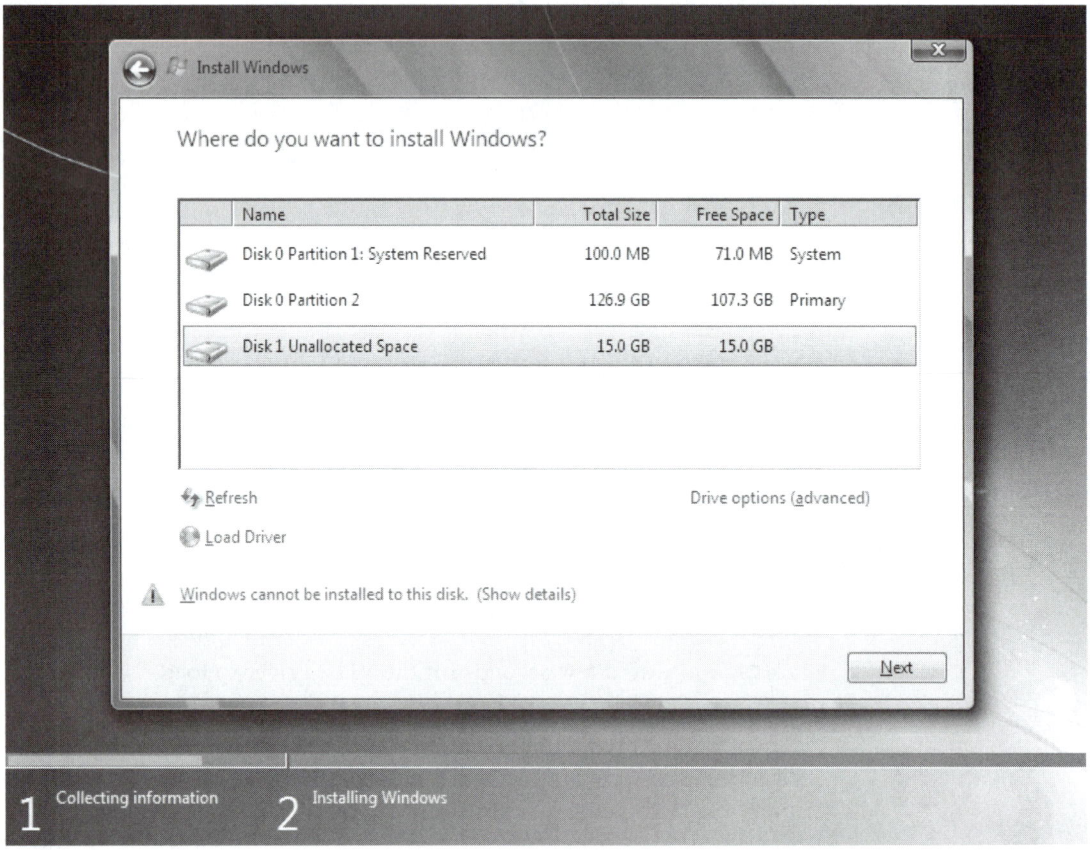

Figure 13-7   Selecting the VHD for install
© Cengage Learning 2012

   e. Ignore the error indicating that Windows cannot be installed to this disk, and click `Next`.

   f. Wait while Windows 7 is installed. This may take 30–45 minutes.

   g. When your computer reboots and the option to select an operating system is presented, leave the setting at its default. The installation of Windows 7 automatically continues.

6. Complete the installation of Windows 7 in the VHD, as detailed in the following steps:

   a. In the Type a user name box, type `Testx`, where x is assigned by your instructor, and click `Next`.

   b. In the Type a password and Retype your password boxes, type `password`.

   c. In the Type a password hint box, type `The easiest` and then click `Next`.

   d. On the type your Windows Product key page, clear the `Automatically activate Windows when I'm online` check box, and click `Next`.

    e. On the Help protect your computer and improve Windows automatically page, click **Use recommended settings**.

    f. On the Review your time and date settings page, pick the correct time zone, time, and date and then click **Next**.

    g. On the Select your computer's current location page, click **Work network**.

    h. Wait until you are automatically logged on.

7. Explore the new operating system instance, as detailed in the following steps:

    a. Click **Start** and click **Computer**. Notice that the 15 GB VHD file you created is listed as the C drive. Partitions on your physical disk are also listed.

    b. Double-click the disk that corresponds to the C: drive in your original installation. You can identify this partition by the size. Notice that Win7Test.vhd is listed as 15 GB.

    c. Close Windows Explorer.

    d. Click **Start** and point to **All Programs**. Notice that no previously installed programs are available. For example, the Windows Automated Installation Kit is not listed.

8. Configure the BCD with descriptions for each bootable drive, as detailed in the following steps:

    a. Click **Start**, in the Search programs and files box, type **cmd**, right-click **cmd.exe** and click **Run as administrator**.

    b. In the User Account Control window, click **Yes**.

    c. In the command prompt window, type **bcdedit /enum /v** and press **Enter**. This displays the current BCD configuration, as shown in Figure 13-8. Notice that the first Windows Boot Loader listed is using the Win7Test.vhd file.

Figure 13-8 BCD configuration
© Cengage Learning 2012

    d. Write down the identifier for the second Windows Boot Loader: _____.

       Type **bcdedit** and press **Enter**. Notice that the first Windows Boot Loader listed now has the identifier {current}. This is a shortcut name for the boot loader entry.

    e. Type **bcdedit /set {current} description "Windows 7 VHD"** and press **Enter**.

    f. Type **bcdedit /set {***IdentifierForSecondWindowsBootLoader***} description "Windows 7 Physical Disk"** and press **Enter**.

9. Set the version of Windows 7 on the physical disk to be the default, as detailed in the following steps:

    a. At the command prompt, type **bcdedit /set {bootmgr} default {***IdentifierForSecondWindowsBootLoader***}** and press **Enter**.

    b. Close the command prompt.

10. View the new boot menu, as detailed in the following steps:

    a. Restart your computer.

    b. When the boot menu appears, press a key to stop the timer. The screen should appear, as shown in Figure 13-9. Windows 7 Physical Disk is highlighted because it is the default selection.

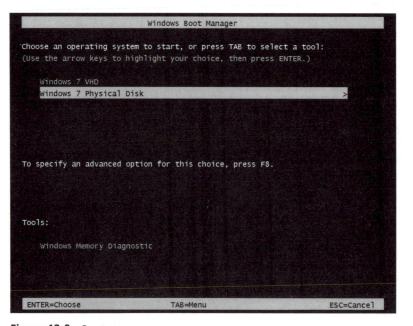

Figure 13-9 Boot menu
© Cengage Learning 2012

    c. Press **Enter** to select Windows 7 Physical Disk. Windows 7 is started from the physical disk rather than the VHD file.

Certification Objectives

Objectives for MCTS Exam #70-680: Windows 7, Configuring:

- Installing, Upgrading, and Migrating to Windows 7: Perform a clean installation
- Deploying Windows 7: Configure a VHD

Review Questions

1. After installing a second copy of Windows 7 in a VHD, which instance of Windows boots by default?

2. You have a 100 GB hard drive with 25 GB of free space. You create a dynamically expanding VHD that is 50 GB and begin installing Windows 7 to that VHD. During the first reboot of the installation, an error appears indicating that the VHD could not be expanded. Why did this occur?

3. Why is it a good idea to give each instance of Windows 7 a unique description?

4. Which key combination is used to open a command prompt at the initial installation screen during the installation of Windows 7?

5. Why did you need to attach the VHD at a command prompt before installing Windows 7?

13

REMOTE ACCESS

Labs included in this chapter:

- Lab 14.1 Configuring a BranchCache Client for Local Caching
- Lab 14.2 Request Remote Assistance with Easy Connect using an Invitation File
- Lab 14.3 Configuring a VPN Connection and Investigating Commonly Modified Settings

Microsoft MCTS Exam #70-680 Objectives

Objective	Lab
Configure BranchCache	14.1
Configure authentication and authorization	14.2, 14.3
Configure remote connections	14.2, 14.3

Lab 14.1: Configuring a BranchCache Client for Local Caching

Objectives

The object of this activity is to configure a BranchCache client for local caching, which is not configurable with Group Policy settings.

Materials Required

This lab requires the following:

- A physical computer or virtual machine running Windows 7 that is configured as User*x*-PC or as specified by your instructor

Estimated completion time: **30 minutes**

Activity Background

A Windows 7 computer can be used by more than one person at a time. The caching ability of BranchCache can be applied to resources on a local computer that are being accessed by multiple users of the same computer. This BranchCache mode cannot be configured through Group Policy and must be configured locally using command-line utilities. This lab investigates how to modify typical BranchCache configuration parameters locally, how to enable local BranchCache caching, and how to reset BranchCache configuration settings back to default values.

Activity

1. Log on to User*x*-PC.

2. Create a new folder that will be used as a local cache location for BranchCache content, as detailed in the following steps:

   a. Click **Start, Computer,** and then double-click the **Local Disk (C:)** icon.

   b. In the menu bar, click the link **New Folder.**

   c. Replace the *New folder* name with **BCACHE** and press **Enter.**

   d. Minimize the Local Disk (C:) file browser window.

3. Open an elevated command prompt window to run system commands in the security context of an administrator, as detailed in the following steps:

   a. Click **Start** and then, in the *Search programs and files* search box, type **CMD.**

   b. In the list of matching programs shown in the Start menu, right-click **CMD** and click **Run as administrator** from the pop-up menu.

   c. When you are prompted by User Account Control for permission to continue with the request, click **Yes.**

4. Confirm the BranchCache system is currently disabled, as detailed in the following steps:

   a. In the command prompt window, type the command **NETSH BRANCHCACHE SHOW STATUS** and press **Enter** to display the basic status report, as shown in Figure 14-1. Confirm that the service mode is currently disabled.

   b. In the command prompt window, type the command **NETSH BRANCHCACHE SHOW STATUS ALL** and press **Enter** to display the full status report, as shown in Figure 14-2. Confirm that the service mode is currently disabled.

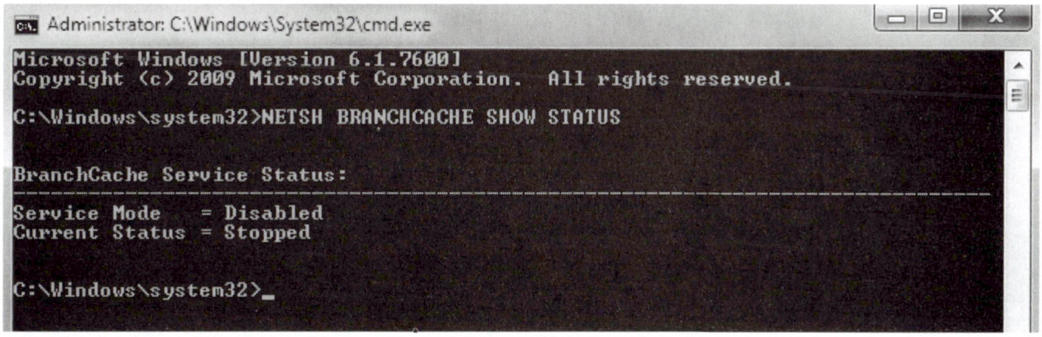

Figure 14-1   BranchCache basic status report
© Cengage Learning 2012

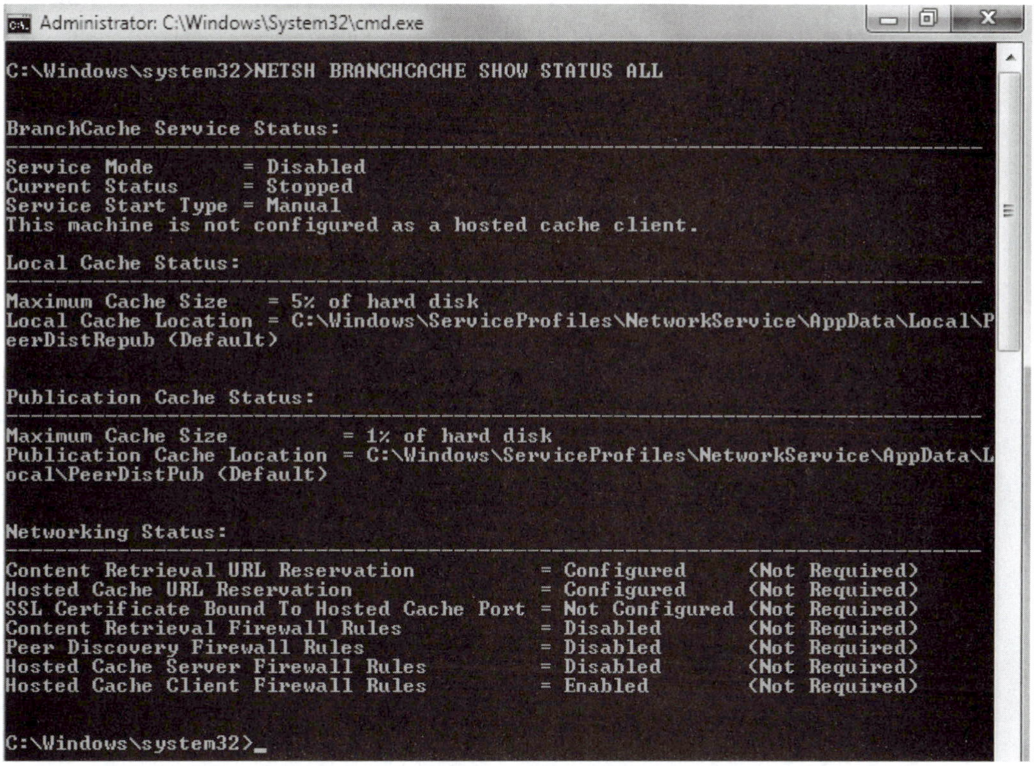

Figure 14-2   BranchCache full status report
© Cengage Learning 2012

5. Update the BranchCache local cache location by typing the command **NETSH BRANCHCACHE SET LOCALCACHE DIRECTORY=C:\BCACHE**, and press **Enter**.

6. Maximize the Local Disk (C:) file browser window. Double-click the **BCACHE** folder and note that BranchCache-related files have been moved to the folder, as noted in the command results from Step 5.

7. Change the local BrachCache cache size, as detailed in the following steps:

   a. In the command prompt window, type the command **NETSH BRANCHCACHE SET CACHESIZE SIZE = 2000000** and press **Enter**.

   b. Type the command **NETSH BRANCHCACHE SHOW STATUS ALL** and press **Enter**.

    c. Record the current value for maximum cache size in bytes, found below Local Cache Status in the report: _____.

    d. In the command prompt window, type the command **NETSH BRANCHCACHE SET CACHESIZE SIZE=12 PERCENT=TRUE** and press **Enter**.

    e. Type the command **NETSH BRANCHCACHE SHOW STATUS ALL** and press **Enter**.

    f. Record the current value for maximum cache size, found below Local Cache Status in the report: _____. Compare this value to the value recorded in Step 7.c, noting the difference in how each limit is described.

8. Activate BranchCache for local caching only by typing the command **NETSH BRANCHCACHE SET SERVICE MODE=LOCAL**, and press **Enter**.

9. Confirm that BranchCache service is operating in local mode, as detailed in the following steps:

    a. Type the command **NETSH BRANCHCACHE SHOW STATUS ALL** and press **Enter**.

    b. Below the heading of BranchCache Service Status, record the value of Service Mode: _____.

    c. Below the heading of BranchCache Service Status, record the value of Service Start Type: _____.

    d. Below the heading of Networking Status, record the value of Hosted Cache Client Firewall Rules: _____. Note which components in the Networking status are reported as required.

10. Configure the BranchCache service to start automatically, as detailed in the following steps:

    a. In the command prompt window, type **SERVICES.MSC** and press **Enter**.

    b. In the Services windows that opens, double-click the service name **BranchCache** listed in the right pane.

    c. In the BranchCache Properties window, as shown in Figure 14-3, click the **Startup type** drop-down arrow and select **Automatic (Delayed Start)**.

    d. Record the service name listed in the BranchCache Properties window: _____.

    e. Click **OK** to save the change and close the BranchCache Properties window.

    f. In the command prompt window, type the command **NETSH BRANCHCACHE SHOW STATUS ALL** and press **Enter**. Note the service start type listed below BranchCache Service Status.

11. Reset the BranchCache client to its default settings and disable the service by typing the command **NETSH BRANCHCACHE RESET**, and press **Enter**.

12. Close all windows and log out as the current user.

Certification Objectives

Objectives for MCTS Exam #70-680: Windows 7, Configuring:

- Configuring Access to Resources: Configure BranchCache

Review Questions

1. Which command-line tool allows you to configure BranchCache?

    a. GPRESULT

    b. SERVICES.MSC

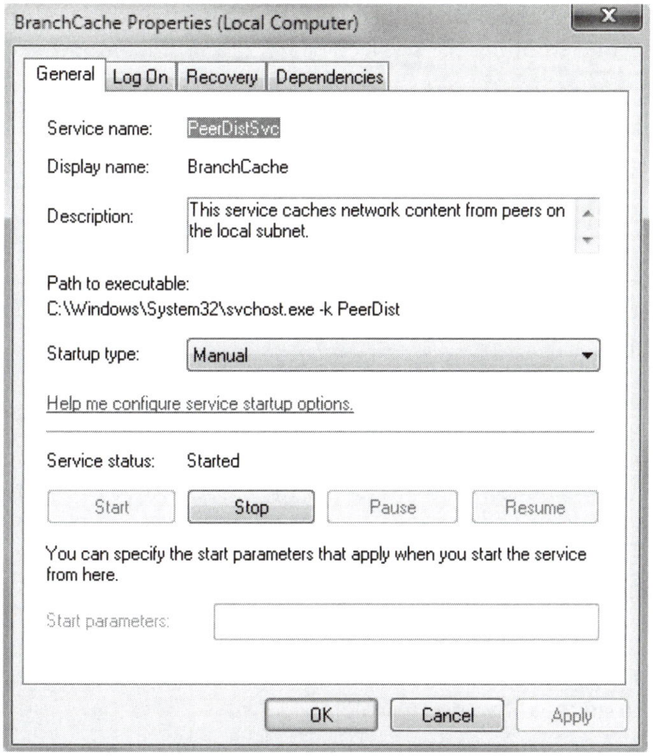

Figure 14-3   BranchCache service properties
© Cengage Learning 2012

    c. NETSH

    d. GPEDIT

2. Which command displays the current BranchCache service mode?

    a. NETSH BRANCHCACHE SHOW HOSTEDCACHE

    b. NETSH BRANCHCACHE SHOW LOCALCACHE

    c. NETSH BRANCHCACHE SHOW PUBLICATIONCACHE

    d. NETSH BRANCHCACHE SHOW STATUS

3. Which command sets the BranchCache client to use the local cache mode and changes the startup mode to manual?

    a. NETSH BRANCHCACHE SET SERVICE MODE=LOCAL

    b. NETSH BRANCHCACHE SET SERVICE MODE=DISTRIBUTED

    c. NETSH BRANCHCACHE SET SERVICE MODE=HOSTEDCLIENT

    d. NETSH BRANCHCACHE SET SERVICE MODE=HOSTEDSERVER

4. Which of the following partial commands can be used as part of the command that sets the BranchCache local cache directory?

    a. NETSH BRANCHCACHE SET CACHESIZE

    b. NETSH BRANCHCACHE SET LOCALCACHE

    c. NETSH BRANCHCACHE SET CACHE

    d. NETSH BRANCHCACHE SET LOCAL

5. Which command resets the BranchCache client settings back to their default values, as well as disabling and stopping the service?

   a. NETSH BRANCHCACHE SET SERVICE MODE=DISABLED

   b. NETSH BRANCHCACHE DUMP

   c. NETSH BRANCHCACHE FLUSH

   d. NETSH BRANCHCACHE RESET

Lab 14.2: Request Remote Assistance with Easy Connect Using an Invitation File

Objectives

The objective of this activity is to initiate a Remote Assistance invitation from the command line, which will use Easy Connect, and also allow the request to be completed by storing and transporting the invitation in a file.

Materials Required

This lab requires the following:

- A physical computer or virtual machine running Windows 7 that is configured as User*x*-PC or as specified by your instructor.

- A portable media, such as a USB flash drive, to transport files between computers

- A lab partner

Estimated completion time: **30 minutes**

Activity Background

Remote Assistance allows a helper to remote control a computer while the user is still logged on. This is often used by help desk staff to perform repairs quickly without the need to visit the user's computer.

Remote assistance can be offered by helper or requested by users. In most cases, a user requests assistance by using Easy Connect. Easy Connect displays a password that must be used by the helper to gain access to the user's computer. The Remote Assistance invitation can also be saved to a file and that file can be communicated using any method of file transfer. This lab reviews essential elements in that process.

Activity

1. Log on to User*x*-PC.

2. Create a new user account on your computer that will be used to test profile updates, as detailed in the following steps:

   a. Click **Start**, click **Control Panel**, and then click **Add or remove user accounts** below the User Accounts and Family Safety heading.

   b. In the Manage Accounts window that appears, click the link **Create a new account**.

   c. Enter the name **lab14usr** as the new user account name. Confirm that the **Standard user** selection is already selected.

   d. Click the **Create Account** button to create the user.

   e. When the Manage Accounts windows reappears, click the **lab14usr** icon.

    f. When the Change an Account window appears, click the **Create a password** link.

    g. When the Create Password window appears, enter **workpass** in the *New password* field.

    h. Enter **workpass** in the *Confirm new password* field.

    i. Click the **Create password** button.

    j. Close the Change an Account window.

3. Log out as the current user.

4. Log in as the user **lab14usr**, specifying **workpass** as the password.

5. In this lab, you and your lab partner will take turns connecting to each other's computer. Stop and do not continue until your lab partner reaches this step. Determine which partner will be first to complete the steps before continuing.

6. Start a session that allows a helper to connect with Remote Assistance using Easy Connect by default, as detailed in the following steps:

    a. Click **Start** and then in the *Search programs and files* search box type **MSRA / geteasyhelp** and press **Enter**. After the Easy Connect session is prepared, the Windows Remote Assistance window will open, as shown in Figure 14-4.

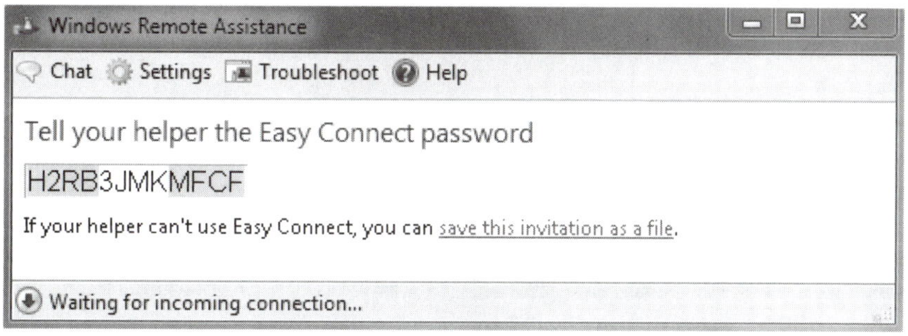

Figure 14-4   Windows Remote Assistance active request via Easy Connect
© *Cengage Learning 2012*

    b. Record the Easy Connect password displayed in the Windows Remote Assistance window: _____.

    c. Click the link **save this invitation as a file**.

    d. In the Save As window that opens, rename the filename from Invitation to **Lab14UsrInvitation_to** followed by the name of the local computer, as shown in Figure 14-5.

    e. Click the **Save** button.

7. Confirm the contents of the Remote Assistance invitation file, as detailed in the following steps:

    a. Click **Start**, **Computer**, and then click **Documents** below Libraries in the left pane of the file browser window.

    b. Right-click the file created in Step 5.d and select **Open with** from the pop-up menu.

    c. In the Open with windows, click the **Other Programs** arrow. This will reveal other programs that can be used to open the file, as shown in Figure 14-6.

    d. Remove the check mark next to **Always use the selected program to open this kind of file**.

    e. Click to select and highlight **Notepad**.

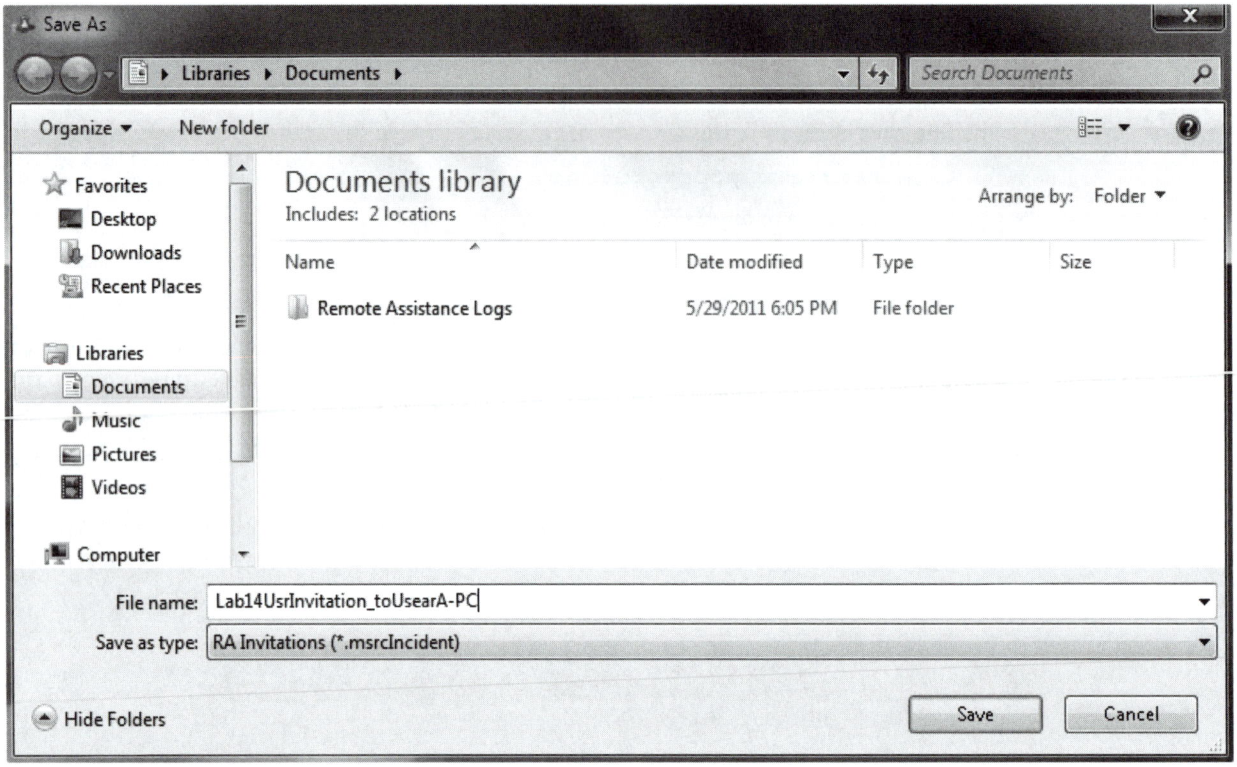

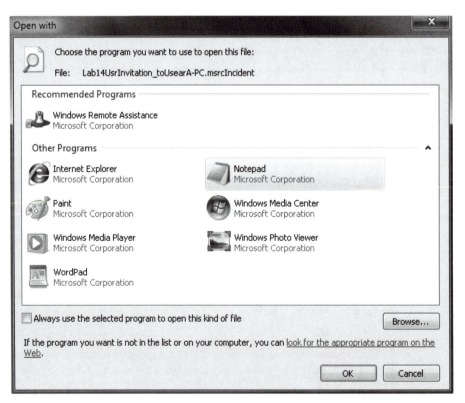

Figure 14-5 Saving a Remote Assistance invitation to a file
© Cengage Learning 2012

Figure 14-6 Opening a Remote Assistance invitation file with a different program
© Cengage Learning 2012

    f. Click the **OK** button.

    g. Record the first line of the file's contents, identifying the data type contained in the file: _____.

    h. Close the Notepad window.

8. Copy the Remote Assistance invitation file to portable media and transfer it to another computer, as detailed in the following steps:

    a. In the Documents file browser window, right-click the file created in Step 5.d and select **Copy** from the pop-up menu.

    b. Insert a USB portable key or other portable media. Once the portable media is ready for use, paste the invitation file to that removable media.

    c. Remove the media and transport it to a different lab computer.

9. Connect from another user's computer using a Remote Assistance invitation file, as detailed in the following steps:

    a. Insert the portable medium that was used to store the invitation file from your computer.

    b. Click **Start**, click **Computer**, and then browse to the device folder containing the invitation file.

    c. *Note*: Do not attempt to connect from your lab partner's computer while the computer is waiting for a connection. Double-click the invitation file on the portable media.

    d. Enter the password you recorded in Step 5.b.

    e. Click **OK** to continue with the connection.

    f. On your lab partner's computer, click **Yes** when prompted for permission to allow the connection.

10. Request control of your remote desktop, as detailed in the following steps:

    a. In the Windows Remote Assistance window, click **Request Control**.

    b. On your computer, when you are prompted to share control of the desktop, click to select **Allow *username* to respond to User Account Control prompts** and click the **Yes** button to continue, as shown in Figure 14-7.

    c. Because your computer is logged in using a standard user, not an administrative user, User Account Control requires you to enter administrative credentials on the computer. Confirm that User Account Control has presented an administrator account for your computer and type the password for that account.

    d. Click **Yes** to close the User Account Control window on your computer and allow sharing of the desktop.

Figure 14-7 Windows Remote Assistance request for permission to share control of the desktop
© Cengage Learning 2012

11. On your lab partner's computer, close the Windows Remote Assistance window.

12. Remove the portable media.

13. Return to Step 5, reverse the roles of each lab partner, and repeat the steps for this lab.

14. Log off the computer.

Certification Objectives

Objectives for MCTS Exam #70-680: Windows 7, Configuring:

- Configuring Access to Resources: Configure authentication and authorization
- Configure Mobile Computing: Configure remote connections

Review Questions

1. Which of these file extensions is used with a file for the purpose of transferring a Remote Assistance request to another person?

   a. .raRequest

   b. .remote

   c. .msrcIncident

   d. .help

2. The contents of a Remote Assistance invitation file are formatted as what type of data?

   a. Binary data

   b. CSV

   c. XML

   d. TXT

3. What command can be used at the command line to start the Remote Assistance utility?

   a. MSRA

   b. RHELP

   c. RA

   d. MSTSC

4. The _____ command-line option will allow a user to start a Remote Assistance request using Easy Connect by default.

   a. /offerRA

   b. /geteasyhelp

   c. /offereasyhelp

   d. /expert

5. The Easy Connect password in a Remote Assistance invitation is how many characters long?

   a. As many characters long as the user types into the password field when he or she creates the invitation

   b. 16 characters long

   c. There is no password used with Easy Connect.

   d. 12 characters long

Lab 14.3: Configuring a VPN Connection and Investigating Commonly Modified Settings

Objectives

The objective of this activity is to configure a VPN connection and update commonly modified properties.

Materials Required

This lab requires the following:

- A physical computer or virtual machine running Windows 7 that is configured as User*x*-PC or as specified by your instructor
- Completion of Lab 14.2

Estimated completion time: **10 minutes**

Activity Background

A VPN connection can be configured to connect to a specific VPN server. The VPN type must be correctly specified and the authentication protocol selected for that VPN server. If the IKEv2 VPN type is selected, the VPN connection can lose its network connection for a period of time and still allow the VPN to reconnect without losing its session state. That network outage tolerance time period is reviewed. This lab then looks at how a VPN connection can have its scope focused to include or exclude IPv4, IPv6, and Microsoft client/server component usage over the VPN connection.

Activity

1. Log on to User*x*-PC.

2. Configure a new VPN connection, as detailed in the following steps:

   a. Click **Start**, click **Control Panel**, and then click the link **View network status and tasks** below the heading Network and Internet.

   b. Click the **Set up a new connection or network** link below the *Change your network settings* heading.

   c. Click **Connect to a workplace** in the Set Up a Connection of Network window.

   d. Click the **Next** button.

   e. If a VPN connection already exists, you will be asked if you want to use that connection. In that case, click **No, create a new connection** and click **Next** to proceed.

   f. Click **Use my Internet connection (VPN)**.

   g. In the Internet address box, type **lab14.testing.local**.

   h. In the Destination name box, type **LAB14-3 VPN Connection**.

   i. Click **Don't connect now; just set it up so I can connect later**.

   j. Click the **Next** button.

   k. Do not enter a username or password; click the **Create** button to continue with the VPN connection creation. Because you are not entering credentials now, you will be prompted for credentials when the VPN connection is established.

   l. Click the **Close** button to close the Connect to a Workplace window without connecting now.

3. Confirm the authentication protocols selected and allowed by default for each type of VPN connection type, as detailed in the following steps:

   a. In the Network and Sharing Center window, click the **Change adapter settings** link to open the Network Connections window.

   b. Right-click the **LAB 14-3 VPN Connection** icon, and select **Properties** from the pop-up menu.

   c. Click the **Security** tab.

   d. In the Type of VPN box, select **Point to Point Tunneling Protocol (PPTP)**.

   e. Record the authentication protocols selected and allowed by default:

   _____

   f. In the Type of VPN box, select **Layer 2 Tunneling Protocol with IPSec (L2TP/IPSec)**.

   g. Record the authentication protocols selected and allowed by default:

   _____

   h. In the Type of VPN box, select **Secure Socket Tunneling Protocol (SSTP)**.

   i. Record the authentication protocols selected and allowed by default:

   _____

   j. In the Type of VPN box, select **IKEv2**.

   k. Record the authentication protocols selected and allowed by default:

   _____

4. Confirm the mobility network outage time limits for an IKEv2 VPN connection, as detailed in the following steps:

   a. Below the Type of VPN box, click the **Advanced Settings** button.

   b. Confirm that the **Mobility** feature is selected.

   c. Record the default Network outage time: _____.

   d. Click the **Network outage time** drop-down arrow. Record the minimum Network outage time: _____.

   e. Record the maximum Network outage time: _____.

   f. Click the **OK** button.

5. Configure the VPN connection to only use the IPv4 protocol over the VPN connection and disallow access to resources using Microsoft resource access protocols, as detailed in the following steps:

   a. Click the **Networking** tab to select it.

   b. Click to deselect **Internet Protocol Version 6 (TCP/IPv6)**.

   c. Click to deselect **File and Printer Sharing for Microsoft Networks**. This will disable the ability of other computers to access resources on your computer using Microsoft network protocols over the VPN.

   d. Click to deselect **Client for Microsoft Networks**. This will disable your computer's ability to access Microsoft resources over this VPN connection.

6. Click **OK** to close the Lab 14-3 VPN Connection Properties window.

7. In the Network Connections window, right-click the **LAB 14-3 VPN Connection** icon, and click **Delete** from the pop-up menu. Click **Yes** when asked if you want to delete the connection.

8. Close the Network Connections window.

9. Delete the user lab14usr as detailed in the following steps:

   a. Click **Start**, click **Control Panel**, and then click **Add or remove user accounts** below the User Accounts and Family Safety heading.

   b. In the Manage Accounts window that appears, click the **lab14usr** account.

   c. Click the link **Delete the account**.

   d. When you are prompted to keep lab14usr's files, click the **Delete Files** button.

   e. When you are asked if you are sure that you want to delete lab14usr's account, click the **Delete Account** button.

   f. Close the Manage Accounts window.

10. Shut down the computer.

Certification Objectives

Objectives for MCTS Exam #70-680: Windows 7, Configuring:

- Configuring Access to Resources: Configure authentication and authorization
- Configure Mobile Computing: Configure remote connections

Review Questions

1. The default VPN type for a newly created VPN connection is _____.

   a. PPTP

   b. L2TP

   c. SSTP

   d. Automatic

2. The default mobility network outage time specified for an IKEv2 VPN connection is _____.

   a. 5 minutes

   b. 10 minutes

   c. 30 minutes

   d. 8 hours

3. The maximum mobility network outage time specified for an IKEv2 VPN connection is _____.

   a. 5 minutes

   b. 10 minutes

   c. 30 minutes

   d. 8 hours

4. The default authentication protocol used for an IKEv2 VPN connection is _____.

   a. EAP-MSCHAP-v2

   b. PEAP

   c. MS-CHAP v2

   d. CHAP

5. A VPN connection can be configured to connect using only the IPv6 network protocol. True or False?

   a. True

   b. False